THE STATUS OF WOMEN IN LAW IN ASIAN COUNTRIES

THE STATUS OF WOMEN IN LAW IN ASIAN COUNTRIES

Usha Srivastava

MD PUBLICATIONS PVT LTD
NEW DELHI
www.mdppl.com

Published by :

MD Publications Pvt Ltd
"MD House", 11, Darya Ganj,
New Delhi - 110 002
Phone : +91-11-45355555
E-mail : contact@mdppl.com
Website: www.mdppl.com

ISBN: 978-81-7533-249-2

Published and Printed by Mr. Pranav Gupta on behalf of MD Publications Pvt Ltd at Mohit Enterprises, Delhi.

Preface

In every state, the legal status of free women depended upon marital status. Unmarried women, including widows, were called "femes soles", or "women alone." They had the legal right to live where they pleased and to support themselves in any occupation that did not require a license or a college degree restricted to males. Single women could enter into contracts, buy and sell real estate, or accumulate personal property, which was called personality. It consisted of everything that could be moved - cash, stocks and bonds, livestock, and, in the South, slaves.

So long as they remained unmarried, women could sue and be sued, write wills, serve as guardians, and act as executors of estates. These rights were a continuation of the colonial legal tradition. But the revolutionary emphasis on equality brought some important changes in women's inheritance rights. State lawmakers everywhere abolished primogeniture and the tradition of double shares of a parent's estate, inheritance customs that favoured the eldest son. Instead, equal inheritance for all children became the rule - a big gain for daughters.

Marriage changed women's legal status dramatically. When women married, as the vast majority did, they still had legal rights but no longer had autonomy. Instead, they found themselves in positions of almost total dependency on their husbands which the law called covertures. Women's rights to real property - the lands and buildings that constituted most wealth in the early national period - were more extensive than their rights to personality. A husband could not sell or mortgage the realty his wife brought to their marriage without her consent. He could use it, but he could not convey it because a woman's real estate, generally inherited from her father, was meant to stay in the family and descend through her to her children.

One of the most important rights of a married woman was dower, which was designed to provide her with support during widowhood. Dower was a legal tradition carried over from colonial days. This and other rules about married women's property rights were meant to support the family as a unit. They worked reasonably well in an economic system based on landed wealth, under which families typically stayed in one place and rarely sold or mortgaged their farms.

Political rights were a function of control over property for men in the republic, but gender alone was the basis for women's exclusion from voting or holding office. Simply put, men with property had the right to vote in the early national period but women, no matter how wealthy, did not, even though women paid the same taxes as men. The reasoning behind this discrimination rested on the assumption that married women were liable to coercion by their husbands; if a wife voted, legislators argued, it meant that a man cast two ballots. Blatantly discriminatory attitudes kept lawmakers from giving women the vote.

I am very grateful to Mr. Pranav Gupta, Director of MD Publications Pvt Ltd, New Delhi, for his kind cooperation and support for this book.

Usha Srivastava

CONTENTS

1

Functioning of the Legal System

Gender issues in South Asia represent a complex challenge. The first round of progress has been significant, with greater recognition of the problem across the region and improved access to services and credit markets in various countries. Yet, dramatic gender inequities persist in the face of these changes and in spite of economic growth. To reverse these inequities will require a deepening of the current focus on service delivery. It also will require greater voice of women in the political decision- making of communities and states. This focus on the, political process demands a more strategic and deft partnership by the World Bank in the gender dialogue with a broad spectrum of key actors.

Our challenge is to internalize and prioritize gender issues across all the sectors we work in, guided by the ongoing diagnostic work in knowledge products like the Country Gender Assessments (CGAs). In addition to identifying determinants of gender inequality, CGAs and other AAA on gender issues offer recommendations that can help the Bank engage governments to undertake policy reforms that provide women greater access and power.

In 2005 and 2006, reports were completed for Afghanistan, Nepal, and Pakistan: *National Reconstruction and Poverty Reduction – the Role of Women in Afghanistan's Future* (March 2005); The Pakistan CGA, *Bridging the Gender Gap- Opportunities and Challenges* (October 2005); and *Unequal Citizens: Gender,*

Caste and Ethnic Exclusion in Nepal (2006), a Gender and Social Exclusion Assessment (GSEA).

As part of Bangladesh's gender program, a CGA is underway and scheduled for completion in Spring 2007. Just as influential as the reports' content, the iterative and consultative process of their preparation has facilitated ongoing debate in client countries and across Bank sectors about how to tackle gender issues. Key process factors include: in-country consultations with stakeholders and country teams at every stage of preparation and dissemination; Country Director Leadership; collection and analysis of original data; and use of qualitative data to enrich analysis of gender-disaggregated quantitative data.

CREATION AND DISSEMINATION OF KNOWLEDGE ON GENDER ISSUES

Preparation and dissemination activities for the CGAs and the GSEA have ensured widespread readership-particularly among in-country stakeholders in government, academia, NGOs, and civil society-and helped focus debate among stakeholders. The reports have shed light on the ground reality of gender disparities in the region.

- Boys outnumber girls in school enrollment in Afghanistan, India, Pakistan, and Nepal; although in Bangladesh girls have caught up with boys, there are concerns about reverse gender inequality.
- Dropout rates for girls across the region are higher than those for boys.
- Women have insufficient access to basic health care, adequate contraceptive services, care during pregnancy and delivery, and other types of reproductive health.
- Girls marry at a young age and about 50 percent have their first child by age 20. In many parts of the region - notably India and Bangladesh - dowry puts pressure on families of girls to marry them early, leading to preference for sons.
- Though most countries in the region have achieved robust economic growth, women's labor force participation rate

is among the lowest in the world. Relative to men, women's voice in decision making at all levels – community, provincial and national – is limited. Where seats in elected bodies are reserved for women, their substantive role is limited.

- At the crux of women's low status is a discriminatory legal system and poor access to justice. Even when laws emphasize equal rights in inheritance of land and property, in practice, these are seldom invoked. Other family law is similarly weighted against women, weakening their position in the family.

Legal and judicial systems, as well as law enforcement mechanisms, have failed to address the high incidence of violence against women in both private and public domains. Having identified determinants of these gender disparities, the reports recommend policy interventions to ameliorate them.

The gender reports have all seen early success in operationalizing recommendations in select sector programs.

- The Afghanistan CGA recommends interventions to enhance female education, health, participation in the labor force and micro-credit schemes, entitlements and protections in Family Law, and the collection of gender-disaggregated data across sectors to document women's and men's involvement and monitor outcomes and investment effects.

The report has influenced follow-up studies on gender and micro-finance and parental attitudes toward girls' education. *Microfinance and Gender Roles in Afghanistan* (2006) offers insights on how to not only increase women's rates of using micro-finance, but also strengthen their control over micro-loan resources. In *Household Decision-Making and School Enrollment in Afghanistan*, four case studies identify interventions that enhance parents' incentives to invest in the education of their daughters.

- One of the central pillars of the Bangladesh PRSP and CAS is actively mainstreaming gender into the preparation process.

Preparation of the CGA has involved a series of in-country consultations, promoting ongoing debate about gender issues. Consultations have cemented Bank partnerships with champions of gender equality in the Government of Bangladesh, other donors such as AusAID, local research organizations such as the Bangladesh Institute of Development Studies (BIDS), independent researchers, and women's rights organizations. Survey and other data collection activities related to the CGA's study of gender norms and outcomes have yielded new sources of both qualitative and quantitative data.

- Co-funded by the Bank and the Department for International Development (DFID), the Nepal GSEA is being followed by joint work supported by a three-year DFID Social Exclusion Action Program (SEAP).

Related studies are monitoring the GSEA's influence on formal policy making and sector programs. Gender mainstreaming has occurred in the Midterm Expenditure Framework and in water resources management projects, in part due to the following findings: groups are an effective modality for empowering women, facilitating their greater inclusion, and creating longer-term development outcomes; inclusive pro-poor budgeting more effectively ensures full access for women than do targeted programs; building water collection and distribution systems in villages saves each woman per village household six hours per day.

- It was the Pakistan CGA that first used primary quantitative and qualitative data to understand the nexus between social norms, female mobility constraints, and other determinants of gender inequality.

Analysis-informed design has improved existing projects, such as programs in Sindh and Punjab that provide stipends to girls enrolled in middle schools. Insights about mobility constraints on middle school attendance have inspired the Gender Network to fund a pilot project response. The report has influenced pre-PRSP discussions, leading to the explicit recognition that PRSP formulation must reflect gender challenges. The CGA was accompanied by a companion volume of background papers by local experts urging amendments to Family Law and law on violence against women. Timely dissemination of both volumes in May 2006 provoked discussion among women's rights groups, whose activism helped effect the National Assembly's passage of the Women's Protection Bill (WPB). Now rape cases will be governed by penal law rather than by the religious-based Hudood Ordinances, one of which requires four male witnesses to prove rape.

BANK CONTRIBUTION AND KEY FACTORS FOR SUCCESS

In addition to providing technical support and funding for the reports, the Bank has facilitated policy/strategy dialogue with stakeholders during the preparation process-itself a vehicle for focusing debate on the need to enhance women's voice as well as access to service delivery. Key among the factors for success is:

- Including stakeholders (e.g., in government, civil society organizations, local research and academic institutions) from the earliest phases of preparation,
- Iteratively consulting stakeholders and country teams to encourage debate, collect data, and ensure stakeholder feedback, buy-in, and ownership throughout preparation and dissemination,
- Identifying and cultivating government champions at all levels,
- Ensuring Country Director Ownership.

LESSONS LEARNED/STRATEGY GOING FORWARD

Gender reports will continue to provide cutting-edge analytical work that-in collaboration with clients- can heighten awareness and in-country debate, as well as enhance political will and consensus in policy implementation. For outcomes to be successful, however, analysis findings must be operationalized. Bank projects and other policy support lending should be guided by the insights of analysis, and the *preparation process* should continue to fuel debate that helps prioritize interventions.

These efforts require complementary government actions, e.g. creating appropriate institutional frameworks to support women's training, market linkages, access to credit and child care facilities, and schooling infrastructure. Ultimately, sustainable improvement of women's welfare requires strengthening their ability to influence decision-making both within and outside the household. Unless women are integrated into the political sphere as critical actors, progress will remain slow. This integration can occur by

1. Facilitating empowerment programs that seek to build women's networks and solidarity around issues such as micro-credit; and
2. Integrating women's voice into local governments. The region's work program to improve service delivery by supporting local governments offers great opportunity to build capacity of newly elected women leaders as part of gender mainstreaming efforts.

Though the practice of the criminal law occasionally may be "coarse," this decision reflects the images and stereotypes that associate the law with masculinity. These images were used to justify the virtual exclusion of women from the prestigious and powerful legal profession in the United States until the 1970s. Despite Justice Ryan's vivid language, the reasons for men's resistance to women lawyers "likely has to do with the law's close relationship to power in our society".

The legal profession structures power relations between groups and classes by shaping the rules and laws that open or limit opportunities without resort to force, making it the quintessential male power role. For many years, by controlling its own membership, the legal community was able to limit both the number of lawyers and the social diversity of those admitted to practice. It did this by exercising both formal control over admissions to law school and bar membership, and informal referral and social mechanisms. These processes enforced the understanding that outsiders such as women and racial minorities would be excluded from the legal community or would be kept on its fringes in low-visibility, low-prestige specialties, serving others like themselves.

Since the 1960s, the legal world has undergone several major changes. The number of lawyers has more than doubled. The nature and organization of legal work have also changed. There are fewer lawyers in solo practice and more who work in large law firms and in salaried positions with corporations and government agencies. Law firms have greatly increased in size and become more bureaucratized and hierarchical. New areas, such as public interest law, have emerged, and the number of women lawyers has mushroomed. Thus, women's growing presence in the law beginning in the 1970s occurred as part of the changing legal context, while the growing representation of women stimulates further change in the organization and activities of lawyers.

Women now comprise more than a quarter of the legal profession and about half of all law students, but their numerical gains have not yielded equivalent increases in power and opportunities. As the report of the American Bar Association (ABA) Commission on Women in the Profession, *The Unfinished Agenda,* concluded, despite substantial progress toward equal opportunity, the agenda [established by this group in 1987] remains unfinished. Women in the legal profession remain underrepresented in positions of greatest status, influence and economic reward.... The problems are compounded by the lack of consensus that there are in fact serious problems.

This chapter explores the history of women in the legal profession, the nature and organization of the work done by attorneys, the changes that have occurred across the legal landscape, and the ways that gendered legal culture and its images have severely disadvantaged women lawyers. In these chapters, we present a general discussion of women's integration into the legal profession rather than focusing explicitly on criminal law because no such specialized data are available and because most of the barriers to women are encountered across legal settings.

BARRIERS TO WOMEN IN LAW BEFORE 1970

In 1638, Margaret Brent became executor of the estate of Lord Calvert, governor of the Maryland colony. Although it is known that she was the first woman to practice law in colonial America, little else is known about women practicing law until the mid-1800s. Women were barred from both law schools and state bar associations. It is possible that a few women appeared in court in their own behalf and others practiced law in the frontier areas. However, few women pursued legal careers. In 1869, Iowa became the first state to admit a woman, Arabella Mansfield, to the bar.

Three years later, Charlotte E. Ray, daughter of leaders of New York's Underground Railroad, became the first African-American woman admitted to the bar. In other jurisdictions, however, women applicants were denied membership. For example, in 1872, Myra Bradwell, who was denied admittance by the Illinois State Supreme Court, appealed to the U.S. Supreme Court claiming that her rights under the Equal Protection Clause of the Fourteenth Amendment had been violated.

The Court, denying her appeal, stated, The natural and proper timidity and delicacy which belongs to the female sex evidently unfits it for the practice of law.... [Additionally] a woman has no legal existence separate from her husband... [so that]... a married woman is incapable, without her husband's consent, of making contracts which shall be binding on her or him, whereas unmarried women are "exceptions to the general rule" of marriage.

The Court's decision in *Bradwell* permitted states to exclude women from practicing law. Since admission to a state bar is the prerequisite for practicing law in that state, women had to challenge their exclusion state by state in order to gain the right to practice law. It was not until 1920, 51 years after women first became lawyers in the United States that women were permitted to practice law before the courts in every state.

Women also were excluded from membership in the ABA until 1918 and from the prestigious Association of the Bar of the City of New York until 1937. Consequently, they were kept from the networks through which lawyers gain contacts, referrals, and power. Between 1870 and 1950, American lawyers as a professional group successfully controlled the market for their services. They developed local, state, and national bar associations; created codes of ethics; and established disciplinary procedures to control the quality of legal services.

They also maintained tight entrance requirements into the profession through control over the standards and admission practices of the emerging law schools. Thus, the ABA and state bars limited the numbers and controlled the characteristics of new lawyers. As a result, despite the vast economic growth during the first half of the 20th century in the United States, the population-to-lawyer ratio was the same in 1950 as it was in 1900, and the legal profession consisted of white men mostly in solo practice.

By the end of the 19th century, the professionalization of legal practice had led to an increasing proportion of lawyers with formal legal education. Until 1900, the most common route to the bar was "reading the law" and serving as an apprentice or "clerk" to a working lawyer. As apprenticeship routes disappeared, even these limited opportunities for women to enter law were reduced by women's exclusion from the academic route.

Although Washington University in St. Louis was the first law school to admit women in 1869, access to legal education remained very limited. Many law schools, particularly the most elite, denied admittance to women altogether. Columbia only opened its doors to women in 1928, and Harvard did so in 1950. Even when women were admitted, quotas and other restrictive barriers kept their numbers small. With a sufficient supply of qualified men applicants and in the absence of antidiscrimination laws, the academic gatekeepers excluded or limited the numbers of men and women of color and white women. For many decades, law classes typically had a maximum of three women. Although academics protested that the low numbers were due to women's disinterest, statistics that appeared in the *Harvard Law Record* in 1965 suggest a pattern of discrimination.

Despite increasing numbers of women applicants, women constituted about 3 percent in each class between 1951 and 1965. Women remained less than 5 percent of the enrollment at ABA-approved law schools until the 1970s. Both faculty and men students made the educational environment inhospitable to women. While all students were subject to ridicule, particularly if they did not provide the right response when called on in class, women were rarely called on, and on such occasions, they were subjected to questions designed to embarrass them (e.g., being asked to explain the details of rape cases) or were humiliated by such comments as "better go back to the kitchen" if they stumbled in recitation. Additionally, women knew they would be expected to respond on "Ladies' Day," which for many professors and men students a show was put on at the women's expense.

For example, one professor sat in the audience asking questions and told all the women in the class to stand at the podium "rather like performing bears". In 1972, passage of Title IX of the Higher Education Act prohibited discrimination based on sex in the enrollment of students and hiring of faculty. Facing denial of federal financial assistance if they continued to discriminate, law schools finally began to admit more women and allow them to compete equally with men. Since that time, women's enrollments have grown dramatically; in 2004, they constituted about half (48 percent) of the students enrolled in law school and 51 percent of those awarded JDs.

The next hurdle for women lawyers was finding a job. Even women with training from elite schools faced employment discrimination that was openly practiced well into the 1970s. For example, a 1963 survey of 430 law firms found that "female status" was the characteristic that got the most negative rating in selecting new recruits. Thus, it is not surprising that in 1965, fewer than 20 percent of the 104 firms responding to a *Harvard Law Record* questionnaire employed any women lawyers. Women who were able to obtain legal work often were offered opportunities in low-status specialties deemed appropriate for women, such as domestic relations and probate law. They received lower pay and were denied partnerships and opportunities for leadership in bar associations.

For example, when former Supreme Court Justice Sandra Day O'Connor graduated third in her class at Stanford Law School in 1953, the only job that she was offered was as a legal secretary. Women also were rarely found on the bench. The first woman justice of the peace was appointed in 1890, but it was not until 1979 that a woman had served at some level of the judicial system in all 50 states. Similarly, the first woman on the federal bench, Francis Allen, was appointed by President Roosevelt to the Circuit (Appellate) Court in 1934. The next was appointed to the U.S. District Court in 1949 by President Truman. By 1977, only eight women had ever served in the federal judiciary at the District or Circuit Court level.

Women were not the only group excluded from the practice of law. In fact, the club-like homogeneity of law firms that hired only white Anglo-Saxon Protestant men has only gradually, and often grudgingly, moved toward greater representativeness. The first step was made by Jewish and Catholic men during the 1950s and 1960s. White women broke through by the late 1970s. Informal barriers against persons of color remain high. The history of the struggle of women in the United States to enter the legal profession was similar to women's struggles in England, other Commonwealth nations, and Europe. In England, the Inns of Court controlled entry into the ranks of barristers (as well as the judiciary that is drawn from this group) and succeeded in excluding women who sued for admission through several judicial interpretations of the law until 1918.

In that year, Parliament passed the Sex Disqualification (Removal) Act largely as a reward for women's performance during World War I. But as in the United States, admission did not end discrimination, and through the 1950s, the number of women admitted to the bar grew even more slowly than in the United States. In Canada, Clara Brett Martin sought but was denied admission to the Ontario Bar in 1891. The provincial government, however, swiftly asked the Ontario legislature to permit the Law Society of Upper Canada to admit women, although it took several years and two separate acts of the legislature in 1897 before Ms. Martin was called to the bar.

In Australia, the various territories admitted women to the legal profession separately but mostly before the mother country did. Women were admitted to the bar in Victoria in 1903, followed by Tasmania (1904), Queensland (1905), South Australia (1911), New South Wales (1918), and Western Australia. Nevertheless, Australian women as late as 1980 were underrepresented in the profession and were consigned to certain areas of practice (primarily family law). In France, much of the argument over the admission of women to the legal profession took place after their admission to the bar in 1900.

Although the government had little difficulty in overturning what it considered a grievous wrong in a court ruling in 1897 that denied a woman the right to admission, the majority of members of the legal profession were not happy about the government's policy. Questions about women's competence lingered, and few women sought legal careers for the next several decades after they were permitted to do so. Across these diverse nations, many of the arguments used to exclude or limit women were similar: the law was and continues to be "constructed as male" (i.e., presumed to be rational, logical, dispassionate, objective, professional, intimidating and demanding), while women are presumed to lack these qualities.

OPENING LEGAL PRACTICE TO WOMEN

In the past four decades, there have been a number of major changes in the legal profession. These include an enormous increase in the number of law schools and lawyers;

an opening of the profession to white women and people of color; a shift in the type and organization of legal employment, including increases in firm size and bureaucratization; increases in the number of hours worked and the salaries paid to lawyers (particularly those in private practice); and a diminution of the legal profession's control over lawyers' behavior. Each of these changes has affected and been affected by the expanded role of women in law.

CHANGING LABOR QUEUES AND DEMOGRAPHICS

From 1960 to the present, there has been a phenomenal growth in the number of lawyers and in the ratio of lawyers to the general population. The number of lawyers in the United States grew from about 222,000 in 1950 to 355,000 in 1971, 542,000 in 1980, 806,000 in 1991, and 909,019 in 2000. The growth rate was about 25 percent during the 1950s and 1960s and rose to about 50 percent in the 1970s and 1980s, but slowed down in the 1990s. The ratio of lawyers to the population of the United States also increased markedly. Between 1950 and 1991, the number of lawyers almost quadrupled, but the size of the U.S. population did not even double. Thus, while there was one lawyer for every 679 people in 1950, by 1991 this ratio stood at one lawyer for every 313 people, and in 2000 that ratio was 264 to 1.

One consequence of this growth is the legal profession's gradual loss of control over its composition. Restrictions on the training of lawyers prior to 1960 led to a shortage of lawyers, expansion in the number of law schools in the 1960s, and willingness to turn to less expensive women lawyers by the 1970s. Greater demand also led to higher starting salaries that, in turn, made the law a more attractive career option. The civil rights, women's, consumers,' and environmental movements of the 1960s expanded new areas of the law and the demand for lawyers. As racial and sexual barriers to entry into law fell, the number of aspiring lawyers more than doubled, while the number of law schools rose by 25 percent.

The number of new lawyers being trained in the mid-1980s was three times greater than that in the mid- 1960s; since then, the expansion of the profession has continued, but the rate of growth is slower. There have been dramatic changes in the demographic composition of the legal profession over the past 30 years. These include a vast increase in the proportion of white women and a small increase in men and women of color. But this increasingly young and diverse profession remains dominated by elderly white men. Since men's enrollment in law schools has remained stable while women's has multiplied, most of the growth in the profession represents an increase in the number of women law students and lawyers.

In 1960, women comprised only 3.5 percent of the enrollees at ABA-approved law schools; in 1970, they comprised 8.5 percent; in 1980, they comprised 33.6 percent; and in 1986, they comprised 40.2 percent. As of 2005, women represented virtually half (48 percent) of all law students in the United States (ABA, 2006). Of the new entrants to the bar in 2003, 46 percent were women, 17 percent were nonwhite (compared to 5 percent in 1970), and 2.5 percent were openly gay or lesbian. Similarly, the number of women lawyers in Canada and Australia in the past 25 years has mushroomed. In 2004, women comprised just fewer than 50 percent of law students in Australia compared with only 20 percent in 1970. In Canada, in 2003 women represented 53 percent of the law school graduates.

CHANGES IN THE TYPE AND NATURE OF LEGAL EMPLOYMENT

The organization of legal work also has changed enormously since 1960. Most lawyers still work in private settings and either serve large corporations or serve small businesses and individuals. However, an increasing proportion of attorneys now work in law firms rather than as solo practitioners, and their work is increasingly specialized. Not only are there more law firms, but they are much larger in size and are increasingly hierarchical and bureaucratic.

For example, the proportion of lawyers in solo practice declined from 61 percent in 1960 to about 34 percent in 2000. At the same time, the number of lawyers in firms with 50 or more lawyers grew from 7.3 percent in 1980 to 18.2 percent in 2000. Increases in size and bureaucratization have occurred not only in private law firms but in corporation counsel's offices and government legal departments. A study of lawyers in Chicago found that the average number of lawyers in the private law firm in 1975 was 27; by 1995, the average firm had 141 lawyers. Similarly, the average size of house counsel offices (lawyers working in corporations and other private organizations) grew from 17 in 1975 to 55 in 1995, and on average, government law offices grew from 64 to 399 between 1975 and 1995.

A result of these changes is an increase in the proportion of lawyers who are salaried workers. More lawyers work for government and private industry now than 50 or 20 years ago. The nature of the work also shifted, as an increasing proportion of lawyers' activities involved work for corporate/business clients rather than individuals. The ideal of professional practice represented in the law firm traditionally rested on service to clients, the production of knowledge, and adherence to an ethical code. Partnerships were granted to associates on the basis of craftsman- ship, the individual's skills in business development, and personal qualities and "fit" within the "brotherhood" of the firm.

The social structure of firms began to change in the late 1970s and 1980s and accelerated in the 1990s as law firms mushroomed in size, hired persons from diverse backgrounds, and began recruiting associates laterally from competing firms by offering more money and a swifter move to partnership. Within the firm, competition and stress replaced "fraternity" and collegiality. Clients, once property of the firm, became property of individual lawyers. To support their rising costs, firms put growing emphasis on the bottom line, and with it came a change in compensation systems from those based on seniority to those emphasizing productivity, particularly client development (i.e., "rainmaking").

This shift advantaged men and disadvantaged women since much of rainmaking activity occurs on the golf course and in extra-work hours activities at bar association meetings and social clubs among persons who give single-minded attention to the job and avoid outside obligations. Firms compete by adding specialty departments in areas of high demand and striving to enhance profitability by increasing the ratio of associates to partners, as well as creating several types of partnerships. With the economic downturn in the early 1990s, law firms for the first time laid off lawyers and decreased the proportion of associates elevated to partner. Currently, both partners and younger associate lawyers face enormous pressures to win and hold client.

In addition, the number of billable hours (i.e., those chargeable to a particular client or account) per year expected of and actually worked by lawyers has increased from 1,800 to as much as 2,300 hours annually to meet the costs of spiraling salaries and growing demands of clients. For example, a study of practicing lawyers in Calgary, Alberta, Canada, found that they average 50 hours per week in the office and that more than half (52 percent) take work home, and their evening and weekend work adds another 5.5 hours, resulting in a median of 53 hours a week of work. These changes in the size, composition, structure, and function of the legal profession have affected its self-governance by breaking down the control formerly exercised by the ABA and state bar associations and subjecting lawyers to more external regulation.

The changes also have increased stratification of the legal profession according to practitioner background, clientele, function, and reward. As sociologist Richard Abel (1986) predicted, and as will be elaborated shortly, increasing heterogeneity within the profession has resulted in differential ranking within the legal profession and segregation associated with racial and gender differences. Changing job queues and expanded demand for women lawyers have enabled them to enter the field, but these changes have occurred at the same time as the legal profession has become more stratified, bureaucratized, competitive, and specialized. Consequently, as will be shown, the legal profession remains gendered despite dramatic changes in the past three decades. To understand why, it is necessary to examine other factors that also have affected both changes in the profession and women's place in it in the past 40 years.

THE CHANGING LEGAL ENVIRONMENT

Civil rights laws have contributed to change in the legal profession by opening the doors to law schools and legal work for women and persons of color. Title VII of the Civil Rights Act of 1964, the 1972 Amendments to Title VII, and the 1972 Educational Amendments Act were of particular importance to aspiring women lawyers. The 1972 Amendments to Title VII extended antidiscrimination provisions to all employers with 15 or more workers, including many law firms, as well as to state and local government agencies and educational institutions. It also allowed the Justice Department to bring "pattern or practice" lawsuits.

When this provision was applied to include the placement offices of law schools that served as employment agencies and made them targets for lawsuits, they radically altered their gate keeping functions. The 1972 Educational Amendments Act prohibited sex discrimination in all public institutions of higher learning receiving federal monies, including major university law schools. This not only opened enrollment to women students, but affected the distribution of scholarships and the hiring and promotion of women faculty members. It also made it illegal for law firms to openly refuse to interview or hire women.

WOMEN LAWYERS USING THE NEW LAWS

Opening employment opportunities in law to women required lawsuits against the legal establishment. These suits have gradually brought about changes in the legal profession's treatment of women in practice, teaching, and the job market. At first, women students at New York University and Columbia Law Schools, with the participation of Columbia Law School's Employment Rights Project, set out to end exclusionary practices in elite Wall Street firms. Pooling information about job interview experiences, they concluded that these firms were not taking their applications seriously. They complained to their school's placement office, and with help from the Employment Rights Project (and funding from the Equal Employment Opportunity Commission), several women filed complaints with the New York City Human Rights Commission against 10 firms on behalf of all women law students in New York.

In 1976, seven years after initiation of their suit, all of the firms agreed to settlements similar to those reached following findings of employment discrimination in two test cases. In the first case decided, *Kohn v. Royall, Koegel and Wells*, the court determined that the firm had systematically discriminated against women in hiring. The firm agreed to a complex formula, including a guarantee that it would offer at least 25 percent of its positions each year to women. In the other case, the court found that Diane Blank's interviewer from the firm of Sullivan and Cromwell had admitted that the firm was biased, discouraged her interest in the firm, failed to examine her resume, and asked about her lawyer-husband's career. Sullivan and Cromwell also agreed to a settlement that included the provision that in addition to hiring women, it would not hold social events in clubs that excluded women. The other eight firms cited in the initial complaint adopted similar guidelines.

Despite antidiscrimination laws, women law students and faculty had to keep up pressure on law school placement offices through the 1970s to force law firms to recruit women seriously or face sanctions. In some instances, women students sued placement offices. By the end of the decade, law firm recruiting had changed; while old prejudices remain, most firms have eliminated blatant discrimination. The next legal barrier was posed by the partnership decision. In *Hishon v. King & Spalding* (1984), the U.S. Supreme Court legally recognized that promotion to partnership is an area covered under Title VII. Earlier, the courts had treated partnerships as voluntary associations that must be congenial for all concerned, because partners are liable for the negligent acts of any copartner.

In *Hishon*, the Court rejected the argument that the choice of partners was protected under the First Amendment right to freedom of association. It ruled that Title VII does not force partnerships to accept less qualified individuals. Nevertheless, consideration for partnership is a "term, condition, or privilege" of the original employment contract covered under Title VII, and, as such, a partnership decision must be made on a fair and equal basis without regard to the applicant's sex. The next hurdle for women was addressing discrimination in the actual decision-making process. Since the decision to admit an individual to a partnership usually involves both objective and subjective factors and a collaborative decision, identifying the "real cause" of such decisions often is impossible.

In a 1989 decision, *Price Waterhouse v. Hopkins* (which actually dealt with issues of partnership in an accounting firm, but the issues raised in this case apply more generally to partnerships), a fragmented Supreme Court failed to establish either clear grounds for determining when discrimination has occurred or the rules of the fight. The facts of the case were clear. Ann Hopkins, a senior manager at the Price Water house accounting firm, was denied a partnership in a "mixed motive" case (i.e., one in which there were multiple reasons for denying partnership, only some of which were related to her gender). Ms. Hopkins had generated more new business for the firm than any of the 85 men who also applied for partnership at the same time; she was also known to be a demanding and difficult supervisor.

In the usual manner, Price Waterhouse solicited comments from partners about candidates who had applied for partnership. Among the 32 comments regarding Ms. Hopkins were 13 supporting admittance and 8 for rejection. The decision was put on hold, and when two of Hopkins' supporters withdrew their support, partnership was denied. The lower courts ruled that once a plaintiff has established that an illegal motive played a significant part in the decision to deny partnership, the burden of proof shifts to the defendant to show that no discrimination actually occurred. In the *Price*

Waterhouse case, the lower court suggested that Ms. Hopkins' management style was a legitimate reason for putting her partnership application on hold.

Nevertheless, the firm still was liable because the partnership process gave unacceptably great weight to negative comments that reflected unconscious sexual stereotypes by male evaluators. Among the suspect comments were statements that Ms. Hopkins needed a "course at charm school" and, from her primary supporter, that she would improve her chances of becoming a partner if she would "wear make up, have her hair styled, and wear jewelry" (at 1116-1117). The Supreme Court overruled the lower courts and raised the threshold for showing discriminatory intent.

The Court was split, with Justice O'Connor in the middle as the swing vote on two issues: the amount of evidence needed to show a discriminatory motive that triggers a shift in the burden of proof from plaintiff to the defendant, and the degree to which discriminatory intent is the cause of the decision. As Madek and O'Brien (1990) predicted, such a split decision led to legislation to resolve these issues. In 1991, Congress amended Title VII of the Civil Rights Act with the provision that stated, an unlawful employment practice is established when the complaining party demonstrates that race, color, religion, sex or national origin was a motivating factor for any employment practice, even though other factors also motivated the practice.

In a recent case interpreting the scope of the statute with respect to the amount of evidence, *Desert Palace v. Costa* (2003), the Supreme Court unanimously adopted a straightforward application of the statutory provision. It ruled that "a motivating factor" means that if race or gender plays any role, however minor, in an employer's decision, the plaintiff has established liability. In that instance, all the employer can do is limiting the amount of award for the plaintiff's full remedies. Thus, the requirement for "direct" evidence of discriminatory intent called for in Justice O'Connor's decision in *Price Waterhouse* was eliminated.

CHALLENGING DISCRIMINATORY PRACTICES

Women lawyers soon encountered discriminatory practices and gendered interactions in the courthouse that threatened their livelihoods. Because these practices often were perpetrated or tolerated by judges, women lawyers could not safely challenge them individually. Instead, attorneys from the National Organization for Women's Legal Defense and Education Fund, in cooperation with the National Association of Women Judges, designed a program to call attention to "gender bias" in the law, decision making, and courtroom interaction in state judicial systems. To make this change strategy palatable to judges and other gatekeepers in the legal system, the program was focused on collecting state-specific information about "gender bias."

Such bias was defined as existing when people are denied rights or burdened with responsibilities solely on the basis of gender;... people are subjected to stereotypes about the proper behavior of men and women which ignore their situations; people are treated differently on the basis of gender in situations where gender should make no difference; [and] men or women as a group can be subjected to a legal rule, policy or practice which produces worse results for them than for the other group. Thus, gender bias includes both overt discrimination and more subtle practices.

The program was designed as part of the judiciary's continuing judicial education efforts and employed a new approach, creation of gender bias task forces, to document such bias in the courts. The first such body, the New Jersey Supreme Court's Task Force on Women in the Courts, was established in November 1982 by that state's Chief Justice to investigate three issues: whether gender stereotypes affect the substantive law or impact on judicial decision making; whether a person's gender affects his or her treatment in the legal and judicial environment; and, if so, how to ensure equal treatment for women and men in court.

Its "First Year Report," published in June 1984, found substantial gender bias and led to creation of similar task forces, similar findings across jurisdictions, general acceptance of the findings, and the introduction of judicial education about gender bias in many states. During the 1990s, several Federal Circuit courts also created task forces to focus on gender bias. However, in response to the Washington, D.C. Circuit Court's report that revealed slights experienced by many women involved in the justice system similar in nature to those identified in other reports, several men judges, upset at the report's recommendations, got Congress to block funding for further gender bias studies that had been proposed in the judiciary budget.

Nevertheless, the tide has clearly turned; as of 2001, 45 states and most Federal Circuits had created similar task forces on gender bias in the courts. Their findings have been both consistent and troubling. A substantial proportion of women lawyers (and a much smaller proportion of men) has experienced various forms of gender bias including sexual harassment and demeaning behavior in courtroom proceedings. These task forces also inspired creation of similar task forces on racial and ethnic bias in many states as well as reports by the ABA's Multicultural Women Attorneys Network.

In addition to the bench, in 1987 the ABA created the Commission on Women in the Profession chaired by Hillary Rodham Clinton to address gender discrimination throughout the legal profession. Its 1988 report to the ABA House of Delegates called on that body to recognize the persistence of discrimination against women in the legal profession and to affirm its commitment to ending barriers that prevent "full integration and equal participation of women in all aspects of the legal profession".

Since putting the legal establishment on record as opposing discrimination more than 20 years after the first surge of women into the profession, the ABA has also amended both its Model Code of Judicial Conduct and the Model Rules of Professional Conduct to include prohibitions on bias. Additionally, it has issued a number of reports that document continuing progress as well as continuing discrimination against women and men of color throughout the legal profession, and has recommend agendas for change.

THE DIVISION OF LEGAL LABOR

Although women comprised 27 percent of the legal profession as of 2000, their numerical gains have not yielded equivalent increases in power, status, and income. In brief, women are proportionally underrepresented in private practice and overrepresented in government, corporate/private industry, and legal aid and public defender (PD) work. Additionally, within each of these organizational hierarchies, women are concentrated in the bottom rungs of prestige and income; they are underrepresented in the ranks of partner, general counsel, and supervisors. This section looks at the organization and work of lawyers as well as their distribution across specialties and workplaces to set the stage for examination of the factors responsible for and the impact of these employment patterns.

THE ORGANIZATION AND WORK ACTIVITIES OF LAWYERS

In complex societies, the critical rules of social life are codified in law, and their meanings are interpreted and enforced by a group of experts on their proper application and use. These specialists in legal rules are lawyers, whose occupational specialty often is traced back to ancient Rome. The work of lawyers is advocacy or action directly or indirectly in defense of a client's interests in the courts and other forms of dispute resolution. Law is a theoretical and abstract discipline, and lawyers' work represents the practical application of legal theory and knowledge to solve real problems or advance the interests of those who have retained them for legal services.

This occurs through the court system, where the rules of the legal system are applied. Legal work revolves around the court setting, where the rules of the legal system interact with specific interests of clients or relationships between clients and the state. The public image of lawyers' activities focuses on the drama of the adversarial process in highly publicized criminal trials pitting the prosecution against the defense, with the judge serving as a referee. However, not all proceedings in court are adversarial. Most laws actually relate to civil matters that involve facilitating, regulating, or channeling activities (e.g., transmission of property, divorce, interpreting tax laws) in a given society. |

In handling cases, the lawyer's role is to adjust the needs, requests, and rights of the client in response to another party's assertion of rights, the rights of the state, or requests of the state for certain behavior (e.g., the payment of taxes). The judge's role is to exercise the authority of the legal system to constrain the activities of lawyers in their role as advocates. In the United States, the division of legal work may be examined along two major dimensions: the specific kind of legal work done and the particular setting of the practice. In each, there is stratification based on the nature of the client served. Criminal law generally deals with the poor, whereas much of civil law has to do with business matters.

More prestige and rewards accrue to lawyers who work for the elite since they become identified with the kind of clientele they associate with. Similarly, types of work settings also involve stratification. Usually, lawyers in solo practice work with poor or middle-class individuals; Wall Street and other lawyers in large and established law firms have powerful corporate clients. In between are smaller group practices, governmental legal activities, and house counsel work. Siemsen (2006) asserts that given the "moral division of labor" among lawyers, the attorneys who do society's "dirty work" by handling criminal defendants and the social problems of the poor and downtrodden are contaminated by their work and given low status; those who litigate (do trial work) with other populations are higher ranked; and at the top of the hierarchy are those who handle civil matters.

Lawyers also are stratified by specialty. Most lawyers enter civil work, and the elite among these go into business-related legal specialties. The work of Wall Street lawyers often involves helping corporate clients manage the private sector of the world economy. However, most lawyers work in smaller firms on the cases involving middle-class individuals and families and deal with wills, accidents (torts), and divorces. In addition to practicing attorneys, a number of persons with law degrees pursue careers in business, politics, teaching, or government and often move from one practice setting to another over their career. In the past quarter century, there has been an erosion of the independence and autonomy of lawyers, resulting in the "post-professional world".

Three key forces have undermined professional control: increasing specialization, the loss of exclusivity, and the growth of technology to access information. As a result, services previously provided exclusively by lawyers now are being delivered by other occupational groups (e.g., accountants and public relations firms), and at the same time, individuals now access legal services and information on the Internet, without having to consult lawyers. The practice of law rests on an institutional foundation, organizational constraints, and professional tasks. Although it is assumed that there are boundaries between a lawyer's work and private life, these are fluid because they are subject to open-ended demands from clients and from processes such as networking.

At the task level, lawyers are expected to be endlessly available to pursue their careers in a single-minded manner. At the organizational level, they are assumed to be willing to work overtime without direct compensation as a sign of "commitment". At an institutional level, professional autonomy rests on a system of private social support that is required to ensure release time from private (e.g., home and family) obligations. In addition to long work hours, professional success also requires some "leisure" time to pursue professional networking to make contacts and garner new clients.

With respect to both work time and "leisure" time, professional men have an advantage over women because they can expand hours spontaneously, flexibly, and informally and thus can more easily meet the organizational expectation of professions that they put work first. The professional model thus rests on men's experience of release from domestic burdens; it gives men an implicit advantage that becomes visible by focusing on the ability to control professional time. This, in turn, rests on a "negotiated release from private time to have access to professional time".

PRIVATE LAW PRACTICE

About three quarters of lawyers are in private practice. However, there is wide variation in the kinds of practice, their positions within firms, the types of legal work they do, and their incomes. Women currently are only slightly less likely to enter private practice than their male counterparts; however, they leave private practice earlier and at a higher rate than their male counterparts in both the United States and Canada. The turnover rate is compounded for women who encounter discrimination and women of color.

A recent study found that from 1998 to 2003, nearly two thirds (64.4 percent) of minority females left private firms within 55 months of being hired (National Association for Law Placement Foundation, 2003). Women are more likely than men to be in solo practice (53 percent versus 47 percent, respectively. Among lawyers in firms, women are more likely than men to enter large firms that offer higher starting salaries, greater prestige, and more advancement potential than small or medium-sized firms.

This apparent initial advantage was offset during the 1990s, however, by the reduction in the percentage of lawyers in private practice elevated to partnership, just as large numbers of women became eligible for elevation. In practice, this change has had a more pronounced effect on women's chances for partnerships than men's. As a result, a disproportionate number of women lawyers have remained at the associate level and the rate at which women have moved from private practice to other employment sectors is higher than that of men.

For example, in a recent survey of law graduates between 1970 and 1999 from five elite law schools, 51 percent of the men but only 40 percent of the women who entered private practice remained with a law firm in 2000, and 55 percent of the men but only 33 percent of the women remaining in firms had become partners. Additionally, women move up firm mobility ladders 37 percent more slowly than men and appear to be increasingly ghettoized within the legal profession.

IN-HOUSE COUNSEL AND CORPORATE LAW

In 2000, about 8 percent of lawyers worked in corporations or for private industry. Women constituted nearly a quarter of this group in the mid-1990s and more than a third in 2000. However, they are not distributed evenly across in-house counsel departments of different sizes or types of business firms. They comprise 15 percent of the general counsels (i.e., top legal officers) in Fortune 500 organizations. Despite similarities in their educational credentials, there are gender differences in the routes by which men and women found such jobs and in their current positions, salaries, and promotion opportunities.

Men employed as in-house counsels disproportionately worked for corporations in the manufacturing sector and in large departments that offer substantial salaries and opportunities for advancement. In contrast, women holding in-house counsel positions were concentrated in the financial services sector and in medium-sized legal departments offering lower pay and fewer mobility opportunities. In the study of graduates from five elite law schools, the women and men in corporate legal departments differed regarding advancement. In 2000, more than half of the men but only one third of the women were general counsels; women were disproportionately represented at the assistant and associate general counsel ranks despite having two years more tenure than the men.

WOMEN AND MEN IN GOVERNMENT WORK

A disproportionately large number of women attorneys are employed in government work, particularly at the state and local levels. In 1980, 17 percent of women lawyers but only 9 percent of men lawyers worked for a government. An additional 4.8 percent of women and 1.2 percent of men worked in legal aid or PD offices. In 2000, the gender gap was reduced, as 10.5 percent of women and 6.5 percent of men lawyers worked for federal, state, or local governments, and 1.7 percent of women and 0.7 percent of men worked for legal aid or PD offices.

As women have increased their representation in law, more have found work in private practice. Nevertheless, more than a third of the lawyers in each of the government and PD settings are women. Women of coloı are especially likely to work in these settings.

Several factors have contributed to the concentration of women in government and PD legal work. It may be attractive to women because it offers more regular and flexible hours, requires little "rainmaking" activity (i.e., bringing in clients), and is a less hostile work environment given the greater presence of other women.

It also may be a "fallback" rather than the preferred option, particularly for African-American women. In a study of black women lawyers in New York, Simpson (1996) found that of the 44 percent who began their careers in government, only 21 percent stated that was their first choice of position they sought. Despite these advantages, women rated the government work environment lower than the environment in private legal settings in terms of opportunities for salary increases, professional development, and achieving career goals than did women in law firms.

Prosecutors constitute the small fraction of government lawyers involved directly in the criminal justice system. National data on the number and positions of women in these offices are not available. Nevertheless, several individual women have achieved high visibility as chiefs of important prosecutor's offices. The best know is Janet Reno, who was Attorney General of the United States during the Clinton administration.

THE JUDICIARY

Because judges have great power and prestige and appointment to the bench usually occurs as a "reward" for a successful legal career, it is not surprising that women comprise a smaller proportion of the judiciary than the legal profession. There were very few women judges before 1970, but since that time, the number of female judges at both the state and federal levels has grown, particularly in the 1990s. Despite recent gains, women still are underrepresented on the bench. At the start of 2001, women accounted for 22 percent of federal district and appellate judges (166 out of the 760 judges serving on the U.S. Court of Appeals and U.S. District Courts.

This is double the percentage in the early 1990s.At the state and local level, there has been similar growth: in 1970, there were only 200 women state court judges, when they comprised 1 percent of the state court judiciary. In 1991, 10 percent of the judges on courts of last resort and 10 percent of intermediate appellate court judges were women. By 2005, women comprised 22 percent of district court judges, 25.6 percent of circuit (appellate) court judges, and 28 percent of the justices on state courts of last resort.

The first breakthrough for women at the federal level came during President Carter's term (1976–1980), when 40 new women, including seven blacks and one Hispanic, were appointed to the bench. President Reagan appointed the first woman, Sandra Day O'Connor, to the U.S. Supreme Court in 1981. President Clinton appointed 100 women judges (29 percent of his judicial appointments), nearly triple the number appointed by Presidents George H. W. Bush and Reagan; he also appointed a second woman, Ruth Bader Ginsberg, to the Supreme Court in 1993.

Additionally, 25 percent of Clinton's appointees were persons of color, com- pared with 15 percent of Reagan's and 12.4 percent of G. H. W. Bush's appointees. Women have also slowly increased their representation on the bench in England, Wales, Canada, and Australia. In England and Wales, in 1998 women comprised 10.3 percent of the judiciary. By October

2004, they comprised 15.4 percent of court judges (and ethnic minority group members comprised 3.4 percent). Nevertheless, the representation of each group decreases the higher one goes in the judicial system. Thus, only 9 of the 107 High Court Judges and 1 of 12 Law Lords (the most senior judges) are women.

In Australia, the first woman judge, Dame Roma Mitchell, was appointed to the judiciary in 1965, but few women were appointed to the bench for another 30 years. A major catalyst for addressing "gender bias in the judiciary" occurred in 1993. A judge of the South Australian Supreme Court, during the course of a marital rape trial, stated that "rougher than usual handling" was acceptable on the part of a husband toward a wife unwilling to engage in conjugal relations. This led to a public outcry, government reviews of practices for making judicial appointments, and several commissions of inquiry. Although the number of women in the judiciary has grown, there currently are no women on Australia's High Court. In contrast, three of Canada's nine Supreme Court justices (including the Chief Justice) are women.

LAW SCHOOL TEACHING

Only 1 percent of lawyers go into full-time law school teaching, yet they have a disproportionate effect on the law as role models, gate-keepers, and shapers of the next generation of practitioners. In addition, their legal writing affects lawyers' arguments and judicial decisions. Initially, the barriers to women achieving faculty positions in law schools were even higher than those facing legal practitioners. In 1950, there were only 5 women law faculty members; they accounted for less than 0.5 percent of tenure-track faculty in law schools. By 1977, the number of women had grown to 391 professors, who made up 8.6 percent of the tenure-track faculty, mostly at a few new and generally low-status law schools.

A decade later, Richard Chused's (1988) survey of law school faculty composition during the 1986–1987 academic year indicated that women comprised 20 percent of full-time faculty, including 45 percent of the professional skills teachers of legal writing and clinical law (who often are not considered regular faculty). His study also provided evidence that women were being denied tenure at high-prestige law schools at disproportionate rates.

While about half of both the men and women law faculty candidates overall were given tenure, schools with a low proportion of women faculty, including a disproportionate share of prestigious schools, granted tenure to women at lower rates (41 percent) than men (51 percent). Additionally, he found that data on the representation of men and women of color on law school faculties suggested continuing discrimination in hiring. In the past two decades, women in legal education have made substantial progress, although they still are not fully represented in leadership positions and are clustered in the least prestigious academic specialties and positions.

As of the 2004–2005 school years, women comprised 35 percent of law school faculty but only 25 percent of tenured faculty. They also were 19 percent of law school deans but 67 percent of the assistant deans who generally have staff positions that are not stepping-stones to deanships. Of the women faculty and deans, 11 per-cent were African-American women, 4 percent were Hispanic, and 3 percent were Asian-American (ABA, 2006). Angel (2000) documented the continuation of the trend earlier noted in Chused's (1988) study that suggests that within legal education a new caste system is emerging.

The majority of legal writing and clinical skills instructors, who usually are not on a tenure track, comprise the new lowest caste in that emerging system, and most of these instructors are women. In both clinical practice and legal writing fields, men are a minority, but they are overrepresented in tenured or tenure-track positions, while women disproportionately occupy the non tenure contract slots and receive lower pay. For example, women comprise 50 percent of clinical skills teachers. However, 55 percent of the men but only 37 percent of these women clinicians are tenured or in tenure-track positions. Similarly, women comprise 70 percent of the legal writing teachers, but men are twice as likely as women legal writing instructors to be tenured.

Angel's (2000) study also indicates a new trend in law schools and universities: a decrease in the percentage of faculty hired for tenure-track positions and the replacement of tenured faculty with contract faculty. Thus, just as women appear poised to make substantial gains in legal teaching and other academic specialties, they encounter new barriers that disproportionately limit their career opportunities. During the 1990s, the gender balance in law faculty hiring changed to women's disadvantage. In 1992–1993, women made up 50 percent of the newly hired associate professors (i.e., those who were presumably on tenure track). In 1997–1998, they comprised only 39.6 percent of those hired.

At the same time, they made up 60 per- cent of the new lecturers and instructors in 1992–1993 and 66 percent of those hired in 1997–1998 (presumably in contract rather than tenure-track positions), suggesting the growth of the "women's ghetto" in law school faculties. As these data suggest, women and men lawyers have different career paths. A study of Chicago lawyers who graduated after 1970 clearly illustrates the ways these paths increasingly diverge over time.

At the start of their careers, women are underrepresented in solo practice and small firms and overrepresented in public sector jobs. These differences grow over the course of the career as women move out of both large and small firms and into non-firm settings in government, legal aid, and corporate work. Conversely, men are less likely to leave large firms and more likely to leave government employment as their careers develop. These patterns suggest that women "choose" to leave firms due to inflexible work schedules that create tension between the competing demands of practice and family.

But Hull and Nelson also question whether this should be characterized as an exercise of "choice" or is, "in significant part, the product of the dynamics of gender inequality within legal employment" (labeled "gender constraints," which we will explore next. The issue of career patterns and "choices" also differs for white and black women. Simpson's (1996) study of black women lawyers in New York found that of the 42 percent who stated a desire to work in a law firm on completion of law school, only 27 percent found employment with a firm.

GENDERED LEGAL OCCUPATIONAL CULTURE AND BARRIERS TO WOMEN

In many ways, the legal culture is a quintessentially male world from which women have been excluded. Professional opportunities are defined by informal social networks, private (formerly all-men's) clubs, and bar associations that order status and power. Each serves as a barrier that reinforces the other. Thus, in circular fashion, the images of the law as "masculine" strengthen men's resistance to including women in informal socializing and bar association activities; their absence from informal networks and professional activities, in turn, supports the view that women do not "fit" in the profession, are not skilled at client development, and lack "commitment" to the practice of law.

Participation in the informal social world of lawyers occurs before or after long hours of legal work and means that a legal career is defined as total commitment to a "workaholic" schedule. Such work-related expectations were created when the prototypic lawyer had a wife taking care of the home and family. Most men regard the expectation of round-the-clock availability as an aspect of the legal culture that simply is one of the inevitable and necessary norms of the profession. While most women lawyers now share these professional norms, for many these work-related expectations generate difficult choices on a daily basis. When women opt not to or cannot create the impression of open-ended availability, their commitment is questioned, particularly that of women with families.

Conversely, men with families are assumed to be committed out of financial necessity and are rewarded with higher salaries. Because the prototype of the lawyer is a man, the characteristics generally associated with masculine dominance are used to explain men's successes; their failures are explained as "bad luck." Thus, men's success is regarded as a function of innate analytic and rhetorical abilities that presumably make them more suitable for practicing law. But women's success is attributed to luck, chance, or inappropriate use of their sexuality; their failures are explained as inability to "think like a lawyer".

Such gender-based schemas affect promotion and salary decisions as well. Women lawyers encounter a number of gender stereotypes and "second generation" gender bias that affect their careers. In contrast to "first generation" patterns of bias that resulted largely from deliberate intentional exclusion, "second generation" bias involves social practices and patterns of interaction among groups within the workplace that gradually exclude non-dominant groups. Often, these behaviors rest on subtle cognitive processes including "homophily preferences" (i.e., tendencies for people to prefer to associate with others like themselves) and "status expectations" (i.e., beliefs about the superiority of some people over others in relation to some task).

Together, these generate barriers for women since the men in the firm prefer to associate with others who are like themselves with whom they can communicate easily and share common interests. They also tend to expect superior performance from men compared with women and from whites compared to persons of color. Because men are valued as having higher status than women, women's competence is often evaluated more harshly than men's regardless of their numerical proportions in work groups, even when they exhibit equal performance. These disparities arise even in the absence of the evaluator's motivation to discriminate; rather, they rest on such stereotypic beliefs as the assumption that women lack aptitude for dealing with complex financial matters, are presumed not to be competent, lack commitment, and tend to overreact to criticism.

Women have to work to overcome stereotypes by which they are evaluated by demonstrating superior performance (confirming women's assertion that they have to work harder to be seen as equally competent). Bias also may take the form of excluding a woman from key social interactions, mentoring, and assignment to "big" cases, or exposure to important clients. Such behaviors individually may appear gender neutral when considered in isolation since they also are experienced by men associates. However, they cumulatively produce a pattern of gender bias when connected to broader exclusionary patterns. For example, even if a woman is willing to work around the clock, often firms make decisions based on stereotypes and assume that she will not be available or believe that she should not be.

Opportunities for such a woman are limited if the partner does not give her an assignment based on the assumption that she does not want to travel or because she is pregnant. These assumptions would not be made about an otherwise equally qualified male associate and cumulatively create a pattern of bias. Scripts prescribe norms of professional interaction such as who can do what, with whom, and under what circumstances. They also reflect the broader cultural beliefs about gender dominance and deference. Men's positions of power and authority as partners and their general status superiority give them the right to control the structure and content of professional conversation.

By controlling the professional context, men behave in ways that show that other men are taken seriously and accorded respect. Conversely, the way men talk about women and their appearance treats women as invisible, devalues them, and affects their ability to perform effectively. For example, when a judge allows the opposing attorney to label a woman attorney's appearance a "distraction," it signals to others that it is acceptable to use a woman's looks as the basis for objecting against other women attorneys. Similarly, a judge may defer to a man attorney who monopolizes argument time or displays an aggressive style, but penalize a woman who displays the same behavior as "shrill" or too aggressive.

Yet, if a woman adopts a less combative, more soft-spoken lawyering style, it is assumed to be because she is a woman, and she is regarded as "not tough enough" and treated as less effective. When a man displays a similarly non-combative style, it is viewed as simply a different style and may be regarded as "negotiating skill." This dilemma was made clear by sociologist Jennifer Pierce (1995) in her study of litigation attorneys. In the adversarial system, where cases have winners and losers, these lawyers' emotional presentation of self is an element of their strategy and a means to dominate and control others. Litigators, who are mostly men, rely on intimidation and "strategic friendliness" to accomplish their professional goal.

As Pierce notes, "Rambo litigators" do masculinized emotional labor since intimidation is associated with domination and control, and strategic friendliness is a form of emotional manipulation in competitive gamesmanship. Women litigators must contend with a situation in which the emotional labor associated with their work clearly conflicts with their gender identity and others' expectations. They face a double bind in doing litigation at the same time that they do gender in the courtroom. If they are aggressive and manipulative as zealous advocates, they risk being seen as pushy and unfeminine; if they adopt a less confrontational style, they risk being seen as too nice and ill-suited to the litigator role.

By not fitting the professional image, women lawyers are highly visible and face constant behavioral dilemmas. They must either model their professional behavior after a masculine image and suppress their femininity, or "act like women" and thus exhibit characteristics incongruent with the professional prototype, which leads to being discounted by men colleagues. Women lawyers who act "like men" are resented for being inflexible or too tough; those who act "like women" are, by definition, not acting in a "professional" (i.e., masculine) manner.

Thus, women lawyers have to seek ways to be "demure but tough". Women are presumed not to be competent while their male counterparts receive the presumption of competence. In addition, feminist legal scholars encounter gendered expectations when they produce legal scholarship that gets labeled "feminist propaganda." Their critics assume that traditional legal canons are value-free, rather than representing a masculine perspective and interests. Mentors are important teachers, advocates, and career launchers for junior associates. They help polish their mentees by giving them expanding responsibilities, opportunities to prove themselves, and exposure to clients.

Many men do not want to mentor a woman because they are uncomfortable interacting with women as peers, are concerned about accusations of sexual intimacy, or do not want to invest time and energy in a woman whom they expect to leave legal work when she starts a family. The few senior women who might become mentors often lack power within the firm and have limited time for mentoring given their work and family obligations. With few mentors available, women have had difficulty learning the norms of informal behavior in the male-dominated community, "fitting in," and forming client and collegial relationships. When women do find mentors, they tend to experience the mentoring process differently from men.

Men's mentoring talk is full of ways that they are helped to belong. In contrast, Reichman and Sterling (2002) found that women describe mentoring as making them feel good about themselves, but the sense of friendship and personal bonding characteristic of the mentoring men experience is largely absent and sometimes based on a parent-child model where traditional gender roles spill over and affect the mentoring relationship. The result of the lack of mentoring is that many female lawyers remain out of the loop of career development. For women who are denied challenging high-visibility assignments, excluded from social events that yield career opportunities, and unaided in efforts to develop marketing skills, the barriers to success often become self-perpetuating.

Senior attorneys are reluctant to spend time mentoring women whom they perceive as likely to resign; women who are not aided are, in fact, more likely to leave, which "perpetuates the assumptions that perpetuate the problem," particularly for women of color. Thus, what appears to be a choice to leave private practice "may be as much about a push away from work as it is about the pull of family". Lawyers meet, socialize, secure clients and business contacts, plan policy, provide leadership opportunities, and set the rules of their profession through informal gatherings and formal meetings of the ABA and in the 1,700 state and local bar associations in the United States.

Through the 1970s, women lawyers were denied memberships in many private clubs and positions of influence within local, state, and national bar associations. These exclusionary practices greatly hampered their legal careers. Today, women are no longer denied membership in clubs, and some hold leadership roles in bar associations (i.e., in 2005 women comprised about one third of the membership, 27 percent of the ABA Board of Governors, and more than a quarter of its section/division chairs and committee chairs; ABA, 2006), but the continued importance of informal networks and mechanisms for securing clients and making informal social contacts with powerful bar members puts them at a disadvantage.

Men and women very early in legal careers show different networking patterns. Men are more likely than women to have breakfast or lunch with partners where they strengthen informal bonds and foster "affiliating masculinities", through "sucking up," doing self-promotion, and giving the partners a chance to get to know them personally and professionally so that they will be remembered when partners assign "big cases." The men join law firm governance committees; women are more likely than men to be asked to participate in less influential firm committees (e.g., recruitment) that provide service to the firm but do not translate into advancement.

In this way, their work "disappears" because it is seen as the so-called "softer" side of organizational practice and not as "real work." In the courtroom, law office, and informal work-related activities, women lawyers encounter an occupational culture uncomfortable with their presence.

Bringing business into the firm is an important criterion for success that generally occurs through participation in informal networks. Women now are permitted to participate in private clubs and bar association activities, but these organizations remain male dominated, and their structures, decision-making logic, and controlling images continue to pose problems for women lawyers. Participation requires that women extend their workday and "socialize" primarily with men who may be uncomfortable with their presence.

Even informal interactions such as making small talk with colleagues pose dilemmas. A woman lawyer who is friendly is suspected of "coming on"; one who is too serious is rejected as unfriendly. Ignoring sexist jokes and comments signals tacit approval; failure to laugh leads to the label "humorless." Women get touched and interrupted more but cannot make "a thing" about this without being labeled "thin-skinned." They cannot simply behave "like lawyers"; they must negotiate their interpersonal power and find an acceptable style. Thus, gender serves as a "screen" for professional interactions so that a woman lawyer is evaluated, above all else, as a woman.

Women perceive that they are "at a disadvantage because they are operating in an alien culture" but have difficulty in conveying their perceptions convincingly to men. For example, between two thirds and three quarters of women lawyers report experiencing bias, but only a quarter to a third of men state they have observed it, and even fewer report experiencing it. Worse yet, the men often trivialize women's complaints. Women's disadvantage becomes cumulative through the organizational logics and opportunity structures in the profession that calls for total career commitment, raising tensions between family and workplace issues.

WOMEN, LEGAL REFORM AND MUSLIM IDENTITY

In Urdu writings of the late nineteenth century, Muslim reformers as diverse as Syed Ahmad Khan of Aligarh (1817-1898), Maulana Ashraf Ali Thanavi of Deoband (1864-1943), and Syed Mumtaz Ali of Lahore (1860-1935) evolved a critique of contemporary Muslim life and culture in response to the pressures of colonial rule. The themes of this critique were threefold. First was the consciousness of the decline brought about by the loss of political power to foreign rule. Second was the analysis of the causes of that decline that included the squandering of power and resources by the military and landed elites, and the loss of religious and cultural vitality. Third was the evolution of a programme of reform that would remedy that decline.

Foremost in this programme of reform was the need for improved education. Whether that education was a Western curriculum that included an Islamic element for the male leaders of the community (Sir Syed), or a reformed Islamic curriculum for the religious guides of the community (Deoband), or else a literary and practical education for both men and women (Mumtaz Ali), was a matter of considerable controversy. There was nevertheless one point upon which all reformers could agree: the status of Muslim women required amelioration. In this, their discourse resembled that of Hindu social reformers of the time.

Both Hindu and Muslim social reformers saw the roots of decline in a subsoil of rituals and customs that they regarded as unnecessary accretions, corruptions of a pure standard embodied in a reinterpreted past. For both Hindu and Muslim reformers, the solution to their current decline included the purification and rectification of religious life, and to that end, the reform of the role of women who were viewed - paradoxically - as both the chief perpetrators of wasteful and invidious customs and as the chief victims of such customs. For the reformers, therefore, women needed to be rescued from ignorance and superstition and also from abuse. Social reform, as articulated in the late nineteenth century, was thus the responsibility of men.

Women were to be the beneficiaries of the actions of men, not actors on their own behalf. Women became symbolic, not only of all that was wrong with cultural and religious life, but also all that was worth preserving. If their discourse was similar, however, Hindus and Muslims looked to different textual sources for their inspiration. For Hindus, the golden age was variously Shastric or Vedic, but certainly pre-Muslim. For Muslims it was scriptural, prophetic and non-Indic. As their discourses concerning the reform of women's intellectual and religious lives evolved, Hindus and Muslims either revived or created certain norms and boundaries for their communities. Reformers thus helped to articulate separate identities, to define what it meant to be either a Hindu or a Muslim, for both men and women.

DISCOURSES OF MUSLIM REFORM

Syed Ahmad Khan, regarded as the father of Indo-Muslim reform, was a champion of Western education for Muslim men. He regarded such education for women as premature, but was in favour of home education for Muslim women and, to his further credit, felt that the custom of *purdah*, as practiced in India, had been carried to extremes. Such isolation, he argued, was the cause of women's ignorance. They were credulous and clung stubbornly to outmoded customs; they made men's lives difficult. In the great days of early Islam, he claimed, women had been educated. They could inherit property and had to be able to manage it.

Hence, they needed to know not only how to read the scriptures, but also how to write and calculate. Islamic civilization had fallen on evil days and thus the status and rights of women had been abridged. This was not true Islam, but the result of adherence to bad custom. Sir Syed's argument found echoes among other reformers, younger men who were even more outspoken about the potential benefits of education for women. Education would break down women's isolation, and combat superstition and bad custom.

This was a line of reasoning heard again and again in Muslim reformist discourse. Muslims thus seemed to accept the British cultural critique that Indian weakness was a result of moral as well as political collapse. But such an argument had been present in Muslim discourse well before the British displaced Mughal power. Shah Waliullah in the eighteenth century, and before him, Shaikh Ahmad Sirhindi in the seventeenth, had lamented the loss of religious compass in the Muslim elite and linked it to the loss of political power.

Re-establishing the authority of God's law (*Shariat*) as opposed to spurious custom in Muslim lives was thus a prelude to regaining political and cultural ascendancy. By the late nineteenth century, women were viewed as an essential part of this process. For Muslims in favour of change, challenges - whether external or internal - had to be met by arguing for a return to a pristine Islam, as variously interpreted. For Muslim reformers as for Hindu, social and religious change did not mean aping the West, but rather arguing for a revitalization of tradition. The *ulama* were very much a part of this effort.

Indian *ulama* in the late nineteenth century, in the absence of a Muslim state, resorted to two main strategies to perpetrate Islamic learnino. The first was to institutionalize founding a number of *madarsas* that were not only repositories of the Islamic curriculum, but that incorporated ideas derived from Western institutions such(as academic departments, examinations and the offering of degrees. The second was to emphasize individual piety and dedication to the faith, based not on custom but on personal knowledge of the scriptures and the laws. That, of course, involved literacy. The *ulama* were heavily involved in publication: popular guides to religious practice, polemical qamphlets, scholarly quarterlies and less scholarly monthlies.

A number of *madarsas* had their own lithographic presses that contributed to the expansion of Urdu as a medium of public discourse. The Deoband *madarsa* was one of the major manifestations of these trends. Deobandis sought to purify personal religious observance and to spread the knowledge of the *Shariat* more widely among Muslims in India. To advance this project, some *ulama* also championed women's education. To purify household rituals, to increase knowledge and observance of scriptural religion as opposed to folk customs, and to improve individual piety in the Muslim community, it was important for women to be educated in their religion.

Maulana Ashraf Ali Thanavi of Deoband accordingly decided to write a compendium of useful knowledge for women, a guide not only to learning, but to the pious life.He began by citing a tradition of the Prophet Mohammad: "It is a duty incumbent on every Muslim man and every Muslim woman to acquire knowledge". This *Hadith* was frequently cited by Muslim educational reformers as evidence that the Prophet himself favoured education for women. Maulana Thanavi then went on to explain the rationale for this book, *Bihishti Zevar* (The Ornaments of Paradise):

> For many years, I watched the ruination of the religion of the women of Hindustan and was heartsick because of it. I struggled to find a cure, worried because that ruin was not limited to religion but had spread to everyday matters as well. It went beyond the women to their children and in many respects even had its effects on their husbands. To judge from the speed with which it progressed, it seemed that if reform did not come soon, the disease would be nearly incurable... [T]he cause of this ruination *is* nothing other than woman's ignorance of the religious sciences. This lack [*sic*] corrupts their beliefs, their deeds, their dealing with other people, their character, and the whole manner of their social life... I have for some time, therefore, realized that in order to manage women, it is absolutely necessary to teach them the science of religion-even if it must be through the medium of Urdu.

Maulana Thanavi here echoes a number of themes articulated by other reformers. Women's ignorance of religion is a problem for the society as a whole, for they infect their children and husbands with a contagion of indiscipline, ignorance and decline. Women are singled out as the carriers of that illness, an imagery suggesting the need to treat not just symptoms, but the root causes of the contagion.

In evidence here is a second idea: that what happens in the home is of importance to the society at large, and that through social relation, women's influence extends well beyond the home. There is also the idea of control. Women need to be 'managed' via proper instruction in Islam. According to this reasoning, women are deficient, but this deficiency can be remedied by discipline and instruction. Women are, therefore, potentially equal to men in their capacity for understanding, and hence their reform and 'management' is central to the religious reform of all Muslims.

Given Maulana Thanavi's egalitarian assumption, which derives from the preaching of Islam, if women have inferior status, it is not due to their inherent inferiority - for their souls are the equal of men's - but because of degenerate custom, falsely identified as religion. *Bihishti Zevar* devotes a lot of space to attacking and rooting out false custom, as did other reformers. Thanavi's concerns are religious, although one also hears echoes of economic concerns about excessive expense and ostentation. The material and spiritual consequences of useless custom are closely allied for both middle class reformers and reformist *'ulama'*. Maulana Thanavi describes marriage customs:

The women of the family gather and confine the girl in a corner... Etiquette calls for the girl to be seated on a low platform, for ointment to be placed on her right hand, and for her lap to be filled with rice and sweets. Rice and sweets are also distributed among those present. From that day on, the women continually rub the girl with ointments. This custom involves much foolishness. The first objection is to the requirement of seating the' girl alone. Whether it is hot, whether it is stuffy, whether all the doctors and physicians in the world say she will get sick... this obligation must not be missed. This entails the evil of strict adherence to set customs.... [P]lacing the ointment on her right hand and felting her lap with puffed rice and sweetmeats seem to be some kind of omens or superstitious acts. If this is so, it is polytheism. What Muslim does not know that that is opposed to the *Shariat*?

The rich composite of Hindu and Muslim observances that evolved over the centuries in the *zenana* in connection with marriage and childbirth is here attacked as both wasteful and un-Islamic. Maulana Thanavi goes on to object to ostentatious charity and to the use of silver implements and silken garments also as wasteful and irreligious, particularly the latter. The mark of a pious Muslim is his or her devotion to God's will, not these vestiges of the nawabi lifestyle which, in his view, convey false status.

Thanavi's insistence on the egalitarian message of Islam has striking implications for the Islamic society as a whole, implications that the Maulana - even with his theme of women's need to become more like men in matters of self control and religious observance - does not fully explore. His emphasis on individual piety meets the needs of a time when an aristocratic culture based on birth was gradually being displaced by a middle-class culture based on individual achievement. This ethic of individual achievement for both men and women was rendered more possible by the culture of print, which made easier the dissemination of works such as *Bihishti Zevar*. But the equal status of all believers when face-to-face with God was, in practice, superseded by the hierarchical relationships of the society. Members of the middle-class service elite, generally speaking, remained preoccupied with status, both among social groups and within families.

One reformer whose views on women's status were egalitarian in practice as well as in theory was Sayyid Mumtaz Ali of Lahore, founder in 1898 of one of the first Urdu journals for women, the weekly newspaper *Tahzib un-Niswan*. It was edited by his wife, Muhammadi Begum. Mumtaz Ale was also the author of *Huquq un-Niswan* (Women's Rights), a treatise in defence of women's rights in Islamic law, inspired by both his early Deobandi education and his experience of debating with Christian missionaries in Lahore. The missionaries criticized Islam, as well as other Indian religions, for the low status accorded to women and blamed these religions for the lack of education among Indian women. Mumtaz Ali knew that the position of women in Islamic law was theoretically higher than their actual current status.

The cause of this discrepancy he felt, was adherence to false customs - in this as we have seen he was not alone. Answering missionaries with theoretical arguments, however, was not enough. Changing Muslim practice had to be the highest priority. Women's adherence to false custom had to be combatted, but so too did the views of men, who felt that keeping women in ignorance and isolation was part of their religion. To attain these aims, he wrote *Huquq un-Niswan*.

Mumtaz Ali denied all English influence upon his writing, arguing that anyone who knew the *Shariat* and who followed the example of the Prophet and his family must be prepared to reject ignorant customs. He thus placed himself firmly within the framework of Deobandi reform, seeking to revalidate Islamic law and prophetic example in Muslim dally life, and to eradicate superstitious customary accretions. The first section of *Huquq un-Niswan* addressed all the various reasons why men are considered superior to women. He showed that the distinctions made between men and women that are justified on religious grounds are, in fact, the products of social custom.

If these distinctions were subjected to the scrutiny of reason, well bolstered by knowledge of the religious sciences, the fallacy and injustice of male supremacy would become clear. Mumtaz Ali points out that even though men and women have different physiques and fulfil different biological functions, both are human and hence equal in God's sight. Mumtaz Ali's arguments, however, go beyond the equality of souls found in Ashraf Ali Thanavi's *Bihishti Zevar* and encompass greater egalitarianism in gender relations as well. While admitting that men have greater physical strength than women, he states that this does not automatically give men the right to rule over women.

A donkey can carry more on its back than a man, but does that mean that donkeys are superior to men? Perhaps in the dark ages, 'might make right', but with the advance of civilization, rulers needed to have more understanding and compassion. Thus the right to rule should belong not to the strong, but to the wise. As for men's supposed greater intellectual capacity, he notes that men and women are of the same species. Any differentiation between the brain powers of the two genders must be something that the society has attributed to them, not chat God has created. Indeed, if the intelligence of women were less than that of men, the human race would rapidly become stupid, for intelligence would be transmitted in lesser degree to each succeeding generation.

Mumtaz Ali argues for a broad, humanistic education for women, not a narrow, household-centred one. Based on the assumption that men and women have equal rational and moral faculties, the education of women needs to be as complete as that of men, with some additional emphasis on household skills. He also discusses *purdah* in Islamic law, maintaining that *purduh* as practiced by Indian Muslims goes far beyond anything that the *Shariat* intended. Such customs have debilitating social results, but, he admits, they are very difficult to dislodge.

Arguing from verses in the Koran that refer to the need for modest behaviour, and from *Hadith* in which the Prophet ruled on various aspects of social interaction, Mumtaz Ali draws a clear distinction between what is customary - and thus subject to change - and what is normative or desirable according to the *Shariat*. He does not argue for the abolition of *purdah*, but rather for a pattern of *Shariat*-inspired modest behaviour on the part of both men and women and for allowing women greater freedom of movement and social discourse, as befits their status as responsible human beings.

Mumtaz Ali then discusses marriage, and here too his emphasis is egalitarian. He notes that the Prophet decreed that a marriage contracted without the consent of the partners is unlawful, but that this consent is usually simply assumed. The boy is cajoled by his parents; the girl is supposed to sit passively during the ceremony, mutely accepting her fate. These customs go completely against the *Shariat*. He also discusses certain reforms in the payment of dower (*mahr*) and in the granting of divorce (*talaq*). In Islamic law, the wife has a right to the payment of *mahr* by the husband, part of which is given upon marriage and part of which can be defected. Parents often demand a huge dower at the outset, in the hope that this will discourage divorce, but this only embitters family relationships.

More beneficial in terms of protecting the wife's interests is the placing of stipulations in the marriage contract (*nikahnama*). For example, the husband might agree to pay a higher amount only in the event of a divorce or a second marriage, and the wife would agree not to demand payment except under such circumstances. In this way, there would be mutual understanding, and both partners would benefit. The wife would have security without demanding ruinous *mahr*, and the husband would know that he would not be liable to a high payment except under certain specific conditions.

Other stipulations in the marriage contract could limit polygamy and give the wife more control over her fate, i.e. the husband could agree to give his wife the right to divorce if he took a second wife. She would thus retain her right to *mahr*, but also the right to initiate divorce under certain conditions. These suggested reforms are fully in line with the *Shariat*. Some benefit the wife, some the husband, but all emphasize the need for mutual agreement and equality in contractual dealings, which are absolutely necessary to ensure equitable and happy marriage based on the free choice of the partners.

Mumtaz Ali's approach to marriage emphasizes close adherence to Islamic law, and human relations based on mutual respect between men and women and understanding between the families concerned. Such considerations carry over into his discussion of relations between spouses. When men recognize that women's rights in Islamic law are equal to their own and grant them an education commensurate with their abilities, then it will not be necessary to consider the problem of marital relations, he maintains - rather too optimistically - since he feels that the problem will disappear of itself.

He admits, however, that this is not currently the case. The cure for injustice is for men to become more enlightened and to realize that their wives are human, he argues. Until women are treated like human beings, it is no use blaming them for not living up to their potential. Mumtaz Ali, who heretofore had emphasized mutual responsibility for improving marital relationships, here places greater responsibility upon men for bringing about social change. He also emphasizes that simply talking about the need for change in public is not enough; men must begin by setting an example in their private lives.

Educated men, government servants, professionals, and the like who talk about the need for self-government in India should realize the connection: if they are unwilling to grant greater education and rights to their women, how can they, in all seriousness, demand greater self-determination for themselves? The educated sections of the community must lead the way in recognizing the rights given to women in the *Shariat*, which have been forgotten. One of the legal reforms that Mumtaz All advocates in *Huquq un-Niswan* is the passage of a divorce law that would recognize a Muslim woman's right to initiate divorce (*khula*). This right is present in the *Shariat*, provided the woman gives up her right to the payment of *mahr*, but it is not in force in India. He thus anticipates by some forty years the Dissolution of Muslim Marriage Act of 1939.

LEGAL REFORM AND MUSLIM POLITICAL IDENTITY

The discourses of Muslim reformers deprecated useless custom, particularly as observed by women, and placed heavy emphasis on the need to observe the *Shariat* in everyday life. The recommendations of these reformers involved changing personal habits and eliminating household rituals. In some cases, however, reformers advocated legislative enactments in order to bring Muslim personal law closer to the spirit of the scriptures, as well as to improve women's rights in the context of family relations. Mumtaz Ali's thoughts on the need for a reformed divorce law were one such instance.

Other reformers were concerned about British legal actions invalidating certain types of waqf (pious endowments) that had been used in the past to support the donor's surviving family members - frequently women. Thus, the revalidation of such auqaf would benefit indigent Muslim women. Another matter that concerned reformers was succession to property. Under the Shariat a daughter is entitled to inherit a share of her father's property - half that of a son, to be sure - but nevertheless her right to property is specified in the Koran and *Hadith*. In many places in British India, however, 'customary law' was enforced, custom that favoured sons to the exclusion of daughters.

This was to the benefit of rural landed magnates, cultivated as political allies by the British, in the interests of keeping landholdings intact. The nature of rural landholdings varied greatly from place to place, but in general, the issue of *Shariat versus* custom among Muslims pitted rural landholders against urban reformers and some *ulama*. In the early part of the twentieth century, therefore, an unlikely coalition of *ulama*, Muslim middle-class reformers, and Westernized politicians with nationalist leanings came together - for very diverse reasons - to enact a series of legal reforms.

The Waqf Validating Act of 1913, the Muslim Personal Law (*Shariat*) Application Act of 1937, and the Muslim Dissolution of Marriage Act of 1939 were laws that specifically applied to Muslims. In this period also the Sarda, or Child Marriage Restraint Act of 1929, was enacted that applied to all religious communities. The latter was heartily endorsed by the All-India Women's Conference (AIWC), founded in 1927, representative of the growing voice of Indian women in the social and educational reform arena.

In addition, a growing body of opinion among Muslim women, whether writing in Urdu magazines or speaking from the platforms of women's associations, objected to polygamy and unilateral divorce, and supported greater property rights for women and the right of a women to initiate divorce when her marriage was cruel or insupportable. Muslim women's resistance to legal inequities included a resolution against polygamy passed by the All-India Muslim Ladies' Conference (Anjuman-i Khavatin-i Islam) at its annual meeting in Lahore in 1918 that caused considerable outrage in the Muslim press.

In addition, a movement in favour of 'delegated divorce' (*talaq-i tafwid*) was spearheaded by Mrs Sharifa Hamid Ali, who served as President of the AIWC in the late 1930s. Mrs Hamid Ali, the wife of a Muslim member of the Indian Civil Service who was a member of the distinguished Tyabji family of Bombay, had a draft prepared of a Muslim marriage contract containing stipulations allowing the woman to divorce under certain conditions. She urged educated Muslim women to see that such stipulations were incorporated into all marriage contracts. Such delegated divorce was permitted under Hanafi law, the school of Muslim law most prevalent among Indian Muslims, and the least latitudinarian in matters of divorce for women.

Under *talaq-i tafwid*, for example, the contract could specify that if a man married a second wife, the first could seek a divorce without forfeiting her *mahr*. This was significant, for if a woman initiated divorce (*khula*), she would lose her right to *mahr*, often her only means of support after divorce. This was a major disincentive to women seeking divorce, even in dire circumstances; whereas delegated divorce gave women a way out of marriage that preserved her right to some support. Such evidence of women's resistance to legal inequities caused some consternation among men and added to pressures in favour of reform.

Mumtaz Ali had anticipated a number of these laws, but it is unlikely that these would have been passed if reformers like him had been their only advocates. Without the evolution of opinion that produced the coalition of men who favoured legal reforms, the chances of an improvement in Muslim women's rights would have been slim. A brief examination of the debates among men that led to the passage of the *waqf*, *Shariat* and divorce legislation is necessary in order to ascertain the impact of those laws both on women's rights and on the emergence of Muslim political identity.

The Waqf Validating Act of 1913, proposed by Mohammad Ali Jinnah, sought to reinstate endowments that benefited the donors' families. This type of *waqf*, as opposed to endowments for public religious and charitable purposes, had been voided by a Privy Council judgment. Jinnah's bill sought to undo what the Privy Council had wrought.

In this effort, Jinnah secured the support of a number of leading *ulama* and Muslim politicians, including representatives of the *madarsas* of Deoband, Firangi Mahal, and Nadwat al-ulama (achieving agreement among such diverse *ulama*was no small featin itself), plus Mian Mohammad Shaft of Punjab (a Muslim Leaguer), Hasan Imam of Bihar (Muslim League and later Congress), and Aftab Ahmad Khan of Aligarh (generally, loyal to the British). Others, however, felt that Jinnah was simply using the issue to further his political career by establishing himself as a spokesman for Indian Muslim opinion, a collectivity that he and other Muslim leaders of the day sought to bring into being.

In a discussion of the passage of the *waqf* legislation Kozlowski points out that Jinnah, like the British jurists whose ruling he sought to undo, emphasized the ancient and unchanging nature of Muslim religious law. As this line of reasoning confirmed British suppositions, it was effective. Muslim politicians thus participated in the tendency, prevalent under British rule, to codify-and hence to rigidify-what was understood as Islamic law.

In the process of negotiating with colonial authorities, Muslim political leaders represented both Islamic law and their own community as more unified than they actually were, or had ever been. But, Kozlowski wryly notes: "Muslim leaders could not be blamed for choosing the line of argument most likely to obtain their goal". He further argues that:

Jinnah and the others might have chosen another away of presenting their case, one which did not depend on so abstract a reading of Islam or the people who professed it. Sir Syed, for example, tried to place the institution [of *waqf*] in the context of changing economic conditions in the Muslim world and India in particular. Sir Syed readily admitted that the use of endowments as family settlements suited the conditions created by British rule.

Jinnah, as a British-trained lawyer, had a considerably more abstract understanding of Islamic law than did Sir Syed. The Shariat Application Act of 1937 also addressed economic conditions created by British rule, particularly in the Punjab. In that important agrarian province, British authority rested firmly upon the recognition and codification of 'tribal' custom, wherein women were deprived of rights to inherit immovable property.

As pointed out earlier, customary law tended to keep landholdings intact, or at least more intact than if daughters could inherit land along with sons. The recognition of custom, by tying the interests of landholders to that of the British administration, was a cornerstone of British policy in the Punjab, but it contravened the *Shariat*, which gave a daughter a share of her father's property, albeit half that inherited by a son. For Muslim women, therefore, support for the *Shariat* had definite, if limited, advantages.

In such a situation, support for the *Shariat* not only denoted ties to the Islamic moral order, but also implied support for nationalist aspirations. In the 1930s in the Punjab, support for customary law was found in the Unionist Party, composed of large rural landholders of various religious communities, who generally spoke in favour of the British connection. Support for the *Shariat* emerged among the Muslim League, which was urban and (relatively speaking) more nationalistic.

The Jamiyat al-ulama, the political party representing many Indian *ulama*, supported legislation to validate the *Shariat* for both religious and nationalistic reasons. A Bill to apply the *Shariat* in the Punjab, which specifically sought to improve women's rights to land inheritance, was blocked by the Unionists in the provincial Legislative Council in the mid-1930s, but the issue persisted, and in 1937, Muslim League members introduced a similar measure in the Central Legislative Assembly, which ultimately passed.

During the legislative debates, the point was repeatedly stressed that this Bill, representing a consensus of Muslims throughout India to have their personal lives guided by the *Shariat*, would grant women greater rights. Speakers as diverse as Sir Mohammad Yaqub from Moradabad, Dr Ziauddin Ahmad from Aligarh, the poet and journalist Zafar Ali Khan from Lahore, the former Khilafat leader Maulana Shaukat Ali, the urbane Congress lawyer Asaf Ali from Delhi, the even more urbane M.A. Jinnah from Bombay, and regional leaders such as Maulvi Syed Murtaza of Madras, Maulvi Mohammad Abdul Ghani from East Bengal and Abdul Qayyum from the North-West Frontier Province all voiced their sympathy for downtrodden Muslim women and their desire to see their lot bettered.

Jinnah was able to secure passage of the Bill, however, only after a number of major compromises left adoptions, wills, and legacies entirely up to individual Muslims. On the inheritance of agricultural land, furthermore, the Bill was silent, for under the Government of India Act of 1935, this was a subject reserved for the provinces and outside the scope of central legislation. The Shariat Application Act of 1937, for all the sympathetic rhetoric of the debate, had an extremely limited effect on Muslim women's rights. It did, however, express a consciousness of Muslim identity in the legal structure of the state and further enhanced Jinnah's claims to speak for that collectivity.

The debate on the Sarda, or Child Marriage Restraint Act of 1929 showed a similar concern to apply the *Shariat* as a generalized scriptural prescription and to represent Muslims as an undifferentiated community. A number of Muslims, including Jinnah, at first opposed the application of the Sarda Act to Muslims, on the grounds that it was irrelevant, as child marriage had no sanction in Islam. T.A.K. Sherwani argued that if Muslims in India did practice child marriage, it was because they were following a Hindu custom - a familiar reformist argument, though not always stated so blatantly. Ultimately, Jinnah and other Muslim representatives were convinced by the select committee's report that child marriages were also common among Muslims, to vote in favour of the Act. Muslim women members of the AIWC also strongly supported the Act, which outlawed marriages under the age of fourteen in all communities.

The legal reform that had the most significant impact on Muslim women' rights was the Muslim Dissolution of Marriage Act of 1939. Major credit for its passage must go to Maulana Ashraf Ali Thanavi whose writings were an enabling factor in assembling the coalition that backed the legislation. As a background, in 1913, Maulana Thanavi had issued a *fatwa* in a case involving a Muslim husband who had applied to a British court in India for restitution of conjugal rights. The wife's family refused, on the grounds that she had renounced Islam and her marriage was no longer valid. The judge asked the claimant to secure a *fatwa* clarifying this point in Islamic law, and Maulana Thanavi ruled that the marriage was indeed annulled as a result of the wife's apostasy.

The Hanafi School of Islamic jurisprudence, followed by a majority of Muslims in the subcontinent, is strictest in matters of divorce and gives a wife almost no grounds for initiating the dissolution of her marriage. In the early twentieth century, the number of Muslim women who resorted to the device of renouncing Islam in order to secure judicial divorces increased alarmingly. This was partly a result of missionary activity, but partly because many Muslim women found no other way out of cruel and abusive marriages. The press took notice of this phenomenon and the influential voice of the poet Iqbal urged Muslim scholars to reform Hanafi law, in order to find a solution within Islam for this problem, so that Muslim women would not have to adopt this desperate tactic.

Ashraf Ali Thanavi, therefore, returned to the subject of his 1913 fatwa and consulted with a number of other *ulama*, including Mufti Kifayatullah of Delhi, Husain Ahmad Madani of Deoband, and various Maliki *ulama* in Arabia. In 1931, he issued a lengthy revision of his earlier *fatwa*: *Al-Hilat un-Najiza li'l-Halitat al-'Ajiza*('A Successful Legal Device for the Helpless

Wife'). He ruled that apostasy did not annul a Muslim marriage, but that a wife might obtain a judicial divorce based on grounds permitted by the Maliki school of Muslim jurisprudence. This device of jurisprudential eclecticism (*takhayyur*) recognized by some legal scholars and commentators, opened the way to a reform of Muslim divorce law.

The Jamiyat al-ulama seconded Maulana Thanavi's view, after which Qazi Mohammad Ahmad Kazmi, a lawyer from Meerut and a Jamiyat al-Mama member of the Central Legislative Assembly, in 1936 introduced the Bill that became the Muslim Dissolution of Marriage Act.

The Bill was first referred to a Select Committee composed of a majority of Muslims, then debated thoroughly in the assembly and finally passed in 1939. The Act provided that apostasy of the wife did not annul a Muslim marriage, a point greeted with some relief by Asaf Ali who was married to a Hindu and was shocked to hear that a marriage between a Muslim and a non-Muslim might be considered invalid *ab initio*.

The Act permitted the wife to seek a judicial divorce on grounds permitted by the Malikis, including the husband's cruelty, insanity, impotence, disappearance, or imprisonment and his failure to perform his marital obligations or to provide maintenance-for specified periods of time ranging from two to seven years. The Act also provided for divorce based on the 'option of puberty', that is: if a woman had been married off by her elders before puberty, and the marriage had not been consummated, she could ask for its dissolution.

It is worth remarking that the legislative debate and the law as enacted were concerned with the suffering of Muslim women that resulted from the inability of men to fulfil their marital duties, or from custom that permitted her to be married off without a choice. This vision of women as victims is familiar and in this context, very useful politically. Begum Hamid Ali, on the other hand, in her campaign in favour of stipulations in marriage contracts was working to empower women, as well as their relations, in marital negotiations.

The Act differed in several respects from the recommendations of the *ulama*, most notably in not reserving jurisdiction in cases of Muslim divorce to Muslim judges. It was also made to apply to all Muslims, not only Sunnis, but Shias as well.

Consequently, Maulana Thanavi and the other divines who had originally urged reform of the divorce law were displeased with the Act in its final form and condemned the Muslim Dissolution of Marriage Act as un-Islamic. More secular parliamentarians, however, including Abdul Qayyum of the North-West Frontier and Asaf Ali from Delhi, were loath to risk governmental defeat of the Act by amending it to reserve jurisdiction to Muslim judges and they accepted its application to Shias as well in the interest of maintaining their claim to represent the interests of Muslims as a whole.

Once again, compromises in the legislature made for a law that was passable, if not strictly shari'i. For all its strange bedfellows, this episode showed that reformers, politicians and *ulama* could work together to bring about the reform of Muslim personal law in a parliamentary context, even where Muslims were in a minority. The evidence of Muslim women's discontent and their resistance to the existing state of affairs, whether within elite organizations such as the AIWC or via apostasy, had acted as a catalyst. Maulana Thanavi's careful scholarship, broad consultation and invocation of the principle of jurisprudential eclecticism had made consideration of divorce reform possible.

The *waqf*, *Shariat* and divorce laws had several results that were cumulative: (1) They recognized that women had certain rights in Islamic law. (One should be careful, however, not to regard these laws as a victory for individual rights, but rather as a recognition of rights that were women's by virtue of their being members of families as well as Muslims.) (2) They created a distinct body of law, within the context of the state, with which both Muslim men and women could identify. (3) They created a fragile political coalition in support of issues that were clearly labelled Islamic.

These laws, with their concern for women in the family, with demarcating boundaries around the Muslim community and defining its legal system in religious terms, and with bringing together Muslims of different ideological persuasions on the basis of their Islamic identity, fitted well into the structure of the British colonial state that allowed considerable latitude for organization around 'private' matters such as religion. It also appealed to the coalition-building skills of the man who shepherded the first two bills through the central legislature, Mohammad Ali Jinnah.

This is not to suggest that Jinnah's political career was mainly associated with the movement for Muslim women's reform, nor still less with the movement for scriptural reform. He was, however, able to articulate issues raised by those interlocking movements within a political and legislative context. It is significant that his most successful efforts at coalition-building among Muslims prior to the Pakistan resolution of 1940 were those focused on legal issues that linked women and family life to Islamic legal identity, and that further linked the concerns of urban and small-town professionals and *ulama* at the expense of rural landed interests.

The defence of the Muslim family and the definition of the Muslim community in India as a legal entity were issues at stake in the enactment of these laws. They were also issues that had linked these two important groups of educated Muslims since the late nineteenth century, groups whose support was essential to Jinnah and the Muslim League's claim to be the political representatives of all Indian Muslims. This linkage among concerns for women's status within the family, Muslim personal law and Muslims' sense of distinctive identity persists into the present.

The writings of Muslim social reformers in the late nineteenth century portrayed women as embodying all that were wrong with their culture as well as all that which was worth preserving. Most of what was wrong could be summed up by the phrase 'useless custom' (*fazul rasum*). Women were its practitioners as well as its victims. The solution to the ambivalence of the reformist message was provided by a return to a purified practice of the faith which, in turn, would improve and preserve the family life that reformers both valued and found deficient. Part of that return to the faith involved a reassertion of scriptural religion over household ritual; another involved the revived observance of the *Shariat* in matters such as the inheritance of property (including charitable endowments), marriage and divorce.

All of the legal reforms that were enacted in the early part of the twentieth century are extensions of this ideology of reform. Scriptural authority, as reinterpreted in the colonial context - increasingly restricted to certain specific texts and clearly defined readings of them - was asserted over customary practice. Since reformers viewed the female and the indigenous as the bases of such customary practice, their educational, social and later legal reforms increasingly asserted male control and values over women's lives.

On the other hand, women were central to the family and their dignity and honoured roles essential both to the preservation of family life and to its improvement. Legal reforms were thus a logical extension of men's concerns to improve women's status and their adherence to the faith of Islam. Women were the symbols of what men wanted their community to be. Women, when consulted, were expected to agree. Concern for Muslim women's rights, as individuals, was another matter. From a feminist perspective one may fault the reformers for doing little to improve Muslim women's rights, but that was not their main concern. Their concern was with establishing norms for community behaviour, and in the process, establishing an irreducible Muslim identity within the political process.

2

Law and the Women

Women all across the globe have come to recognise gender violence as a symptom of unequal power between men and women. Gender norms are determined by social and cultural norms demarking what they think are appropriate places for women and men. Such norms perpetuate gender hierarchies, which are entwined in the foundations of the structures of family and community and restrict decision-making and access to resources, leading to a multitude of other restrictions and social taboos. Social interpretations of the 'man's place' and 'male privilege' are used to justify such restrictions on women and also to justify violence against women. In South Asian countries, the culture of patriarchy is deeply entrenched, making a strong foundation for gender biases. In this region, gender biases are perpetrated not only by men, but also by women as part of the social order.

A complicated web of social, cultural and economic factors traps women and girls in its meshes, rendering them vulnerable to various forms of violence. These factors, coupled with rigidly defined and enforced gender norms create a vicious cycle of deprivation, low self-esteem and discrimination against women. Women and children are generally undervalued in South Asia. There are even laws which put 'women and lunatics' in one class. Discrimination against women in many families in South Asia begins even before birth with sex-selective abortions.

The preference for sons is still strong, while daughters are considered an economic liability. Once the girl child is born, she faces discrimination in the areas of nutrition, health care and eventually in the area of education. Even though women in South Asia all suffer from various forms of gender-based violence and discrimination, are socially disadvantages and are given a low status in society, they are not a homogenous category. Social and cultural norms in various countries in the region create slight differences. For example, while an upper caste urban Hindu woman in India and a rural Muslim woman in Bangladesh may both suffer from domestic violence, the factors that contribute to the violence may vary. This may be the same for women of the same nationality, but from different economic levels.

However, some things remain homogenous. According to the 1996 Human Development Report for South Asia, 'several factors that transcend class, religion, culture and locality affect the lives of all South Asian women. These include responsibility for housework and childcare, vulnerability to domestic violence and the economic vulnerability that reflects women's unequal legal and social status.' The report goes on to mention that these commonalities are based upon a shared history of colonialism and religious, cultural, economic and political structures shaped by a strong patriarchal values that deny women power.

In South Asia, British colonisers used communalism as a ploy for their policy of divide and rule. Hindus and Muslims were divided along religious lines for political gain. Historically, women have been treated as war booty and have been humiliated, raped and abused by invading armies and warring factions. The history of the Partition of the subcontinent is no stranger to this. It is rife with accounts of women being raped out of revenge by each religious community against the other. The same history is repeated in Bangladesh's war for independence, where many Hindu women were raped and assaulted by the Pakistani army. The more recent carnage in Gujarat, where scores of Muslim girls and women were raped and sexually assaulted by Hindus is another instance of how women become symbols of community shame and honour.

This sort of religious fanatism both by those of the Muslim and Hindu faith are hotbeds for the recruitment of young men and adolescents to sustain the movement, creating a continuous chain of violence. However, India, Pakistan and Bangladesh are not the only sufferers of such violence. In the Kingdom of Nepal, the Maoist movement has also had an impact on women. The looting, extortion, harassment, torture, seizure of homes and land, rape and kidnapping effects women both physically and mentally.

Women's movements and organisations for 'the betterment' of women have existed for over 100 years. In the subcontinent, such small organisations can be traced back as far as the late 1800's. In modern times, in the growing gloom of violence against women, many strong women's movements have grown and spread across the sub continent in a strong bond of sisterhood, especially in the area of trafficking and migration. However, even though the women's movements are growing, there has been little change in social attitudes and traditions towards women.

Women in Pakistan have yet to be rid of the curse of 'honour killings', in India, brides are burnt in secret, Dalit women are abused as caste culture reigns strong and in Bangladesh acid violence victimises more than 300 women every year. It is true that women's movements have brought about amendments in the law and the introduction of new laws and that women now take active part in government affairs and women lead many human rights organisations. Such women play an important part in ensuring that women and their demands are made visible and heard.

However, women's entry into the market and public domain is fiercely challenged and women who dominate South Asian governments almost always reach the top wearing the badge or bearing the legacy of deceased male relatives. Women still lack access to resources and justice and lack of information about legal remedies, coupled with poverty, fear and a social system that insists that issues like domestic violence and rape must not be aired in public, further inhibit the process to safeguard women's human rights.

How about the governments of South Asia? Some instances of violence are country-specific. For example, the curse of karo kari or honour killings plagues Pakistan, acid violence is most widespread in Bangladesh that in the other countries of the region, the problem of caste is found in India and Nepal. However, the governments of the region are trying to deal with the issue of violence against women and create mechanisms for the advancement of women. Bangladesh, Nepal and Pakistan have separate Ministries for this issue, like the Ministry for Women and Children Affairs of the Government of Bangladesh, created in 1978.

The Ministry of Human Resource Development of the Government has a Department of Women and Child Development. Furthermore, all have policies and activities geared towards the development of women, especially in the areas of health and education. Some of the countries have a National Human Rights Commission where cases of violence against women are also dealt with. Unfortunately, despite the setting up of exclusive ministries and department cells and despite the laws and the legal system and the setting up of family courts and special tribunals, it is a common fact all over south Asia that violence against women has had no significant drop.

The main reason for this is lack of implementation of the laws due to various reasons, including corruption - and the disinterest of the governments. Furthermore, most of the government officers who work in these specialised departments are not trained or sensitised in how to approach the issue and have little idea of the concept of gender and development. According to a 1994 study on judicial attitudes to women in India, 48% of judges agreed that it is justifiable for a man to slap his wife on certain occasions, 74% endorsed the view that preservation of family should be the primary concern for women even when there is violence within the marriage.

Advocacy for legal reforms, implementation of the law and other related issues have always been on the agenda of human rights organisations, especially women's rights organisations. To date, many grass-roots level women know that there are laws to protect them from various forms of violence, but when the issue becomes a domestic one, culture, tradition and family bar the way for any attempts to seek justice. Economy is also a factor, coupled with the fear of becoming an unwanted burden in a father's or brother's home. Reporting of violence against women has increased and spans the region and several relevant regional meetings are held every year on the issue. What more can the NGOs do, short of running the government?

Changing the way people think is central to addressing gender based violence. Policies and laws cannot be implemented unless there is community support. Emphasis needs to be made that the issue of violence against women needs to be tackled by both men and women and that the media should refrain from sensationalism and stereotyping. Media is vital to create awareness right to the grass roots level and a sensitive media is a powerful tool.

The bottom line, however, is that gender violence cannot be dealt with unless one also addresses the fundamental issues of basic health, education, nutrition and livelihood, all of which play a role to reduce the risk of violence. Women in the region now work just as hard as the men and are an integral part of the development of the countries. In all, gender violence in South Asia needs to be given much more attention to than what the governments are currently giving the issue.

Generalizations about women in Asia, perhaps like all other sweeping statements, are risky in spite of similarities; it is a continent of vast varieties. There are differences of ethnicity, class, socio-political systems, religion and urbanization. The Asian countries reflect the world's major cultures, systems and beliefs. Their populations vary - so do their levels of development. Japan has a per capita GNP of over $6.000; for a few others this figure is a little over $100. As exemplified by the case of the People's Republic of China, India and Pakistan, for example, the political systems are diverse. There are about a dozen Moslem countries, some with militant and others with conservative views.

And Turkey is a secular state among them. The recent resurgence of Islam in countries like Iran, Pakistan and Malaysia is a reminder undesigning the importance of religion in defining women's status. In some countries where the Confucian and Hindu traditions are still strong, multitudes of women, though not all, 'obey their fathers when unmarried, their husbands when married and their sons when widowed'. Such religious diversity cannot be found in any other-continent. Hinduism (India), Buddhism (Sri Lanka, Japan), Christianity (the-Philippines) and Islam (Turkey, Iran, the Arab countries, Pakistan, Indonesia) are all represented in Asia. These reminders on variation may be sufficient.

One encounters the same variety in the world of Asian women. One finds women such as Mrs. Bandaranaike, Mrs. Gandhi and Mrs. Aquino in powerful political positions. In the leading cities, one also sees thousands of well-educated professional women. But especially in the rural areas, there are high rates of female mortality at child birth, low life expectancy, hunger, ill-health, illiteracy and overwork. Although there are important differences from one country to another or even between regions, millions are caught up in the vicious circle. Male dominance is frequent. But the condition of women is improving substantially as a result of modernization and economic growth.

One should be reminded that patriarchy, whether in parts of Asia or elsewhere, has been the product of historical development rather than an indication of man's natural superiority. (How many men can jump as high as Lyudmiia Andemnva?) If Aristotle believed that men were by nature superior or if later prominent thinkers such as Arthur Schopenhauer, Auguste Comte and Georg Hegel maintained that a woman should only rear children and obey the husband, they merely reflected the institutionalized role of the sexes.

Findings prove that at the dawn of society the leading role belonged to women. Since it was impossible to establish fatherhood, descent was traced through the maternal line.

As tools developed, men took the leading place in society, becoming the hunter (breadwinner) and the soldier (defender). Their functions increasingly limited to managing the household, women were kept from participation in social production and hence became economically and morally dependent on men. Even the simplest societies, such as the Intuits (Eskimo), became men-dominated. Even participation in formal religious activity by women was infrequent. Although there were sole conspicuous examples of the power of women, even among them actual power was in the hands of men.

The elevated social status of individual women was accidental. For instance, the position of the queen mother in West Africa or the chieftains in Samoa was not related to any fundamental concept of the high placement of women. If there was a Russian female officer who took part in the 1812 war against the armies led by Napoleon, such cases were infrequent. As the technological changes of the Industrial Revolution transformed production, women were drawn into the factories. They had already become a part of the French Revolution - to such an extent that a god calling for the destruction of the old order was the symbol of Freedom. It is no surprise that women's rights came to the fore first in the industrializing states.

Charles Fourier, a prominent French utopian socialist, was perhaps the first among those who said that the degree of emancipation of women was a yardstick for the degree of a general emancipation in a society. Later assertions for a supposed biological inferiority were a screen for the oppression of especially the working women. The Chartists included woman suffrage in their program. In the United States, higher education for women began with the opening of Oberlin College as a co-educational institution (1833). In England Gorton College (Cambridge) was established (1869) as the first women's college of university rank. But no woman was qualified to practice law in England until 1922.

Women were not permitted to matriculate in Germany until Heidelberg and Freiburg granted them that right (1901). It is worth to remember that the National Socialist Government in Germany decreed in 1934 that women may not exceed 10 percent of the total student body in a university. Throughout history class lines have cut across sex lines. Women have enjoyed privileges denied to same men and some women, but within each class, women have been generally at a disadvantage. Similarly, women of dominant races had privileges withheld from men or women of other races. Even in some advanced societies women are deprived of the right of equal pay for equal work, and they play a very modest role in state administration.

For instance, a U.S. researcher, Kirsten Amundsen, writes in The Silenced Majority: Women and American Democracy that American womem, which constitute 40 percent of the total labour force, were underpaid and overworked. Professions in the scientific and technological fields are generally monopolized by men. Economic crises and the introduction; new technologies generally lead to a decrease in jobs for women. The application of cybernetics will cause a further decrease in the number of working women. The situation is extremely serious in same parts of the world, such as the south of Africa, where the racist South African regime endangers the peaceful development of Namibia, Angola, Mozambique, Zimbabwe, Zambia, Botswana and Lesotho.

Women in those countries additionally suffer since scarce resources have to be used for defense or for political emancipation. The status of women throughout Asia is undergoing a drastic transformation. Republican Turkey was perhaps the first country in that continent to abolish legal inequalities and recognize women's rights to participate in public life - in any case earlier than in a number of European states such as Belgium, France, Switzerland, Italy, Greece or Portugal. Mustafa Kemal Ataturk, the founder of the Turkish

Republic, was preoccupied with the idea of radically changing the status of Turkish women. Indeed, his sweeping reforms in all walks of life made the Turkey of the 1920s and the 1930s a forward-looking society.

Turkey was then one of the very few countries in the world with a republican regime, As to women's rights voting privileges in England were not extended to women on the same terms as to men until 1928.Attempts to enfranchise women were defeated in the upper house in Sweden until 1921.Turkey, on the other hand, abolished the Caliphate and promulgated the Law for the Unification of Instruction (both in 1924), the latter bringing all religious schools under unified control.

The introduction of the Turkish Civil Code (1926), which made no discrimination between the sexes, as well as a secular, co-educational system, was "revolutions" for a society with traditional Islamic norms. It is true that most of the major progressive reforms, including those in favour of Turkish women, were given rather than fought for. Bat it is fair to remember that reforms in the 'superstructure' facilitate qualitative changes in society. Extraordinary organizers may also perform essential functions. This fact refers not only to scientists, writers and artists without whose work the development of science and culture would be inconceivable, but also to men like Ataturk engaged in public affairs.

It is true that the course of history is determined by the struggle of large social groups. But the great men of history are those outstanding figures whose deeds further the development of society and who serve the use of progress. Fazýl Hüsnü Daðlarca, a leading contemporary Turkish poet, says in one of his couplets that "nations breathe with their major sons". Truly, their activity can accelerate the course of history and alleviate the birth pains of a new and a better; society. Although problems still beset the Turkish women of today, the trans- formation started by a new legal system cannot be minimized.

Under Turkey's conditions, the cases of Sabiha Gökçen, Turkey's first female military pilot (of the 1930s), and of

Kerirnýan Halis, Miss Turkey elected Miss Universe (1932)', were symptoms of a basic change. Turkish women enrolled in schools, became professionals, entered politics and earned fame as writers and artists in the earlier part of the Twentieth Century. The status of women throughout Asia has undergone a drastic trans formation, either on account of modernization or change in the political system. Women in general are more zealous in strive for equal participation in economic and social development.

Following the United Nations declaration of the Decade of Women and Development, many Asian governments have set up special executive agencies bent on women's issues and concerns in the Central Asian Soviet Republics and in China a new ideology and political system and in Japan economic growth gave women a higher status than instituted by tradition. The ideology of the Soviet Union and China counter-balanced the traditionally inferior status of women. Countries like Turkmenistan, Uzbekistan, Kirghizstan, Tajikistan, Kazakhstan, Azerbaijan, Armenia and Georgia, as Republics within the Soviet Federation, are governed in accordance with their own constitutions which guarantee equal rights to women in all spheres of economic, government, cultural and other public activity.

Women are expected to take part in governing the state, receive equal pay for equal work and have equal opportunities for jobs. Since the state all at funds for building nurseries and kindergartens, boarding schools, laundries and service shops of all kinds, which help relieve women of a part of house work, women have opportunity to study, learn a trade or profession and choose an occupation to their liking. In the Central Asian outskirts of the Tsarist Russian Empire, women were generally victims of arbitrary rule.

Older people, who for years had closely adhered to the traditions of their ancestors, were also largely hindered by prejudices even under the new Soviet regime: Younger people naturally broke away from the laws of the past more readily. Turkmenistan, for instance, was a poverty-ridden, backward looking area in the 1920s. Today, it has twice the ratio of students per inhabitants compared to the Federal Republic of Germany. The status of Turkmen women has radically changed. They now have the same opportunities for education and employment as men. One of the Turkmen female deputies in the USSR Supreme Soviet is a Vice-Chairwoman of the Soviet of the Union.

The Presidium of the Supreme Soviet of the Turkmen SSR has five women members (35 percent of its membership), and three women in the Council of Ministers. Women are represented in the local Soviet of People's Deputies, making up nearly 45 per cent of their membership. 360 women occupy leading posts in executive committees of regional, city and district Soviets: They have free excess to all domains of creative activity, production, education, science or culture. 42 percent of all working people engaged in the national economy are women. They make up 40 percent of the scientists, 50 percent of its medical personnel and 45 percent of its teachers.

The facts and figures are about the same in the other Soviet Central Asian Republics. In Uzbekistan, for instance, 183 deputies of the Supreme Soviet of the Republic are women. Uzbeks women have equal rights with men legally and in everyday life. Every third engineer and scientific worker is a woman, three out four' doctors are women and 45 percent of the teachers are likewise women. The social status of Azerbaijani women (Caucasus) has also changed drastically. Today, woman account for 53 percent of all the specialists in public education and for 59 percent of those in health care. They are firmly established among the engineers at various industries where they make up 26 percent of all experts.

On the whole, Azerbaijani women represent 43 percent of the labour force. They participate in all spheres of life, including the management of state and social institutions. They are in charge of large industrial enterprises, learns, educational establishments and research centers. The position of women in China, as portrayed in Pearl Buck's The Good Earth, was abandoned in the early 1950s since women were now needed for agrarian and industrial production. Doubtless, their status improved significantly in the last four decades. Yet, there were several shifts in their position as the "Great Leap Forward" or the "Cultural Revolution" advanced or regressed.

As a matter of fact, the women's liberation movement in China, from the end of the last century, passed through various stages. It was always connected with other causes, such as nationalism, the war against Japan and the Revolution in the past, Chinese women were assigned an inferior status under the Confucian canon. Although the' torturous foot-binding custom was not attributable to Confucius, but the result of a kind of "masculine aesthetic standard", women were placed in a fixed hierarchy in favour of a "stale" society. But continuous and humiliating defeats in the hands of foreigners forced the reformists to think of promoting women's education as an insurance against the decline of China's sons. Some urban gentry' class daughters, who studied abroad, came home with feminist ideas.

They even joined secret revolutionary societies, a significant figure of this period being Qiu Jin, who was a feminist educator and who had died as a revolutionary martyr. The 1911 Revolution spread women's schools from coastal' cities into provincial capitals, and the "May Fourth Movement" (1919), which started as a protest against the Paris Peace Treaty, evolved into a cultural crusade embracing ideas of a new status for women. Double standard of morality, arranged marriage, foot binding and the like were condemned, and monogamy, political participation, equal heritage rights and women's education were advocated. Under the "Nationalist" rule, the only achievement "was the Civil Code (1931), which improved the legal position of women. They gained equal property inheritance and were entitled to choose their husbands. But the "Nationalists" were more entangled with military affairs and less with the implementation of the new laws.

When Chiang Kai-shek launched the "New Life Movement", the emphasis was again on women as wives and mothers only. Until 1949 Song Meiling (the wife of Chiang Kai-shek) was the only female figure, who was the first lady, not a political leader. Mao Zedung, on the other hand, qualified women as a potential revolutionary and productive force. Consequently, the first Chinese Soviet (of the Jiangxi province, 1931-34) promulgated the most radical marriage laws China has ever known. But this caused a hostile reaction from the male population. It was the Communists who turned back their policy to avoid alienation from the male masses.

Efforts were renewed to win over the women for production when the anti-Japanese war broke out (1937). The establishment of the People's Republic of China (1949) gave the new government a chance to promulgate the final version of the marriage law, supposed to deal the last blow to the traditional family structure. The majority of Chinese women were assigned to the labour force, going to the factories and the fields. Maa Zedung had said: "Women hold up half of the sky". But in 1955 there was an unemployment crisis and women again turned to housekeeping duties.

They were once more needed for production with the "Great Leap Forward" (1958). In spite of the several other shifts in later years, women's role has undeniably improved. Many household tasks being collectivized, they constitute a solid percentage of the work force. Yet the traditional norms within the family are difficult to break. In same circles, marriage is still "arranged", and the tradition of paying a dowry to the girl's family is maintained to same extent. Changes in the political systems elsewhere in Asia inescapably brought about important transformations in the lives of those communities.

For instance, the life of an Afghani woman was within the confines of her home prior to the April 1978 Revolution. Even today there are Afghani families sharing obsolete views as to the position of women, but there are also female mechanics and specialists, who view their role in the society in a different way. The 1979 Revolution in Iran proved that women can bring their weight in favour of radical changes in a country hitherto torn by contradictions. In 'Iraq and Syria, where the different branches of the Arab Ba'th Socialist Party are in power, official order believe that the society remains in chains unless its women are liberated, enlightened and educated.

Women take part in party work and in mobilizing the people as well as in fields such as the judiciary, teaching, the arts, literature and journalism. In North and South Korea women today enjoy a great deal of freedom and privileges, discrimination against whom was justified by the Confucian doctrine and the customs based on them. While the North experienced the conversion on account of a new political system, the South owed the change to steps towards modernization. It was perhaps much more in Japan that the rapid socio-economic changes put women in a place.different than the bottom of the social order of the feudal and the Tokugawa periods.

The status of Japanese women improved immeasurably especially since the end of the Second World War. The Constitution (1946) guaranteed legal equality for all, regardless of sex: The Japanese Civil Code abolished the traditional household system. The Education Law stated that every 'child, boy or a girl, was entitled to advance into all strata of learning. The, Election Law gave women the right to work. Consequently, the voting rate of women exceeded that of men since 1968. Finally, as the Japanese economy made remarkable advances since the 1960s, there was an increased demand to recognize women as part of the labour force.

Although there is a gap between men and women with respect to wages and promotion, the number of female employees has increased and the range of their occupations has expanded. The Japanese Government is bringing further efforts to promote the participation of women in decision-making bodies and to eliminate discriminatory practices. Although there are important variations worthy of remark between the South Asian countries, there are similarities, such as low female participation in labour force. Successive censuses show that the participation rate for women is only 11 percent in India and lower in Pakistan and Bangladesh. Doubtless, all South Asian countries wish to modernize.

But this process displaces women in same societies from the traditional work in agriculture and in cottage industry. They do not become idle, but they withdraw from the labour force and turn to poverty induced marginal occupations. The problem of the state of women had begun to exercise the minds of the pre-Partition Indian reformers in the early years of the Nineteenth Century. They agitated against child marriage, *purdah*, enforced widowhood and the denial of education to girls. The Nineteenth Century battle for reforms was inconclusive. The reforms would reach only a part of the urban middle' class. Gandhi's views on the status of women were radical. He held that women ought to be treated as individuals in their own right with full potentialities for self-development.

Engaged in the fight against alien rule, Indian women had a moral right to equality. It was left to Jawaharlal Nehru to provide the constitutional and legal framework for equality between the sexes. That outstanding leader of the Indian national liberation movement paid considerable attention to the problem of women's emancipation. He threw his weight against discrimination. He endeavored to embody the principle of equality in the Indian Constitution. But there was criticism of the early bills introduced in the Indian Parliament to grant Hindu women' limited rights to secure divorce and inheritance of property. Before the enactment of the new Hindu 'Code, Muslim women enjoyed advantages over their Hindu sisters in matters of divorce, remarriage and inheritance.

They had also joined hands with their men for the struggle against alien rule and for the creation of Pakistan. Fahma Jinnah and Ra'na Liaquat' Ali represented Muslim women leadership of the 1940sand the early 1950s. Career women of Pakistan in the following decades, such as Abida Hussein in politics, Shaista Ikram in diplomacy or Zubeida Agha in arts proved that work and employment were not necessarily disruptive of the family. The scene in India and its neighbors is certainly changing, even though the rates may be uneven.

Attitudes and roles are' in a flux in India, Pakistan, Bangladesh and Sri Lanka. Women's legal status is generally guaranteed through progressive legislation related to child marriage, divorce, polygamy and inheritance. Hundreds of thousands of women now work out of economic need rather than to get even with men. The educated women in all these countries acquired' remarkable confidence. Female literacy in India, for instance, is rising at a faster rate than male literacy. But the demographic and socio-economic data for countries with extensive territory and large diversified population is bound to differ from one area to another. Hence, female literacy is 65 percent in Kerala (India), but 11 percent in Rajasthan.

Although the most important role of South Asian women may still be motherhood, they are not "nailed to their own' crosses". Conditions vary between regions and classes, and there are government plans to attack the problem. The Government of India see to promote the social progress of working women, above all those living in the rural areas. A Women's Division of the Government of Pakistan was established in 1979, two years after the process of Islam conversion was initiated. This Division launched about 4,000 multi-purpose projects such as centers for literacy, vocational training, health and legal aid. A Women's Rights Wing strives to represent women's interests in public policy formulation.

A number of national conferences on the theme have been organized by this Wing. In Bangladesh, where the legal status of women is determined by the Sharia laws, the Parliament has a reserved quota for women members, a separate Women's Affairs Ministry has been established and a quota of 10 percent of jobs is set aside for them. The status of women varies according to the ethnic (Sinhalese, Tamil, Moors), religious (Buddhist, Hindu, Christian, Muslim), caste, class and legal disparities in Sri Lanka. But that country produced the world's first woman Prime Minister. Female literacy is 70 percent, life expectancy is -67 years and women form 40 percent of all university students.

They, nevertheless, constitute 27 percent of the total work force. Except teachers, doctors and clerks, they receive unequal pay. They still work on plantations - longer than men. Women of South-East Asia have traditionally enjoyed a higher status. For instance, they do not practice seclusion. Filipinos frequently point out how well of their women are. Indeed, they obtain as much education as the men and arable to pursue a wide array of occupations. Female urban literacy is 92 percent and rural literacy 77 percent. But women have higher rates of unemployment, they receive the lower ranks of the occupation in the distribution of level of responsibility and when they are employed, they earn about 44 percent less than men of comparable education.

Although the President is Mrs. Aquino, very few (0.6 percent) of them become executives. The traditional society of Indonesia (with its kinship system) still exercises an important influence on women's position. But the universal marriage law, promulgated in 1974, sets a minimum age (16 for women) for marriage, restricts polygamy as well as men's right in respect to divorce. Inheritance, however, is still determined by customary law. Although there are also segregated Muslim and Catholic private religious schools, the system of learning is co-educational. Having ratified the ILO Convention, the Indonesian Government has thus accepted the principle of equal pay for equal work.

Those who have reached 17 or are already married have the right to vote. Indonesian women have been elected to the Constituent Assembly and have worked as Cabinet Ministers. Progress is closely linked with the role women play in society. The attitude to various aspects of their position differs from country to country depending on the social system and the level of economic development.' It is clear, however, that problems relating to their life can no longer wait for a solution. The position of women is a "barometer of democracy" in any country. The statements of all Asian leaders, when combined, make up a program of the social emancipation of women.

The first provision of this program is their complete equality as an inalienable part of the transformation of society for the better. Women are a powerful social force without whose participation it is impossible to solve fundamental problems.

One of the primary conditions for the emancipation of women is the wide use of female labour in social production. Free, conscious and creative female labour in such production helps the around development of the woman's personality, relieves her from secluded life and stimulates her general activity. Increasingly active part in the administration of enterprises and of state is included in the performance due to women.

JAPANESE DOMESTIC LAW

Historically and up until mid-1950, only the western nations have been in the centre of international organisations, creating leagues, organisations and pacts among themselves on the European continent. African and oriental nations, on the contrary, tended to be situated in and defined on the periphery of European organisations. However, after World War II and more conspicuously in 1960s and thereafter, Asian nations have started to establish their own associations and groups. Among the several United Nations agencies established in Asia Pacific area since 1940s, most conspicuous organization is the Economic and Social Commission for the Asia Pacific (ESCAP).

The Commission was originally established in Shanghai, China, on 28 March 1947 as the Economic and Social Commission for Asia and the Far East (ECAFE). The location of its headquarters relocated to Bangkok, Thailand in 1949, and the name was changed in 1977 to ESCAP, reflecting both economic and social aspects of development and the geographic location of its members. According to a UN press release, ESCAP has grown from 10 to 60 member and associate member countries, representing some 60 per cent of the world's population, or 3.5 billion people.

Its membership ranges from small Pacific island countries such as Niue, to the most populous countries of the world, China and India. In commemorating the Commission's fiftieth anniversary, the Shanghai Symposium was held from 18 to 20 March 1997. It is reported that the participants to the symposium, including Qian Qichen, China's Vice Premier and

Foreign Minister and Adrianus Mooy, Executive Secretary of the Commission, unanimously agreed that ESCAP must continue to play a catalytic role in spreading the growth momentum more evenly, and play a multifaceted role as the only intergovernmental forum for the exchange of national economic and social development views and experiences.

In addition to UN organisations, the Association of Southeast Asian Nations (ASEAN) is perhaps the most important regional organisation, established in 1967 at Jakarta, Indonesia, and has been leading other regional organisations in Asia. Other regional organisations followed. Now, in alphabetical order, there is Asia Pacific Economic Cooperation (APEC), Asean Regional Forum (ARF), Asia-Europe Meeting (ASEM), Closer Economic Relations-Trade Agreement between Australia and New Zealand (CER), Indian Ocean Rim Association for Regional Cooperation (IORA), Korean Peninsula Energy Development Organisation (KEDO), and Pacific Economic Cooperation Council (PECC), to name a few. Each of these organisations has its own sub-groups either as expert or advisory groups.

APEC, for instance, has advisory groups such as ABAC, EPG, and PBF, four committees of BAC, CTI, EC, PLG-SME, and several other working groups including TID, TP, IST, HRD, REC, MRC, TEL, TPT, TWG and FWG. ASEAN has similar sub-groups, committees and working groups. By looking at these groups and committees totally, one can be perplexed to see the multitude of organisational structures in the Asia Pacific. In addition to the above "official" and large international organisations, non-governmental and smaller organizations have been playing important role in international governance.

The Charter of the United Nations, in article 71, stipulates that the benefit of NGO activities in economic and social matters can be utilised by Economic Social Council (ECOSOC) in its jurisdiction. According to Charnovitz, Director of Global Environment and Trade Study at Yale University, the decade of the 1990s has provided new opportunities for NGO participation, although NGOs have almost two centuries of experience since 1775. Therefore, not only the official international organisations but also NGOs will have to be considered as important international organisations.

REGIONAL ASSOCIATIONS RELATING TO LAW AND LAWYERS

There are several regional associations relating to law and legal activities in the Asia Pacific area. In addition to the most active Law Association for Asia and the Pacific (LAWASIA), lawyers' organizations such as Asian-African Legal Consultative Committee (AALCC), Human Rights Watch Asia (HRW Asia), International Jurists Organization, Asia (IJOA), and Inter-Pacific Bar Association (IPBA) focus their activities mostly in the Asia Pacific, while Amnesty International, International Association of Lawyers (IAL), International Bar Association (IBA), International Commission of Jurists (ICJ), and Lawyers Committee for Human Rights (LCHR) cover the region as part of their international activities.

In particular fields of law, United Nations Commission of International Trade Law (UNCITRAL, created in 1966) works mostly on trade and investment laws, while International Institute for the Unification of Private Law (UNIDROIT, created in 1926) has a long history for the unification of private laws, such as Principles of International Commercial Contracts (1994). Although mostly concerned with commercial activities, International Chamber of Commerce (ICC) works on International Commercial Terms (1990) and the Uniform Rules on Documentary Credits of 1993. ICC's new arbitration rules, adopted in April 1997 in Shanghai, China, will play an important role with the global increase in the use of arbitration as a mode of dispute resolution.

In 1980s, as a result of UN Conference on Contracts for the International Sale of Goods (UNCCISG), the Convention on Contracts for the International Sale of Goods (CISG) entered into force in January 1988, thus providing several countries such as Australia, China, New Zealand and Singapore a common legal document for international contracts. In relation to international law, particularly on human rights, there has been no regional mechanism or machinery (such as human rights commission or human rights court) in the Asia Pacific region, unlike Europe, Americas, and Africa and Arab nations. The matter has been the subject for the continued discussion at ESCAP and LAWASIA in recent years, and several proposals including the Pacific Charter of Human Rights have been presented by participants to the ESCAP and LAWASIA seminars and by other NGOs.

Currently, it seems that the only available means for referral to an international body by an individual is through communications from the complaining citizen directly to human rights committees such as under the International Covenant on Civil and Political Rights (ICCPR). Along with ICC, the International Centre for Settlement of Investment Disputes (ICSID) functions as a tribunal for arbitration under the Convention on the Settlement of Investment Disputes between States and Nationals of Other States (Washington Convention). Finally, ASEAN's Ministers of Law Meeting (ASLOM) should be mentioned. In April 1986, in Bali, ASEAN Ministers of Justice and Law, and Attorneys-General met for the first time, and agreed on the organization arrangement for cooperation in legal field. Legal cooperation initially comprised the three aspects of exchange of legal materials, judicial cooperation, and legal education and research.

In April 1993, in Kuala Lumpur, the Second ASEAN Ministers Meeting noted the desirability of judicial and legal cooperation and called upon the ASEAN legal fraternity to enhance the understanding of each other's legal systems, highlighted the need to disseminate reports of studies and research on law and recommended increased bilateral and regional cooperation in legal training, continuing legal education and exchange of study visits. A feasibility study for developing an ASEAN Legal Information System was considered. In September 1996, at the third ASLOM in Manila, study visits by law officials, continuing legal education programmes, exchange of teachers and experts in the field of law were also discussed and encouraged. The fourth meeting will be held in Singapore in 1999.

PROBLEM

The problem here in terms of law is threefold: first, even though the activities of these regional organisations or regional functions of international organisations have direct or indirect impacts on Japanese domestic laws, these impacts have been under virtually no legal scrutiny by Japanese courts and also, when interpreting international standards and legal norms, Japanese courts have faced difficulties in appreciating and evaluating the norms. This is conspicuously expressed in a Supreme Court decision in 1995. The majority opinion (10 to 5) in the Grand Bench decision on 5 July 1995, held that article 900 of the Civil Code, allowing discriminatory treatment against illegitimate children or children born out of wedlock, was not unconstitutional.

Prior to this decision, the Human Rights Committee of ICCPR had specifically recommended that the article in question was against Article 24 of the Covenant, and that the Japanese Government should take measures necessary to remedy the situation in question. Second, the impacts of international and regional organisation on domestic laws should be explored more fully by practicing and academic lawyers. There are a couple of court decisions in Japan, citing international obligations under treaties and conventions. These and others reflected the efforts by attorneys for the particular cases, particularly from the Osaka Bar Association and the Japan Federation of Bar Associations, with assistance from academic lawyers. However, the study should be conducted more fully and systematically.

Third, international and comparative legal studies in this field need more attention, such as by this NZACL special issue on regional impacts on the domestic legal system. By a single inquiry on the internet by Yahoo, Alta Vista or Infoseek which the author tried in February 1998, "Asia pacific and law" search produced 316,725 Alta Vista web pages for the words, and 3,343,423 Infoseek pages containing at least one of these words. These and other Web sites and related organisations should be orchestrated in this kind of research.

As Professor Echols of the Howard University Law School suggests, "the increases in [regional] arrangements and in the numbers of countries involved, coupled with their expanded substantive scope, are creating new bodies of law and presenting new challenges to the multilateral system". The system of law and politics in the Asia Pacific region should not be ignored. This is true with regard not only to attorneys who counsel clients concerning international transactions, but also to citizens whose daily transactions are now more or less governed by these regional bodies of law and politics. Without full or substantial analysis and consideration of their activities and products, we will perhaps be unable to see the position of Japan among nations of the Asia Pacific, not to mention the position of Japanese law in the globalizing age.

PROLIFERATION OF ORGANISATIONS AND TREATIES

It may be of some assistance to look at Japan's international relations after 1945, first, and examine Japan's relations with Asia Pacific area. Since 1945, Japan has been maintaining strong relations, both politically and economically, with the United States. Politically, Japan has been pursuing the dual purposes of the internationalism and globalism on one hand, and bilateralism, that is bilateral relations with the United States on the other. The former principle of internationalism or pacifism was introduced into the Japanese constitutional regime under the General Headquarters (GHQ) directives and later in accordance with the Peace Treaty between the Allied Powers and Japan (1951), and was executed in the Ten Principles of the meeting of twenty-nine African-Asian nations in Bandong, Indonesia (1955).

The latter regime was inaugurated by the security treaty between Japan and the United States of 1951, and has been maintained in 1954 by the Mutual Defense Assistance Agreement between the United States and Japan, and in 1960 and thereafter by the Treaty of Mutual Cooperation and Security between the United States and Japan. Since 1951, the security treaty, Anpo Joyaku, has become a catchword for both those for or against the Japanese Government's foreign policies, thus dividing sharply the political orientation of the people up until 1990s. Although the nature or characteristics of the US-Japan security treaty has substantially changed in the past 46 years, this nature is still maintained or reinforced in the late 1990s when Japan is trying to hold its political and military relations with the United States under the Joint Declaration on Security Alliance for the 21st Century.

Economically, Japan's dependence on the United States continued until 1960s when Japan's annual growth rate was more than 10% every year. The economic growth of Japan developed out of Japan's international relations with and assistance from the United States, but it is important to see that it has been based not on bilateral but on multilateral base, that is GATT.

Under GATT, it was not necessary for Japan to claim its position for open, liberal and free international trade before the international and regional fora, since GATT has been playing a foster parent role for Japan. Perhaps Japan has been one of the best beneficiaries of the GATT trading system, and even with its huge amount of economic gains Japan could still maintain its position of multilateralism or open regionalism under the GATT/WTO regime of international trade and commerce. This policy was made clear and is still maintained with the United States by the Japanese Government in its Joint Statement on Framework for a New Economic Partnership in 1993.

Japan's Relations with Asian Countries

In the 1940-1950s, Japanese Government policy toward Asia was not so clear. Political relations with China, Korea and Soviet Union have prevented the Japanese Government from making its positions clearer for these important nations than its relations with Southeast Asian nations. However, one basic policy was clearly enhanced in relation to Asia as a whole: the policy of "dividing politics from economic activities", which successive LDP governments have taken primarily as a means of economic development of Japan. This is, in a sense, in contrast to the political-economic mix policy of the Japanese Government with relation to the United States.

In the 1950-1980s, by a series of voluntary reductions of exports, ranging from apparel to machinery products and later from automobile to computer chips, from Japan to the United States, Japanese companies have actually shifted their location of production and consumption of products to Southeast Asian countries since 1960s. In other words, the economic problems of Japan with the United States have been solved by political measures, while political problems with Asian countries have tried to be avoided or have been settled by the economic means of ODA assistance and overseas production.

Normalization of diplomatic and political relations with Korea under the Korea-Japan Basic Treaty in June 1965 and with China under the Joint Statement of China and Japan in September 1972 and the resulting Peace and Friendship Treaty between China and Japan in August 1978 added further economic opportunities to the Japanese economy. However, a peace treaty with Soviet Union, now the Russian Federation, has never been concluded. It was only after the APEC Summit meeting in Blake Island, Seattle, USA in November 1993 when the Japanese Government seemed to have clearly recognised the situation that the host country of the Summit, the United States, was actually interested in the Asia-Pacific region in economic terms, and that Japan needed its clear policy, political or otherwise, for the Asia-Pacific.

There was a precedent for this: Nixon's recognition in 1972 of China without any prior consultation with the Japanese Government. In 1972, Japanese Government followed the unilateral practice of the United States for China in political terms; and again in 1993, the both governments published their

Joint Statement on Framework for a New Economic Partnership in 1993 in economic terms as mentioned above, this time particularly for Asia Pacific and generally for the rest of the world. However, as long as APEC continues to be a forum of independent nations rather than involving multilateral institutions, coupled with its history based on initiatives of Australia and Japan, the United States will not be able to exert its political powers over APEC.

Japan's Policy for Asia and the Pacific

According to Kagami, Consul General to the Consulate General of Japan in Detroit, Michigan, the Pacific Rim area still: (1) has some de-stabilising elements politically; (2) is economically interdependent in trade and investment, (3) is characterised by diversity in population, income, culture, religion and ethnic make-up, (4) has the problem of Chinese reform and opening of its economy; and (5) greatly depends on the economic and political presence of the United States. He also cites economic cooperation and ODA, and concludes that regional cooperation should not result in regional blocs, and that three pillars of trade and investment liberalisation, their facilitation and economic and technical cooperation should be enhanced as agreed in Osaka in 1995.

These and other views verify the Japanese government attitude against such a regional grouping as East Asian Economic Group (EAEG). Under these circumstances, Japan considers APEC the most important forum for economic cooperation in the Asia Pacific. "Furthermore, it strongly supports the APEC commitment to open regionalism, which contributes to regional and global economic growth in a manner that complements and reinforces the multilateral free trade system."

Japan stresses the following key functions and responsibilities for APEC: (1) promoting and liberalizing trade and investment; (2) acting as a forum for consultation on economic cooperation; (3) monitoring regional economic trends; (4) ensuring its consistency with GATT, and seeking to complement and strengthen GATT; (5) striving to enhance understanding with non-members, international organisations and others. In the 1960s, a concept of a Pacific Free Trade Area (PAFTA) was advanced by Professor Kiyoshi Kojima, a Japanese economist, as a regional economic cooperation for the United States, Japan, Canada, Australia and New Zealand in 1965.

The idea later developed into a series of regional conferences, called the Pacific Trade and Development Conference (PAFTAD). In April 1966, the first Southeast Asian Ministerial Conference for Economic Development was held. In August 1967, ASEAN was established. In May, 1968, the Pacific Basin Economic Council (PBEC) was formed. PBEC has national conferences, and PBEC (US), for instance, had the annual policy conference in February 1998 in Washington, DC under the theme of "Riding Out the Storm", examining the impact of the recent Asian financial crisis on business around the Pacific Rim and holding a symposium under the co-sponsorship of PBEC committees of Canada, Mexico and the United States.

Then, in the 1970s, came the idea of an Organisation for Pacific Trade and Development (OPTAD), similar to OECD in Europe. The idea is credited to Sir John Crawford of Australia and Dr. Saburo Okita of Japan. Although the concept was never realized, in 1979, the then Japanese PM, Masayoshi Ohira, proposed the Pacific Basin Cooperation Concept as a common policy for the Asia Pacific. In 1980, the Pacific Community Seminar was held in Canberra, Australia. Eleven Pacific basin countries participated, leading to the establishment of the current Pacific Economic Cooperation Council (PECC), the name of which was formally adopted at its Honolulu meeting in January 1992.

PECC also has national committees. The Japan National Committee for Pacific Economic Cooperation (JANCPEC), for instance, has its secretariat at Japan Institute of International Affairs (JIIA) in Tokyo, consisting of 100 members and advisors from industry, government and academia. JANCPEC has nine sub-committees on Pacific Economic Outlook (PEO), Transportation/Telecommunication/Tourism (TTT), Trade Policy forum (TPF), Food and Agriculture Forum (F&A), Minerals and Energy Forum (MEF), Fisheries Development, Pacific Island Nations (PIN), Science and Technology (S&T), and Human Resources Development (HRD).

In the 1980s, there were concurrent movements in North America and in the Asia Pacific for the formation of regional trade areas. In North America, the pros and cons for free trade area agreements with Taiwan, Republic of Korea and ASEAN, or the Pacific Rim region were examined by the International Trade Commission (ITC) of the US Federal Government. In North America, the Canada-US Free Trade Agreement and its extension to North American Free Trade Agreement (NAFTA) came to be implemented. In the Pacific, also in January 1989, Australian PM Robert Hawke proposed the formation of a consultative system for the Asia Pacific region. In November 1989, APEC was established at its first Ministerial Meeting in Canberra, Australia. Member economies have their own office at each government. Japan, for instance, has its responsible office in the Ministry of Foreign Affairs (MOFA).

In the 1990s, APEC's second Ministerial Meeting was held in Singapore in July 1990, third Meeting in Seoul, South Korea in November 1991, fourth Meeting in Bangkok, Thailand in September 1992, fifth in Blake Island, Seattle, USA in November 1993 (where the first Economic Leaders Summit was held), sixth in Jakarta, Indonesia in November 1994, seventh in Osaka, Japan in November 1995, eighth in Subic, the Philippines in November 1996, and ninth in Vancouver, Canada in November 1997.

In the 1990s also, a concept of an East Asian Economic Group (EAEG) was advanced (but not implemented) in December 1990, and in October 1991, ASEAN reached agreement on creating the East Asian Economic Caucus (EAEC). In January 1992, ASEAN determined to establish the ASEAN Free Trade Area (AFTA), while in North America negotiations over NAFTA reached a settlement.

ORCHESTRATING LEGAL IMPLICATIONS OF ASIA PACIFIC ORGANISATIONS

A brief examination of organisations and associations in the Asia Pacific will lead to one immediate concern: orchestrating the system for the analysis of legal implications of them in each country. Although certain groupings of the regional organisations and associations may be made in three large categories such as ESCAP (UN), ASEAN, and APEC, or according to subjects such as contract law or human rights, what is required for legal analysis today is to untie the legal ramifications of complex and overlapping institutional outputs and practices.

Taking the law of contract, for instance, three levels of study will be necessary: (1) legal institutional such as AALCC, UNCITRAL, UNIDROIT and ICC along with UCC and European Code of Contract, (2) non-legal institutional such as APEC's BMN, CTI, IPR, PBF, TP and similar sub-groups of ASEAN, PECC and SPF; (3) traditional doctrinal study with new contract patterns or forms in mind, such as 1997 UN report on Consumer Guidelines of 1985, or contract of new services including services for telecommunications and financial services. As John Barton suggests, it is important maintaining "sensitivity to potential inter-cultural issues," when implications of international legal integration are to be examined. Therefore, socio-cultural and inter-cultural studies should supplement the relevant study of law in the Asia Pacific area.

3

Law as an Instrument of Change in Asia

The law regulates the social interests, arbitrates conflicting claims and demands security of persons and property of the people and is an essential function of the state. It could be achieved through instrumentality of law. Undoubtedly, there is a cross cultural conflict where living law must find answer to the new challenges and the courts are required to mould the sentencing system to meet the challenges. The contagion of lawlessness would undermine social order and lay it in ruins. Protection of society and stamping out criminal proclivity must be the object of the law, which must be achieved by imposing appropriate sentence. Therefore, law as a corner stone of the edifice of "order" should meet the challenges confronting the society.

The social impact of the crime, e.g. where it relates to offences against women, dacoity, kidnapping and other offences involving moral turpitude or moral delinquency which have great impact on social order and public interest, cannot be lost sight of and per se require exemplary treatment. The law in order to be legitimate and legal must also satisfy the mandates of the Constitution of India. The Constitution of India is not intended to be the arena of legal quibbling for men with long purses. It is made for the common people. It should generally be so construed as that they can understand and appreciate it. The more they understand it the more they love it and the more they prize it. It is really the poor, starved and mindless millions who need the court's protection for securing to themselves the enjoyment of Human Rights.

The Constitution precedents cannot be permitted to be transformed into weapons for defeating the hopes and aspirations of our teaming millions, half-clad, half-starved, and half-educated. These hopes and aspirations representing the will of the people can only become articulate through the voice of their elected representatives. If they fail the people, the nation must face the death and destruction. Then, neither the court nor the Constitution will save the country. The Constitution, unlike other Acts, is intended to provide an enduring paramount law and a basic design of the structure and power of the State and rights and duties of the citizens to serve the society through a long lapse of ages.

It is not only designed to meet the needs of the day when it is enacted but also the needs of the altering conditions of the future. It contains a framework of mechanism for resolution of constitutional disputes. It also embeds its ideals of establishing an egalitarian social order to accord socio-economic and political justice to all sections of the society assuring dignity of person and to integrate a united social order assuring every citizen fundamental rights assured in part III and the directives in part IV of the Constitution. In the interpretation of the Constitution, words of width are both a framework of concepts and means to achieve the goals in the preamble. Concepts may keep changing to expand and elongate the rights.

Constitutional issues are not solved by mere appeal to the meaning of the words without an acceptance of the line of their growth. The intention of the Constitution is, rather, to outline principles than to engrave details. Thus, law should sub serve social purpose. Judge must be a jurist endowed with the legislator's wisdom, historian's search for truth, prophet's vision, and capacity to respond to the needs of the present, resilience to cope with the demands of the future and to decide objectively disengaging himself/herself from every personal influence or predilections. Therefore, the judges should adopt *purposive interpretation* of the dynamic concepts of the Constitution and the Act with its interpretative armoury to articulate the felt necessities of the time.

The judge must also bear in mind that social legislation is not a document for fastidious dialects but a means of ordering the life of the people. To construe law one must enter into its spirit, its setting and history. Law should be capable of expanding freedoms of the people and the legal order can, weighed with utmost equal care, be made to provide the underpinning of the highly inequitable social order. In this background we will discuss the "need" of amending the Information Technology Act, 2000(Act).

THE NEED OF CHANGE

The Act has been enacted "primarily" to deal with e-governance and e-commerce. The "legislature" was, however, cautious and wise enough to incorporate provisions dealing with "contraventions" and "offences" using the information technology. A "Constitutionally ideal amendment initiative" must consider the following aspects:

a. *Nature of amendment*: The concept of "indepth review" suggests that the present Act is "improper" rather than "imperfect". The stress seems to be on "complete change' rather than "necessary minor modifications". This is a wrong strategy that has unfortunately been adopted by the government.

b. *Need of amendment*: The need of amendment is not based on "germane reasons" but is primarily guided by the recent "MMS controversy". The law is meant for the "People of India" and not for any particular "segment". The most embarrassing moment of the Indian Legal System was not the "arrest" of the CEO of the Bazee.com but the "interference of the USA in the sovereign governance of India". It must be noted that the managing of e-commerce business requires certain safeguards to be followed by those who are deriving benefits out of it. If these 'minimum safeguards" are not followed than the law will take it very seriously. The "rule of law" does not recognise any appeal of a "foreign country" or "domestic pressures". Thus, the amendment of the Act must be guided by germane reasons only and it should not be based on irrelevant, arbitrary, unreasonable and extraneous considerations.

c. *Areas of amendment*: The law exists to serve the needs of the society, which is governed by it. If the law is to play its allotted role of serving the needs of the society, it must reflect the ideas and ideologies of that society. It must keep time with the heartbeats of the society and with the needs and aspirations of the people. As the society changes, the law cannot remain immutable. The early nineteenth century essayist and wit, Sydney Smith, said, 'Then I hear any man talk of an unalterable law, I am convinced that he is an unalterable fool."

The law must, therefore, in a changing society march in tune with the changed ideas and ideologies. At this stage the words of *Justice Bhagwati* in the case of *National Textiles Workers Union v P.R. Ramakrishnan* need to be set out. They are: "We cannot allow the dead hand of the past to stifle the growth of the living present. Law cannot stand still; it must change with the changing social concepts and values. If the bark that protects the tree fails to grow and expand along with the tree, it will either choke the tree or if it is a living tree it will shed that bark and grow a living bark for itself.

Similarly, if the law fails to respond to the needs of changing society, then either it will stifle the growth of the society and choke its progress or if the society is vigorous enough, it will cast away the law, which stands in the way of its growth. Law must therefore constantly be on the move adapting itself to the fast-changing society and not lag behind. The Act requires amendment to fill in the following "grey area" on a priority basis:

i. The "right to information" as flowing out of Article 19(1)(a) of the Constitution,

ii. The "right to know" as flowing out of Article 21 of the Constitution,

iii. The "right to privacy" as flowing out of Article 21 of the Constitution,

iv. The need of protecting the "electronic data property". The "paper based data property" can be sufficiently protected by the Indian Copyright Act, 1957,

v. The need of providing a "sound e-governance base" that should include effective e-justice administration facilities,

vi. The need for providing a more stronger e-commerce base,The need to strengthen the "Internet Banking" infrastructure,

vii. The need to strengthen the " Cyber Insurance Business infrastructure",

viii. The need to protect people of India from "Cyber Terrorism" in India,

ix. The need of adoption of the "techniques of aggressive defence" in India, etc.

These are the issues that need an immediate attention of the "legislature" and not other "self serving changes" which will leave the Act more vulnerable to "unconstitutionality".

d. *Place of amendment*: One of the thriving needs of change is in the field of "cyber forensic". The Act, however, is not the right "place" to make the change. In India we have both "substantive" and "procedural" laws. The Indian Penal Code and Information Technology Act are "substantive laws" whereas the Indian Evidence Act and Criminal Procedure Code are "procedural laws". Thus, the inter-mingling of procedural laws into substantive laws is not a desirable exercise. This mandates the amendment of the "Evidence Act" rather the "Information Technology Act".

e. *Ancillary matters*: The ancillary matters like "cyber-café regulations", "blocking of web-sites", etc are not the fit subject for "amendment". As far as the regulation of the cyber-café is concerned, the respective "State Governments" can do so through "notification method". Similarly, the authority for the blocking of web sites has already been constituted under the provisions of the Act; hence duplicating the efforts and wasting the valuable resources will serve no useful purpose.

If these areas are "ignored" either in the zeal of amendment process or due to pressure tactics, then the law in this regard would be a "remedy worst than the malady" hence its amendment should not be undertaken at any cost. If such an amendment were proceeded with, then it would definitely be tested on the touchstone of the provisions of Constitution of India and will not survive the test of "constitutionality".

ALTERNATIVE STRATEGY

The cumbersome, time consuming and expensive process can be avoided by issuing "simple notifications" by the government that will clear the mist surrounding the present atmosphere. Similarly, the matter is before the court the same can also be taken care by the courts in India. Legislatures are not best fitted for the role of adapting the law to the necessities of the time, for the legislative process is too slow and the legislatures often divided by politics, slowed down by periodic elections and overburdened with myriad other legislative activities.

This task must, therefore, of necessity fall upon the courts because the courts can by the process of judicial interpretation adapt the law to suit the needs of the society. Thus, Courts in India can provide a much better solution to this situation by adopting the "purposive and updating modes of interpretation' of the provisions of the Act. It is presumed that the Parliament intends the court to apply to an ongoing Act a construction that continuously updates its wordings to allow for changes since the Act was initially framed. While it remains law, it has to be treated as always speaking. This means that in its application on any day, the language of the Act though necessarily embedded in its own time, is nevertheless to be construed in accordance with the need to treat it as a current law.

The role model for governance and decision taken thereon should manifest equity, fair play and justice. The cardinal principle of governance in a civilized society based on rule of law not only has to base on transparency but also must create an impression that the decision-making was motivated on the consideration of probity. The government has to rise above the nexus of vested interests and nepotism and eschew window-dressing.

The act of governance has to withstand the test of judiciousness and impartiality and avoid arbitrary or capricious actions. Therefore, the principle of governance has to be tested on the touchstone of justice, equity and fair play. Though on the face of it the decision may look legitimate but as a matter of fact the reasons may not be based on values but to achieve popular accolade that decision cannot be allowed to operate. Any decision of the government ignoring these "mandates" will be declared to be unconstitutional, no matter how much pressure is put on it.

The concept of gender justice has a variety of meanings. In the area of liberal philosophy, it is focused on thinking about subjective agency, rights and capacities; whereas in political science it is concerned with the constitution, processes of democracy, and citizenship. In the area of law, the concept of gender justice can mean formal equal rights between men and women. As well, it can relate to uncovering gender biases that are integral to the legal process and which affect the ways women come to experience the law. In the legal terrain, the concept of gender justice is contingent on location-within the family, the class and/or religious community as well as within the definitions of the nation-state. Law is not the only site for the pursuit of gender justice. But given law's location as an authoritative discourse, it does have a critical role to play in shaping the meaning and content of gender justice.

The review of literature on gender justice and the usage of the term in the context of this essay is set out. In particular,

I include a discussion on how liberalism has been quite central in influencing our understandings of gender justice in law, especially with its focus on the autonomous, liberal subject, who exists a *priori* to social relations. This section examines how the legal arena has shaped our understanding of gender justice, with its constant reiteration of the rights of 'man', its focus on the autonomous, liberal subject, and the belief that law is an objective external, neutral truth. In the second section, there is an analysis of the meaning and practice of citizenship and rights as it has emerged in South Asia through the colonial encounter and taken shape in the postcolonial era of nation-states.

The third section highlights the key areas of struggles for gender justice in South Asia. The fourth section summarizes some of the challenges faced by donors, the women's movements and other human rights and social justice groups in the pursuit of gender justice in and through law. The final section sets out recommendations for future research.

DEFINITIONS AND REVIEW OF LITERATURE ON GENDER JUSTICE

The literature on gender justice as understood in law reflects several different understandings of the concept in the South Asian context. There are at least three distinct perspectives that are discernible in the literature, which in turn affect understandings of law and development, citizenship and entitlement. These three approaches are: protectionism, equality and patriarchy. Each is described in the following section, and I offer examples highlighting how the literature on gender justice fits into each category. These categories are flexible, and clearly not all writings on gender justice in the arena of law fit neatly and unequivocally into a single category.

PROTECTIONISM

Perhaps the most problematic articulation of gender justice in law is the one that posits the relationship between women and law as one of protection. Scholars who endorse this approach have reinforced an essentialist understanding of gender difference, assuming that women are naturally weaker than men. For example, in a chapter entitled 'The Weaker Sex', author J.P. Atray notes:

> This position of helplessness is so much visible among women in general that it has ceased to be any longer of much significance even to them.

The protectionist approach accepts the traditional and patriarchal discourses that construct women as weak, biologically inferior, modest and incapable of decision-making. Such so-called feminine characteristics are perceived as natural, immutable and thus, as the appropriate starting place for legal regulation. Writers within this approach often extol the role of women within the family-roles which are assumed to be natural, selfless and sacred. Atray writes:

> A woman's position as a wife has been given the highest place over all other roles which she is required to play because it is here that she is required to perform the most arduous of duties and the most difficult of responsibilities... As a wife, she is beyond everything else and sits on a pedestal as high and as glorious as the imagination can reach.

Women's roles as mothers are similarly celebrated, and naturalized as an inevitable consequence of the biological differences between women and men. In this literature, the role of law is unproblematically asserted as protecting women. Laws that continue to treat women differently than men are accepted as a necessary part of this protection. This protectionist approach is often reflected in judicial approaches to the question of the relevance of gender difference. Since women are seen as weak and subordinate-and thereby in need of protection-they must be treated differently in law. Any differential treatment of women is deemed to be intended for women's protection and, therefore, for their benefit.

Some recent examples of law enacted ostensibly for women's benefit include the imposition of minimum age limits on female workers going abroad for employment by

Bangladesh, India and Nepal. In 1998, Bangladesh banned women from going abroad as domestic workers.[1] In 2002, the government of Bangladesh announced it was considering removing the ban. However, the ban appears to have remained in effect. In the same vein, although not entirely prohibiting migration by women, the Nepal Foreign Employment Act, 2042 (1985) prohibits issuance to women of employment licences to work overseas without the consent of the woman's husband or male guardian.

Although the Bangladesh Constitution declares equal rights for men and women in all spheres of public life Article 28(1), Article 28(4) also provides that the article shall not prevent the state from making special provisions in favour of women and children, or for the advancement of any 'backward section of citizens.' Given that women are included together with that group, there is an assumption incorporated into the Constitution that women are in need of greater protection than men and that the state or a male guardian is in the best position to afford her protection. This provision has justified a number of measures enacted by the state in the name of women's equality rights that actually reinforce a protectionist approach by the state towards women.

Some of these include the Factories Act 1934, The Tea Plantation Labour ordinance of 1962 and The Shops and Establishments Act of 1965. These restrict women's rights to movement or choice of employment. These laws prohibit employment of women and children between the hours of 8 p.m. and 6 a.m., provisions which are justified on the grounds that women are vulnerable at night and require state protection from possible harm or abuse. Women's ostensibly natural differences are deployed to justify any differential treatment in law, and in effect, operate to preclude any entitlement to equality. This approach is firmly located within patriarchal discourses. It does not problematize the way in which law treats women, nor does it consider women's subordinate status. Gender justice is located exclusively within a protectionist framework, whereby laws are enacted in order to protect women as they are unable to decide and act for themselves.

The effect is to infantilize women and pursue an agenda that merely reinforces this infantilization as it is contingent on male or state protection. While it is concerned with women as subjects of law, and even as subjects of rights, this literature is not within a feminist theoretical tradition. It is an approach that tends to essentialize the difference-that is-to take the existence of gender difference as natural and inevitable. It is an approach that affirms the legal relevance of gender difference and thus risks re-inscribing this difference along with the underlying social relations that produced it.

The legal recognition of this difference-within a protectionist approach-tends to both reflect and reinforce the common-sense understanding of this discrepancy as natural and inevitable. This conception of gender justice is reproduced in the discourse of progressive groups, such as women's groups as well as the discourse of the religious and conservative groups as I will illustrate later. It is a conception that is highlighted as it continues to be relevant in the contemporary moment and because it has had a significant effect on how gender justice has come to be understood in law.

EQUALITY

A second and perhaps more familiar approach to gender justice in the literature is one that is based on promoting equality. The literature has primarily focused on providing empirical reviews of laws that affect women. Writers within this approach have tended to provide comprehensive reviews of a range of legal provisions affecting women, from personal laws to criminal and labour laws. This literature highlights both laws that continue to discriminate against women and successful challenges to such discriminatory laws.

Writers within this approach have also tended to emphasize problems in relation to the under-enforcement of existing legal provisions governing women's equality rights. Implicit in much of this work is the assumption that law can play an important role in advancing women's equality by removing the legal obstacles that have limited women's full and equal participation. While this work recognizes there is still some distance to go before women's rights are adequately protected in law and gender justice fully achieved, there is a general optimism regarding the extent to which much of this road has already been travelled. Again, the positive role of law has more often been assumed than questioned.

An important feature of this approach is the conception of law upon which it is based. The depiction of law that emerges within this literature is its role in social engineering. For example, the 1975 *Report of the Committee on the Status of Women in India* placed considerable importance on the role of law: 'One of the main characteristics of modern society is a heavy reliance on law to bring about social change.' This role is highlighted in postcolonial states:

The tasks of social reconstruction, development and nation building all call for major changes in the social order, to achieve which legislation is one of the main instruments. It can act directly, as a norm setter, or indirectly, providing institutions which accelerate social change by making it more acceptable.

While the Report includes recommendations for sweeping legal reforms, this emphasis on the role of law in social engineering is not unqualified. For example, the Report also notes some of the limitations of law in this process. 'But legislation cannot by itself change society. To translate these rights into reality is the task of other agencies. Public opinion has to be moulded to accept these rights.' The Report, while noting the role of the judiciary and the executive levels of government in this process, further observes that neither level of government has fulfilled this role. With regard to the Courts, the Committee notes that legislation has often been narrowly interpreted, and that the courts have often 'failed to give effect to the principles underlying the legislation.' The subsequent focus of the Report is on revealing the areas in which the implementation of the law falls short of the principles it articulates.

Other government reports have also echoed this view of the limits of law. The *National Perspective Plan for Women* on India has observed:

> It is...necessary to realize that there are limits to the extent to which changes can be effected by law. Attempts at bringing about changes in women's status through either legislation or judicial activism can achieve little success without a simultaneous movement to change the social and economic structures and the culture of society. (Government of India 1988:135)

The view that emerges from both the *Report of the Committee on the Status of Women and the National Perspective Plan* is that law is a necessary but insufficient part of a more general strategy of bringing about social change. These reports, along with other literature in which the role of law is qualified, go some distance in recognizing the limitations of law in bringing about social change. However, they remain firmly located within the law as a social engineering thesis. As such, this literature does not question law's commitment to social change, nor does it consider the role of law in the subordination of women, beyond the discriminatory character of some laws. This understanding is important as it has been influential in shaping programmes for pursuing gender justice in different parts of South Asia.

There is an assumption that equality can be achieved through mere reform of the law and enforcement, which is a vision of equality for women found in the context of liberal feminism. Such feminism begins from the basic premises of liberal theory: individualism and equality. Accordingly, the focus of liberal feminism has been on women as individuals-in particular, the extent to which women have been denied the status of individuals, and denied the liberal goal of equality. Liberal feminism has placed considerable attention on law in pursuing gender justice. According to this approach, law has contributed to women's oppression by exclusion.

Women's oppression is understood largely as a result of discriminatory treatment. Thus, law can contribute to overcoming oppression by the creation of a legal order that includes women on an equal footing. Liberal feminist perspectives focus on eliminating statutory provisions and language that explicitly discriminate on the basis of sex, and which reinforces sexual stereotypes. According to this perspective, in order to achieve gender justice, women should be treated the same as men, and gender difference should be irrelevant in law. Liberal feminist perspectives on law have also developed a concern with ensuring equality for women through equal opportunity. In order to create conditions of equality for women, liberal feminists may argue in favour of affirmative action, that is, for rules that treat women preferentially in order to create substantive equality.

Liberal feminism provides some important insights into the legal regulation of women. It has focused on and identified the various forms of discrimination against women in law, and has provided a major impetus for waves of law reform establishing formal legal equality for women that have taken place throughout South Asia. However, it is also limited in some very significant respects. There is, for example, no analysis within liberal feminism of the underlying structures of oppression. The focus on the individual, and in particular, on the equal treatment of the individual in law leaves the economic, social, cultural and political institutions that produce and reinforce women's oppression uninterrogated. There is, accordingly, no consideration of the role of law in transcending this oppression-the role of law is simply assumed rather than problematized.

The liberal feminist approach is based on a very specific conception of equality-that is, it is based on the prevailing conception of equality as sameness. In this vision of equality, women are understood as the same as men-so, for the purposes of law they are the same, and must be treated the same. According to this version, any legislation or practice that treats women differently than men is seen to violate guarantees of equality. This sameness approach has been used to strike down provisions that treat women and men differently. It has, however, also been used to preclude any analysis of the potentially disparate affect of gender-neutral legislation. In some ways, this approach to equality is a reaction to the protectionist approach, which reinforced gender difference, instead of realizing gender justice. Thus it simply reproduced the processes of subordination under which women lived.

Some feminist approaches have endorsed this conception of equality. According to them, gender difference ought to be irrelevant, and women ought to be treated exactly the same as men. Advocates of this approach argue that so-called 'special treatment' has historically been a double-edged sword, because under the guise of protection, it has been used to discriminate against women. They point to the use of gender difference in the past in prohibiting women to vote, to be elected to government, to be admitted to the legal profession, and other such participation in the economic, political and cultural dimensions of society.

Similarly, in South Asia, an emphasis on equality as sameness is characterized by the same insights and limitations as liberal feminism. There is a focus on laws that treat women differently, and the need to reform such discriminatory laws. The starting assumption is one of equality, not difference. Like liberal-feminist perspectives to law, more generally this approach has been important in challenging prevailing assumptions about women, in revealing the extent to which women continue to be discriminated against in law, and in demanding that laws be reformed to better reflect and promote women's right to full and equal participation in the world around them. The role of law is assumed, while the underlying structures of oppression are given little attention.

It is also not enough to draw attention to the under-enforcement of law, as this approach does, and recommend ways to ensure more efficient enforcement. The emphasis of this approach is on increasing women's access and enforcement through such means as sensitizing the judiciary to women's issues, legal aid, family courts and increased legal awareness for women. Similarly, it assumes that if law is effectively enforced, it can remedy the social problems for which it is designed. This emphasis on enforcement obscures the role that law plays in women's subordination: that it cannot simply be deployed at will with the belief that it will produce progressive outcomes for women and gender justice. Eliminating discrimination and improving enforcement are not insignificant reforms. However, without a deeper understanding of the role of law in women's subordination, these reforms may only lead to further disillusionment with the legal system.

PATRIARCHY

A third approach in the literature on gender justice is one in which law is seen as an instrument of patriarchal oppression. In this approach, the focus of gender justice is to challenge the patriarchal assumptions on which law is based. Laws throughout South Asia continue to reflect patriarchal oppression and discriminate against women. These laws, and the judicial interpretations of these laws, are connected to the patriarchal social relations in which women have been oppressed.

Fareeda Shaheed's work is an example of the law as patriarchy approach. She argues that patriarchy in Pakistan results in inequalities to women. Law is used to entrench social and behavioural codes that are labelled as Islamic and used to counter Westernization, including feminism. She argues that law is used as a way of vindicating patriarchy. The three sources of such laws are customary law, religious law, and British civil and criminal law. She discusses how customary and religious laws currently endorse Muslim practices that promote the superiority of men and rejection of Islamic teachings promoting women's rights.

Customs such as the practice of *purdah* are designed to restrict women's participation in economic and political life. They simultaneously reinforce the control of men in the public domain. Lina Gonsalves' analysis in her study *Women and the Law* is also an example of scholarship within the law as patriarchy framework. Gonsalves focuses on the enforcement (and lack thereof) of laws that were intended to benefit women, and argues that 'law enforcers...discriminate between women and men and unconsciously tend to reflect traditional and rigid attitudes towards women'.

She attempts to highlight the extent to which 'the police, public prosecutors and the judges, who are products of patriarchal society, are by and large biased against women, and help to perpetuate and preserve the oppression of women. Gonsalves examines a broad range of laws affecting women-succession, maintenance, custody, divorce, rape and dowry-and attempts to illustrate the patriarchal biases in the courts' interpretation of these laws.

The outcome of trials and the unwillingness of the police to probe violence against women at home and in society have led to a situation in which the law as a whole can easily be taken to be an instrument of patriarchal oppression.

This literature views law as an instrument of patriarchy. It can be seen to loosely correspond to a 'dominance feminist perspective' on law. Dominance feminism attempts to provide a more structural analysis of women's oppression, based on the concept of patriarchy. As Supriya Akerkar succinctly describes 'the context of dominance feminism is that gender inequalities are the outcome of an autonomous system of patriarchy and that gender inequalities are the primary form of social inequality.'

The law as a patriarchy (or dominance feminism) approach tends to examine the ways in which gender justice in law is informed by and serves to reinforce patriarchal social relationships. A primary concern includes the way in which law reinforces male control over women's sexuality, together with the way in which law continues to exclude or marginalize women's values and needs in the legal processes. Law is regarded as being based on male norms, male experience and male domination. The focus of analysis is often on the legal regulation of sexuality and of violence.

Dominance feminism has made an important contribution

in attempting to locate women's oppression within broader structures of gender oppression, as well as in exposing how even the most intimate space of the home and family is political. In the context of law, it has been crucial in revealing the importance of the legal regulation of sexuality and of violence in the oppression of women. However, it is a perspective that is also limited in some important respects. It has been criticized for its understanding of patriarchy as a historical, decontextualized and universalistic; for its essentialist construction of women only as victims, rather than as agents of resistance and change; as well as for its focus on gender oppression to the exclusion of other forms of oppression.

The exclusive focus on sexuality as the site of women's oppression leaves out other sites that contribute in significant ways to gender injustice, such as the family and the economy. The complex and specific nature of relations of oppression tends to be reduced to monolithic and highly general explanations. Dominance feminist perspectives on law have been important in highlighting the negative and deeply problematic stereotypes of women that inform law and law enforcement. Further, such perspectives are also an important contribution in directing attention to the deeper structures of law and legal discourse, and suggesting a connection between these structures and women's oppression.

However, this framework does not go far enough in explaining the role of law in women's oppression nor in women's struggles. It is not sufficient to simply assert that law is patriarchal, or that the lawmakers are sexist. The vision of law as an instrument of patriarchy tells us very little about the precise workings of the law, and even less about if and how women can use law. These three approaches to gender justice influence the ways in which this issue is addressed in law. Each has shortcomings as set out in this section. There is a need to further problematize the concept of gender justice from a postcolonial perspective and to contextualize the role of rights and legal discourse in promoting specific understandings of gender justice.

CITIZENSHIP AND RIGHTS

In this section the meaning of citizenship and rights and their relevance to the pursuit of gender justice, are analysed in the context of South Asia.

CITIZENSHIP

The conception of gender justice affects the ways in which claims to citizenship and entitlement are pursued. Citizenship has been traditionally understood in a formal sense, that is, it is based on equal and formal citizenship for all adults born within the territory of a state. With the ending of colonialism in the context of South Asia, all adults were to be included in suffrage, and political inequality thus eliminated. However, feminists have challenged these formal understandings of citizenship, asserting that women still have a secondary status in political and public life. Women are also paid less than men and seem to be less respected than men in public life. They are often characterized as 'second-rate citizens'.

The analysis of gender justice suggests that citizenship is intimately connected to understandings of gender difference and whether women are included on the same terms as men, are treated as naturally weak and inferior, or as sometimes requiring different treatment and sometimes similar treatment in order to enjoy full access to their rights as citizens. If a woman, for example, is merely considered as naturally and inherently different from a man, then as evidenced in South Asia and elsewhere, difference in treatment in terms of the rights and privileges accorded through citizenship and the claims to entitlements will be justified merely on the basis of that difference.

If however, women are considered to be the same, and gender difference largely ignored, then citizenship will be understood in terms of formal equal treatment and similar treatment. This will not enable women to claim special rights, an entitlement to special treatment in order to accommodate the differences between men and women that do exist. For example, pregnancy or childcare is largely ignored in the sameness approach. Women are treated the same as men and any special treatment based on women's role in child bearing and rearing is regarded as a violation of the equality clause or as an exception to the principle of equality rather than integral to it.

Finally, if gender justice is viewed from the perspective of patriarchy, any claims to citizenship always will be exposed as deeply flawed, as inherently based on oppressing women through their sexuality and holding some undefined, omnipresent system of patriarchy responsible for women's oppression. Thus, citizenship is not just about membership and the rights and responsibilities that membership bestows. It is also connected to the way in which women are included or excluded based on the assumptions about gender difference on which citizenship is based.

In the legal arena, the literature reflects very different understandings of citizenship, and influences the ways in which gender justice is pursued. In the context of South Asia, the definition of citizenship was heavily influenced by the legacy of the colonial encounter. Citizenship was something that the 'white man' invented and was focused on the idea of the citizen as someone who was virtuous and rational, who had no kinship ties. In contrast, the colonial subject was viewed as lacking citizenship, as chaotic, different and incapable of taking on the responsibilities demanded of citizenship. This conception of citizenship, as linked to notions of reason, capacity to choose, as well as civilizational development was quite prevalent.

It was reminiscent of the attitude towards women, both in the subcontinent as well as in the west, who were regarded as infantile, incapable of decision-making and in need of protection. The law was employed as a means for defining citizenship in terms of an unstated Eurocentric norm. It was, at its core, a definition based on racial distinctions, on exclusions and the techniques of 'othering'. At the same time, the colonial power desired to redefine the colonial subject through a move to universalize and rationalize laws as well as to create a native population through Western education and create elites that mimicked the West. Thus the disciplining of sexuality in the colonial context which was perceived as corrupting and excessive, as well as the representation of the Western citizen to the colonial subject as good, decent, enlightened and civilized through the technologies of law and education were integral to the definitions of citizenship and of who could be incorporated into such definition and in what ways.

A uniform criminal legislation was enacted in 1833, which inaugurated the process of 'disarming' Indian society and moving towards the creation of a universal legal subject. The moral compass of the colonial power was inserted into the legal agenda, and used to justify the banning of a litany of practices-infanticide, sati, child marriages-in the name of rational law and civilizing the native into a recognizable and more familiar subject of liberal rights discourse. The image of citizenship as pure, virtuous and rational has been challenged in the feminist and postcolonial scholarship. It has also been contested on the ground, in the context of the early struggles for freedom and rights fought by anti-colonial movements, the struggle for rights and equality by women and other disadvantaged groups, and the contemporary conditions of globalization.

Anti-colonial struggles opened up new definitions of citizenship, as an identity that enables rights claims. Women have claimed rights to citizenship in Pakistan, India and Nepal; along with freedom from non-discrimination and freedom from violence. Religious minorities have claimed rights to retain special temporary measures as well as the right to be governed by their personal laws, in order to retain their integrity and freedom from majoritarianism. These claims have challenged the West's notions of universality and exposed the notion that the universal subject, or idea of the pure citizen, had built into it an exclusionary potential.

In the contemporary period, citizenship has been subjected to new concerns and challenges. The conflicts between different religious and ethnic groups, as in India, Bangladesh and Sri Lanka, have resulted in an increased strain in the boundaries of citizenship, where different groups are pitted against one another in their claims for recognition. Challenges have been made by religious and conservative forces against claims to citizenship by minorities in their own countries. Some examples include the claims of Ahmadiyas in Pakistan, the Nepali refugees in Bhutan, or the Muslims in India.

Citizenship is increasingly being informed by xenophobia, exclusions and other forms of alienation, that treat 'the other' as a threat to national and social cohesion and national identity (and security). It is for this reason that a review and understanding of the colonial constructions of citizenship are critical in order to appreciate the current shifts and contemporary constructions of citizenship. In the contemporary period, citizenship is increasingly essentializing identities, contingent on static definitions of caste, religion, age as well as class, as more groups compete for access to the scarce state resources and benefits. In other words, citizenship is being used as a tool for inclusion as well as exclusion, and cannot be understood in purely universalistic terms or as having equal applicability to all.

In the context of women, claims to citizenship have at times been based on the recognition of their gender difference. Historically, women have been denied rights to citizenship in their individual capacities and their citizenship determined by a male member such as a father or husband. Such exclusions were based on essentialist assumptions about women. They were not deemed capable of exercising rights to self-determination or engaging the public democratic or political process by virtue of their inferiority to men. This, in turn, has tended to essentialize gender identities: women are cast primarily as caretakers, mothers and wives in need of protection. Such an assumption has led to law-reform proposals that actually curtail rather than advance women's rights to gender justice.

An example is the previous Indian government's law reform proposal on domestic violence that was more concerned with the protection of the institution of the family and marriage, and women's roles within this institution. It sanctioned the right of men to beat their wives with reasonable cause, which included instances where a wife made a grab for her husband's property. A second example includes the recent interest in sexual harassment in Nepal and India, which has come to be informed by moralistic assumptions about women's sexual conduct and the need to sexually sanitize the workplace. At the same time, ignoring these differences does not address how difference has been used to discriminate against and subordinate women. The critical point is that the ways in which differences are understood and defined have a considerable influence on the way in which citizenship comes to be understood and defined.

The contemporary conditions of globalization have further altered understandings of citizenship. Since the 1980s, the processes of globalization have resulted in increased economic privatization and deregulation. Simultaneously, we have witnessed the emergence of new non-state actors, groups and communities who are migrating and no longer identified exclusively within one nation. There is an increased dependence on the market to provide essential services such as health or childcare. The unequal distribution of wealth leaves some citizens with less purchasing power to access these services and contributes to the impoverishment of marginalized groups such as women.

Feminist academics, advocates and women's organizations argue that unless development planning and practice take into account unequal power relations on the basis of gender, women's position-as well as that of other marginalized groups-will remain unchanged and might even worsen. Finally, undocumented migrants, of which women constitute at least fifty percent, are crossing borders and gravitating towards the large metropolitan centres, setting up a new strata of informal citizenship that destabilizes further 'pure forms' linked exclusively to one nation.

RIGHTS

Feminist legal studies and practices have begun to explore the question of the role of law in feminist struggles from a multiplicity of perspectives, many of which defy simple classification. A new perspective on the role of law and rights in the context of South Asia is emerging, one based on post-colonialism. I now review some of the recent literature in this area, which exemplifies the emergence of this approach. It is important to pursuing a gender justice project specifically in the context of South Asia, although it has ramifications well outside of this region. Postcolonial approaches to rights and law are varied and defy any simple classification. One common position, however, is that they do critique the basic philosophical tenets of the enlightenment-rationality, objectivity and subjectivity.

Post-colonialism rejects the concepts of objectivity and neutrality that are ostensibly the central characteristics of law, insisting the law is always based on biases and a point of view. Quite specifically, that law is based on inclusions and exclusions that are determined invariably from a majoritarian perspective. This view is based partly on the historical experiences with law, where the sovereignty of the Asian subcontinent was denied in the name of the imperial project and justified on the grounds that the colonial subject was so culturally and socially different, that he or she was not entitled to sovereignty or rights.

Difference was a ground for denying rights, and was not an argument posited in opposition to the notion of universal rights, but inherent in the universal project. Rights could only be conferred on those who had reached a certain stage of civilizational maturity and the colonial ruler was best situated to determine when that stage had been reached. Feminist legal studies have begun to develop increasingly complex and nuanced analyses of law's role in women's oppression, and its potential role in challenging that oppression. Interestingly, some of the most insightful work that has initially been written comes from disciplines other than law. Feminist historians have played a leading role in the articulation of a more complex understanding of the role of law in social change. Lata Mani, Radhika Singha and Tanika Sarkar are among the feminist historians who have critically examined the complex relationship between law in colonial India and women's subordination.

Singha, for example, considers the ways in which law-making was a cultural enterprise, where the colonial state could draw upon differences such as rank, status and gender. She explains how the state re-ordered these identities in ways that produced an exclusive definition of its sovereign rights, so as to define who was or was not entitled to benefits conferred. In addition to feminist historians, feminist work on law has begun to emerge within the social sciences and humanities more generally. In their ground-breaking discursive analysis of the Shah Bano case, Zakia Pathak and Rajeswari Sunder Rajan have examined law as discourse, and the way in which this discourse constitutes subjects.

More recently, Rajeswari Sunder Rajan has examined the relationship between the postcolonial, Indian nation-state, law and Indian women's actual needs and the contradictions produced through this relationship. She argues that law and citizenship define not only the scope of political rights for women, but also their cultural identity and everyday life. Postcolonial legal scholarship has only recently begun to develop these feminist perspectives. Archana Parashar, in her study of family law reform, examines and evaluates some of the insights of debates within feminist legal studies. She uses the insights of these debates to further her understanding of the role of law in social change, while rejecting those aspects of the debates that do not fit the Indian context.

In developing her analysis of the role of legislation and the promotion of gender justice, Parashar argues for the importance of law reform in women's struggles. However, her view of the nature of the role of law reform is informed by a consideration of the limits of law. She argues, for example, that 'instead of dismissing law reform as a means of achieving equality for women, it is more productive to realize the limitations of law and have appropriate expectations that law reform by itself will be insufficient to change society and end women's oppression.' She argues that law can serve an important symbolic value: 'Symbolic legislation can be of liberating value as it can provide a focus around which forces of change can mobilize.'

In this respect, Parashar's work marks an important shift in feminist legal analysis, in its integration of rigorous and detailed legal analysis with a feminist perspective attentive to both the limitations and possibilities of law. Other scholars have similarly begun to complicate feminist understandings of law. Nivedita Menon has explored questions of the conceptualization of rights within the context of women's struggles around abortion, sexual violence and reservations. Menon's work can be seen as a discursive analysis of the women's movement's engagement with law.

In the context of abortion, for example, she argues that the women's movement has demanded that women have a right to choose and have control over their bodies. Yet, within the context of sex selection, the same groups have argued for a limitation on the same right. Menon attempts to illustrate the contradictions within the liberal discourse of rights for feminism. She argues that rights are discursively constituted-that rights only acquire meaning within specific contexts and specific discourses. In other words, rights may have a radical potential within feminist frameworks, but once they are put into the context of the broader political economy, their meanings may change and their contradictory character exposed.

Flavia Agnes' work has also been an important contribution to the development of more complexes and nuanced analyses of feminist engagement with law. Throughout her work, Agnes interrogates the effect of law reforms on women and questions whether laws intended for women's benefit have lived up to their promise. Her work on violence against women, for example, addressed the failure of law to adequately address the reality of violence. Through a detailed examination of laws addressing rape, dowry, domestic violence, prostitution, indecent representation of women, sati (the practice which relates to the immolation of widow on her husband's funeral pyre) and sex discrimination tests, Agnes explores the broader questions of why law has had so little effect in women's lives, and whether law can bring about social change.

In her analysis of rape laws, for example, Agnes reveals the ultimate failure of the campaign for reform in the early 1980s to bring about a transformation in the definition of rape. She illustrates the extent to which 'the same old notions of chastity, virginity, premium on marriage and fear of female sexuality are reflected in the judgements of the post-amendment law.' Agnes' analysis of the other legislative provisions intended to protect women against violence similarly attempts to reveal the extent to which the reforms did not fundamentally challenge and transform the underlying assumptions about women's identities.

She exposes how law is susceptible to being appropriated by a reactionary politics, illustrated in her analysis of the debates on the Uniform Civil Code in India, and how these are located in a highly charged communal context. She reveals how communalism seeps into some recent judicial decisions, exposing the contested nature of law and rights (Agnes 2001; Agnes 2004). Agnes is also critical of both the women's movement's failure to develop an explicitly secular agenda, and the resulting-though unstated-Hindu norm that has come to characterize the movement.

The postcolonial literature that is emerging in the context of South Asia reveals that law is no longer viewed in terms of an either/or dichotomy. It is neither a mere instrument of social change nor of patriarchy. What is emerging is a much more complex analysis born from postcolonial location and experience. Law was received in the Asian subcontinent as already exclusive and subordinating. It was introduced into the subcontinent as a mechanism for denying the colonial subject rights and freedoms that could only be acquired through civilizational maturity and the development of the capacity to reason.

During the freedom struggle, it is clear that rights also served a progressive end, because the freedom fighters invoked civil and political rights in order to acquire independence. Yet the struggle itself speaks to the contradictory nature of law and rights, and how it is a contested terrain. In the context of women, there is evidence that law has been used as both a subordinating tool as well as a liberating one. Women have won the right to vote, to education and also have succeeded in law reform in the area of sexual violence. But as the literature indicates, such achievements cannot be read as clear victories. They have at times been achieved by reinforcing gender difference. In the case of rape for instance, a woman may succeed in her claims if she is willing to present herself as chaste, pure, virginal and modest.

This representation is deeply entwined with the demands of nationalism and for feminism to position itself at times as anti-Western, so that they do not compromise their nationalist credentials. The new literature is exposing how certain assumptions about women are embedded in legal discourse and how gender and the constitution of women's subjectivities need to be understood against the backdrop of the colonial encounter. At one level, it would seem that rights discourse is ultimately unable to represent the interests of marginalized and disadvantaged groups. However, this position would be met with considerable resistance from women, Dalits (lower castes), Muslims and other disadvantaged communities who have used rights in their struggles for social change.

Rights remain important to people who have never had them, and a perspective that argues against rights can only come from a privileged position, from those whose rights are already secure. At the same time, there is a need to move beyond the limitations of what I have described above as 'a rights-based approach.' Remaining confined to a universal understanding of rights, does not attend to its potential to be exclusive (as demonstrated by the history of colonialism) and also to be appropriated by more reactionary agendas (as demonstrated by the use of rights discourse by right wing nationalist entities, such as the Hindu Right in India). The rights based agenda can be used in pursuit of gender justice, only so long as it remains attentive to historical antecedents and fact that rights can be appropriated by the more powerful and can entrench notions of gender difference in ways that are not necessarily liberating for women.

KEY ISSUES

In this section, three key issues that have arisen in the context of the pursuit of gender justice in law are addressed. First, there is the issue of equality: this has been a central concern of women's movements in South Asia and has had important implications for the struggles for gender justice. Second, violence against women is a concern, given that most law reform campaigns on women's rights in the contemporary period have focused on issues of sexual violence. Third, religion particularly highlights the precarious position of women in minority communities, especially in Bangladesh, Pakistan and India.

EQUALITY

The Constitutions of Bangladesh, India, Nepal, Pakistan and Sri Lanka include the right to equality and a provision that does not regard special measures enacted for the benefit of women and children as violative of the equality provision. Before discussing the meaning of equality and its effect on gender justice, I must add a note of caution. Despite the legal interpretations to the meaning of equality, its understanding and effect is also shaped by the very different political, religious and cultural contexts of each South Asian country. All-with the exception of Nepal-were once colonies, and won their independence in the first part of the twentieth century. Yet each has developed in very different ways. While feudal relations continue to influence power at the local levels, India and Sri Lanka are distinctively different from Pakistan and Bangladesh, which have experienced long periods of military rule.

Bhutan is a monarchy and a closed society. It is currently using 'authenticity' criteria for conferring citizenship. Nepal was once a monarchy, and is now a relatively new democracy.

This democracy is currently (at the time of writing) being threatened by the Maoist insurgency and its political struggle with the monarchy. India and Sri Lanka are democracies, but have experienced considerable political turmoil in the form of self-determination movements, ethnic and religious strife. Thus, by pointing out the commonalities in the pursuit of gender justice through equality discourse, it is important to keep in mind the diverse political, social, economic and cultural formations of these different countries.

Equality has eluded any simple or uniform definition. In the context of constitutional law and equality theory, two approaches to equality are clearly identifiable in political and legal discourse: a formal and a substantive approach. In the formal approach, equality is seen to require equal treatment-that is, all those who are the same must be treated the same. It is based on treating likes alike. The constitutional expression of this approach to equality has been in terms of the similarly situated test-the requirement that those who are similarly treated should be treated similarly.

Within this approach, equality is equated with sameness. Only individuals who are the same are entitled to be treated equally. Any differential treatment of individuals or groups who are the same is seen to constitute discrimination. The first step in the similarly situated analysis is to determine who is to be compared to whom. If the individuals or groups in question are seen as different, then no further analysis is required, because the difference justifies the treatment. Accordingly, when groups are not similarly situated, then they do not qualify for equality, even if the differences among them are the product of historic or systemic discrimination.

In contrast, the focus of a substantive equality approach is not simply with the equal treatment of the law, but with the actual effect of law. The explicit objective of a model of substantive equality is the elimination of the substantive inequality of disadvantaged groups in society. As Parmanand Singh observes, it 'takes into account inequalities of social, economic and educational background of the people and seeks the elimination of existing inequalities by positive measures'. Substantive equality is directed at eliminating individual, institutional and systemic discrimination against disadvantaged groups, which effectively undermines their full and equal social, economic, political and cultural participation in society.

The dominant understanding of equality in South Asia is heavily influenced by the liberal tradition, and based on assumptions of sameness. In other words, if you are the same you are entitled to equal treatment. Sameness becomes the pre-requisite to a challenge of discrimination. At the same time, the equality clause in each of the constitutions makes specific exceptions to the dominant understanding of equality as sameness. Reservations for scheduled castes and tribes, and special treatment for religious minorities and women have generally been regarded as exceptions to the dominant understanding of equality, rather than as integral to equality. Yet, these exceptions have rendered the universal understanding of the concept at times ambiguous and highly polarized. For example, the way in which gender difference is understood has a profound effect on the entitlements and rights that women are accorded.

If gender difference is irrelevant and all persons should be entitled to formal equal rights, what happens to differences that have actually disadvantaged or historically been used to subordinate women, such as pregnancy or child care? If gender difference is regarded as an exception to equality, it can justify highly protectionist legislation. If gender difference is read as integral to equality, then historical disadvantage, rather than sameness or difference, becomes central to the understanding of equality. Three approaches to the question of gender difference can thus be identified: protectionist, sameness and compensatory. A protectionist approach assumes that women are different from men-women are understood as weaker, subordinate and in need of protection.

In this approach, any rule or practice that treats women differently than men can be justified on the basis that women and men are different, and that women need to be protected.

The second approach is an equal treatment or sameness approach. In this approach, women are understood to be the same as men, that is to say, for the purposes of law they are the same, and must be treated the same. Any legislation or practice that treats women differently from men is seen to violate the equality guarantees. This sameness approach has been used to strike down provisions that treat women and men differently. It has, however, also been used to preclude any analysis of the potentially disparate effect of gender neutral legislation. In the third approach, women are understood as a historically disadvantaged group, and as such, in need of compensatory or corrective treatment.

Within this approach, gender difference is often seen as relevant and as requiring recognition in law. It is argued that a failure to take difference into account will only serve to reinforce and perpetuate the difference and the underlying inequalities. There are competing understandings of equality as well as to gender difference that exist in different countries in South Asia. The judicial approaches have been overwhelmingly influenced by a formal approach to equality, and a protectionist approach to gender difference. This formal approach to equality, in which equality is equated with sameness, and the protectionist approach to gender difference, in which women are understood as weak and in need of protection, has operated to limit the efficacy of these constitutional challenges.

Some examples of a protectionist approach to gender difference include the provisions of the Nepali Constitution, which preclude Nepalese women from passing their nationality on to their children or to a spouse of foreign nationality (Article 9(5)), presumably on the grounds that women are incapable of assuming a nationality independent from that of their husbands, coupled with the simultaneous concern over national and cultural purity. Similar to it is Section 488 of the Indian Code of Criminal Procedure, 1872 (now Section 125). It requires men to pay maintenance to their wives, but imposes no corresponding duty on women to maintain their husbands.

The provision is based on the assumption that women are economically dependent on their husbands. The amount of maintenance is usually minimal, reflecting how women's contribution to the household is regarded as supplemental or nominal. Section 488 was challenged as violating the equality clause in the Indian Constitution (Article 14) The Court upheld the section, stating that it applied to all women in similar circumstances, that is to all women deserted by their husbands and that such legislation favouring this class of people was not arbitrary.

Although the decision was beneficial from the perspective of the individual woman seeking maintenance from her husband, the reasoning was based on a formal approach to equality. It suggests that those who were similarly situated could be treated the same. The court also emphasized the issues of gender difference, treating the difference between men and women as natural, stating explicitly that woman were weaker than men and thus, in need of special treatment. The language suggests a protectionist approach to gender. In Pakistan, in 2003, the Supreme Court of Pakistan overturned a 1997 verdict of a High Court that voided the marriages of adult Muslim women without the permission of the woman's father or guardian.

The decision challenges the protective assumption that informed the High Court's decision, and adopts the sameness standard when it comes to consensual marriages by either adult men or women. The case illustrates that formal equality remains an important goal for securing gender justice, while at the same time, emphasizing that formal equal treatment does not necessarily redress the underlying structural and systemic conditions as well as assumptions about gender difference which reinforce gender discrimination and women's subordinate status. The role of equality rights litigation in challenging laws that allegedly discriminate on the basis of sex is contradictory. Judicial approaches have operated to limit the extent to which differential treatment of women is seen to be discrimination.

And even where such differential treatment is perceived as tantamount to discrimination, the results are not always unequivocally positive. For example, while some cases have either struck down laws that have created legal obstacles to women's equality, the reasoning on which the results are based often reinforce assumptions about women as the weaker sex and vulnerable. Conversely, cases in which courts uphold laws that are designed to address women's substantive inequality may be done on the basis of similarly problematic reasoning. The analysis belies the assumption that legal engagements can 'solve' the problem and produce gender justice in result, even though on the face of it, the law appears gender-neutral.

The language of equality has played a central role in the struggle of the women's movement to bring about gender justice. And yet the language of equality is also used by those who oppose efforts to improve women's social and economic position. In its guise as formal equality, it has been used as a shield against efforts to develop programmes that are specifically directed at improving the conditions of women. It is also a concept that can and is being used by the Hindu Right or Muslim fundamentalists, in their attack on minority rights. One example of this in India is the case of Shah Bano, where a 73-year-old Muslim woman, who was divorced by her husband to whom she had been married for 40 years, brought a petition demanding maintenance from her husband under Section 125 of the Indian Criminal Procedure Code.

According to Muslim personal law, she would only have been entitled to maintenance for the period of the *iddat*, that is, three months after the divorce. In April 1985, the Supreme Court held that she was entitled to maintenance under Section 125, and that allowing this maintenance would not violate the Koran. Conservative and orthodox forces within the Muslim community were outraged: they regarded the decision as an encroachment on the authority of Muslim theologians. An independent member of parliament introduced a Bill to save Muslim personal law. The women's movement, along with progressive Muslim organizations, campaigned against the Bill. The Hindu Right also campaigned vigorously against the Bill, which in its view was simply another example of the Congress government 'pandering to the minorities'.

The government ultimately supported the enactment of the *Muslim Women's (Protection of Rights on Divorce) Act* in May 1986, which provides that Section 125 of the *Criminal Procedure Code* does not apply to divorced Muslim Women. According to the Act, which effectively codifies Muslim personal law of maintenance, a divorced woman's husband is obliged to return her *mehr* (dowry) and pay her maintenance during the period of *iddat*. If the divorced woman cannot support herself at the end of that period, her children, parents or relatives who would be entitled to inherit her property, are responsible for her support. If they cannot support her, the responsibility then falls to the State Wakf Boards.

As a result of this controversy, Shah Bano and Muslim women as a group ended up with fewer rights than they had at the beginning of the controversy. At the same time, feminists and the Hindu Right ended up on the same side of the fence-arguing that the law violated women's equality rights (although the hidden agenda of the Hindu Right was to represent the Muslims as discriminatory in their treatment of women). The case provides an excellent example of how equality rights can be used in a way that may undermine gender justice, especially of women belonging to religious or caste minority communities.

The issue of equality remains a central pursuit of the women's movement. However, clearly an absolute focus on gender equality may set at odds women in majority and minority communities. There is clearly a need for greater clarity in legal strategies and arguments for pursuing equality goals that do not end up harming more women than they help, or reinforcing a majoritarian agenda.

VIOLENCE AGAINST WOMEN

Since the nineteenth century, social reformers and women's rights activists have sought to extend the legal intervention of the law, particularly the criminal law, into the realm of the family. These proposals have sought a renegotiation of the public and private spheres, through an incremental encroachment of the 'public'-the state sanctioned criminal law-into the 'private' sphere of the family. Despite these repeated challenges to the public and private distinction, and the steady expansion of the scope of criminal intervention into previously private spheres, the distinction has not been eliminated. Certain acts continue to be constructed as private family issues, and beyond the purview of law. The exclusion of rape in marriage from the purview of the criminal law of all South Asian countries continues to perpetuate sex roles and the obligations of men and women in marriage.

The Hindu Right is a coalition of organizations and political groupings whose avowed aim is to establish Hindus as the master race in India and as normative for citizenship. The Hindu Right has been increasingly influential in contemporary politics in India and its political wing, the Bhartiya Janata Party (BJP, or Indian People's Party) headed the union government for much of the 1990s, until the last general elections in 2004. The Rashtriya Swayamsevak Sangh (RSS, or Association of Nationalist Volunteers), is the ideological body, while the Vishwa Hindu Parishad (VHP, or World Hindu Council), is a mass front of the party.

This public and private distinction also continues to inform the enforcement of criminal law. Despite provisions within the *Penal Codes* of South Asian countries condemning various forms of violence within the family, this distinction undermines the enforcement of such provisions. As part of the continuing hangover from the nineteenth century colonial encounter, the family continues to be constructed as a private sphere, beyond the legitimate intervention of the law. This factor is important to address in trying to evaluate the success or failure women's movements in South Asia have had in dealing with violence against women. Several issues, such as adultery, dowry, honour killings and rape continue to be informed by assumptions about women's moral identities within the family.

Legal interventions in these areas, in the name of protecting women, have frequently resulted in reinforcing the moral regulation of women in and through familial ideology. Violence against women has been at the forefront of the contemporary women's movement in India, Sri Lanka, Pakistan and Bangladesh. It has also been raised in the context of Nepal, though it has been part of a much broader project to reform gender insensitive and unequal laws. In most countries, there has been considerable focus on issues of rape. In India, the contemporary women's movement was galvanized at the end of the 1970s largely through two campaigns for law reform-rape and dowry (Agnes 2001). A national campaign emerged around the rape case of Mathura, a young tribal woman who was raped in police custody. The lower court held that she was 'of loose morals', and acquitted the two police officers.

The High Court overturned the decision. But, on appeal to the Supreme Court of India, the decision of the lower court was reinstated because the Supreme Court held that there was insufficient evidence that Mathura resisted the sexual intercourse. There was a public outcry over this decision and a national campaign launched to reform the rape laws. There were protests throughout the country and women's groups across the country joined in the protest, organizing marches and demonstrations to denounce the decision, and to bring attention to the issue of sexual violence against women.

For example, the Constitution of Bangladesh accords priority to the harms and discrimination that women may experience in the public arena. Abuse and discrimination in the home and family fall outside the purview of equality. The State cannot intervene in the home even if a women experiences domestic violence, marital rape, and other forms of harassment. Thus the public and private distinction operates to sequester some central women's rights concerns from the purview of equality. The women's movement and the legal community in Nepal have been struggling for a complete overhaul of the law as regards women's rights to equality and the promotion of gender justice.

The enactment of the Country Code (11th Amendment) Bill, 2002, introduced major reforms for women, including the right of daughters to inheritance rights to the ancestral property from birth. The new law also establishes a wife's equal right to her husband's property immediately after marriage. A further reform is the repeal of the provision that a widow attaining the age of 30 must live separately before taking her share of property. The new law provides that a widow is entitled to use her share as she wishes even if she gets remarried. The amendment also removes the condition that women must attain the age 35 and complete 15 years of marriage before she can live separately and take her share from her husband.

The amendment provides equal rights to unmarried daughters and sons in cases of intestate succession. The Bill further provides that daughters have the right to be provided with food, clothing, appropriate education and health treatment to the same extent as sons. Despite the broad range of reforms, there are still a number of discriminatory measures that continue to operate against women. A number of the changes in the law continue to reinforce women's roles as wives and mothers and their access to rights is frequently contingent on the extent to which they conform to these roles. The notions of chastity, virtue and selflessness continue to inform the laws intended for the benefit of women.

In the subsequent campaign, the women's movement sought to challenge the prevailing legal and social understanding of rape and consent. In fact, consent could be implied from the absence of injuries or passive submission, in which only the 'utmost resistance' could demonstrate that she did not consent, or, in the case of a woman of 'loose morals', where consent would simply be assumed. The campaign was firmly entrenched in the language of patriarchy-that is, the feminist campaign against rape attempted to connect this violence against women with the idea of systemic oppression of women by men. In the words of one feminist organization: 'For us rape is an act of hatred and contempt-it is a denial of ourselves as women, as human beings-it is the ultimate assertion of male power'.

Gradually, the campaign began to influence the public debate and even politicians spoke with outrage of the increasing attacks on women, and of the shame and dishonour brought on women and their families. Their language was embedded in the notion of protectionism-that is, of the need to protect women's honour and chastity from violation. Subsequently, the Law Commission was appointed to study the issue. It recommended comprehensive reforms to the rape law, echoing many of the demands of the women's movement. Recommendations included shifting the onus of proof regarding consent to the accused, and excluding the relevance of a woman's past sexual conduct from a rape trial.

The Bill subsequently introduced by the government fell considerably short of these recommendations, and included some regressive provisions demanded neither by the women's movement nor the Law Commission. The amendments to the rape law were finally enacted in 1983, recognizing the crime of custodial rape in which consent was not relevant as well as the establishment of mandatory minimum sentences for rape. While the feminist campaign was successful insofar as the issue of police rape was placed firmly on the public agenda and legislation was passed to address it, the broader struggle over the meaning of rape was less successful. The reforms had very little effect in challenging the traditional definition of rape, based on assumptions about chastity and virginity and women's sexual conduct.

The women's movement was not able to displace these assumptions. Rather, its demands for the reform of rape laws was taken up and supported by other, more conservative political voices, and cast within the more traditional discourse of shame and dishonour. There was some disillusionment after the law reform campaign because it seemed so little had been achieved. Some women's organizations shifted their focus away from law reform, towards taking up the individual cases of women in courts. Litigating these cases became a more significant focus for some women's organizations, which sought to provide legal assistance and other forms of support for women going through the judicial system.

Simultaneously, many feminists became concerned with the lack of institutional support for women. As a result, many women's centres were set up in the early 1980s, designed to provide women with legal assistance, health services and counselling. Marital rape is not recognized as an offence in most countries in South Asia. In India, marital rape was one of the issues taken up during the campaigns to reform the rape law in the early 1980s. The Law Commission recommended that the marital exemption to rape be removed, and that the criminal law recognize marital rape. This recommendation was not taken up by the government, and thus not included in the *Criminal Law Amendment Act*, 1983. But, the Act did narrow the marital exemption somewhat. Section 376A of the *Indian Penal Code* provides that the rape of a woman by her husband from whom she was judicially separated constitutes rape, and is punishable by up to two years imprisonment.

While Section 376A can be seen to begin to challenge the exemption of the marital relationship from the purview of the criminal law of rape, the challenge is a fairly minimal one. A husband is only to be held criminally responsible where there has already been a judicially recognized rupture in the marital relationship. Presumably, it is this judicially sanctioned rupture that revokes a wife's assumed consent to sexual intercourse with her husband. Thus, Section 376A does not challenge the assumption that the act of marriage gives rise to an unqualified and unconditional consent on the part of the wife to sexual intercourse with her husband. Rather, it simply recognizes that the act of judicial separation revokes this consent.

In Sri Lanka, the rape law is similar to that of India. In 1995, amendments were introduced to the penal code to specifically address sexual abuse and exploitation. The rape law was modified to create a more equitable burden of proof and make punishments more stringent. Marital rape was also made into a punishable offence in cases of spouses living under judicial separation. In Nepal, a charge of rape can only be filed against a man, but not a husband, who has had sexual intercourse with a woman under sixteen with or without consent, or who has forced the act upon a woman over 16. Punishment ranges from 6 to 10 years imprisonment for the rape of a girl below 14, and 3 to 5 years for the rape of a woman above 14. In May, 2002, the Supreme Court ruled that sex without a wife's consent was rape. The judgement was the result of mobilization by the women's movement and a petition filed by the Forum on Women, Law and Development.

In Pakistan, the law is much more complicated and the women's movement has made little headway in challenging the laws or bringing about law reform. Under the existing law, a woman's own evidence is not admissible in a court considering a charge of rape. A conviction may be obtained only on the evidence of four reputable male witnesses, or upon the confession of the rapist, repeated on four separate occasions. If a woman complains of rape and the charge is not proved she is liable to the same punishment as an adulterous woman or convicted rapist: public flogging or death by stoning. In 1979, under the rule of General Zia-ul-Haq, Pakistan enacted the Hadood Ordinance.

This ordinance was passed as an effort to Islamicize Pakistan's legal system. As a provision of the Hadood Ordinance, the Zina Ordinance defines 'rape' in terms of Islamic law; that is as being sexual relations between individuals who are not married, whether by force or consent. However, neither statutory rape nor marital rape is considered a crime under the Zina Ordinance. All sexual relations outside of marriage are essentially considered a criminal act. The death penalty for gang rape was also added to the provisions of the Zina (Enforcement of Hadood Ordinance, 1979, while the Zina Ordinance was created to impose a conservative sexual morality upon society and, in essence, to protect women from rape, it has become a discriminatory law against women.

It leaves victims of rape without justice or, in some cases; it puts the victims themselves in jail. There are very strict evidentiary requirements under the Zina Ordinance. A woman who accuses a man of *zina-bil-jabr* (rape) must prove without a reasonable doubt that the man (or men) raped her. If a victim cannot prove that she was raped, she could end up in jail for adultery or non-marital intercourse. By reporting the rape, a woman admits that either extra-marital or non-marital intercourse has occurred. In addition, Article 151(4) of the Qanun-e-Shahadat Order of 1984 allows the 'immoral character' of the victim to be admitted into evidence (Human Rights Watch 1999:7).

The Zina Ordinance is divided into two categories, zina and zina-biljabr. Zina is the crime of non-marital sexual relations and adultery while zina-bil-jabr is the category of forced intercourse. Those found guilty of either category can receive harsh punishments, including flogging and death. The death penalty however has never been carried out against a perpetrator under the Zina Ordinance.

The women's movement in Bangladesh has lobbied vigorously to amend laws to address the increasing problem of violence against women, as well as to improve women's social status. The Dowry Prohibition Act of 1980 was enacted forbidding anyone from giving or receiving dowry. However, despite the legal enactments, the practice of dowry remains prevalent. The Nari-O-Shishu Nirjatan Daman Ain 2000 (Law on the Suppression of Violence against Women and Children 2000), was a radical piece of reform that expanded the definition of rape considerably, although it did not include marital rape or domestic violence. In it, sexual harassment is defined as a criminal offence punishable by law. Section 10(2) of the Women and Children Act states:

Any man who, in order to satisfy his lust in an improper manner, outrages the modesty of a woman, or makes obscene gestures, will have engaged in sexual harassment, and for this, the above mentioned male will be sentenced to rigorous imprisonment of not more than seven years and not less than two years and beyond this will be subjected to monetary fines as well. Although the law has been, in part, a product of intense activism by the women's movement, the definition assumes that what is at stake is a woman's modesty, presumably sexual modesty. Such traditional notions about women's sexual conduct and behaviour can have adverse effects on women's rights, as interpretations as to what constitutes modesty and 'appropriate' female behaviour are highly subjective.

Moreover, the legal protection of modesty can end up limiting rather than expanding women's freedom. Other recent acts to prevent violence against women include the Acid Control Act, 2002, and the Acid Crime Control Act, 2002. Some of the women who are found to be victims of or threatened by rape, acid throwing, and dowry related violence, sexual harassment or fatwa-instigated violence, can be placed in 'safe custody' in shelter homes, for their protection, even if it is without their consent. Although this provision has been reviewed, it exemplifies a protective approach towards women that continues to inform the law. It illustrates how legal interventions in the area of violence against women-which has been at the core of gender justice strategies pursued by women's groups-can sometimes, serve to reinforce gender difference and undermine women's rights.

The laws in the different South Asian countries continue to reinforce the assumption that a woman surrenders her right to consent to sexual relations at the time of entering into a marriage and the husband is given an unconditional, unqualified right of sexual access to her. Every act of sexual intercourse is deemed to be consensual, as such consent is deemed to have been given at the time of marriage. The continuing exemption of marital rape from the purview of the criminal law sustains the assumption of the wife as exclusive property of the husband. It remains a central obstacle to women being conceived of as full citizens and reproduces a colonial and Victorian assumption that women are infantile, passive and lacking decision-making abilities.

Nonetheless, the considerable attention accorded by the women's movements in South Asia to amend the rape laws, has in some instances led to a change in the law. It has also led to the creation of greater public space to demand legal reforms and the formation of institutions to deal more effectively with rape. And there is no doubt that the reporting of incidents of rape has gone up, though the rates of conviction in all South Asian countries remain low. The efforts of the women's movement to resort to the criminal law to intervene in the family and to protect women against abuses perpetrated against them within this private realm have produced contradictory results.

The various legislative enactments and amendments, as well as the progressive impulse of the women's movements throughout South Asia, have not succeeded altogether in displacing the public and private distinction. The idea of the family as private, and the construction of women as wives and mothers, weak, passive and in need of protection, are still very much apparent in the judicial interpretations of the laws intended to benefit women. And even when the courts do convict an accused under one of these criminal provisions, the grounds on which they do so are often shaped and sustained by assumptions of women as weak, passive and in need of protection.

Rape has also been an important issue for the women's rights movement in Nepal. The amendments to the civil code strengthen the law and increase the punishment for rapists. According to the new provisions, a rapist can be imprisoned for 10–15 years, if their victim is below 10 years of age; 7–10 years of imprisonment, if their victim is between 10 and 16 years of age; and 5–7 years of imprisonment, if the victim's age is above 16 years. In each category, an additional five years of prison can be given if the victim is a pregnant or a disabled woman. Yet once again, the amendments have not necessarily increased the number of convictions. Indeed, judges are loath to convict if the sentences are too high. At the same time there has been no challenge to some of the normative assumptions about gender that inform the rape law.

Although violence against women has been a key issue in women's movements in South Asia, it is time to re-evaluate whether the legal strategies pursued to counter such violence have produced gender-just laws at the end of the day. The failure at times to bring normative challenges in legal campaigns has resulted in reinforcing assumptions about gender difference and resulting in the production of protective legislation. Although violence against women continues on a staggering scale in South Asia, and even though the women's movement has been intensely involved in combating such violence, legal campaigns have not necessarily produced progressive outcomes.

RELIGION

Religion remains a contentious issue in the area of women's rights and has become particularly so with the increase of fundamentalism in the South Asian region. The women's movement has pursued an approach towards religion from a purely secular standpoint. However, this approach has not necessarily produced outcomes that advance gender justice. The case of Shah Bano exposes the paradoxes produced by religion and equality rights for women. With the creation of Pakistan in 1948, the legislation relating to Muslim family law introduced under British rule continued to govern personal status. The state was declared to be Muslim, founded by Muslims of the subcontinent who wanted to build up their lives in accordance with the teachings and traditions of Islam.

In 1961 the Muslim Family Laws Ordinance was passed, outlining the codes of marriage divorce and other matters pertaining to the family. The ordinance was based on the recommendations of a commission that polygamy should be discouraged, divorce restrictions be tightened and women's right to divorce acknowledged. Further, the ordinance stipulated all marriages and divorces should be registered, adequate maintenance be enforced and the age of marriage raised to sixteen for girls. In 1963, the Fundamental Rights Bill, the first amendment to the Constitution, specified that the Muslim Family Laws Ordinance was not open to judicial review. The Ordinance drew much criticism from religious leaders.

Since the 1960s, Pakistan has undergone several changes of government, and been primarily subjected to military rule. Islamist groups such as the Jama'at-i-Islami have gained increasing influence, especially in the Northwest Frontier Province and Sindh. In 1979, President Zia ul-Haq passed the so-called 'Hudood Ordinances', discussed earlier, as part of a larger programme to make Pakistan's legal code and system of government more Islamic. In 1991, President Nawaz Sharif passed a law giving religious courts the right to overrule existing laws. More recently, other factors have intensified the conflict between gender equality and the right to freedom of religion. The Northwest Frontier Province has adopted the *sharia* law as part of the states personal law.

Women are confronted with a situation where the adoption of such a code is read as a counter to the influence that the US is exerting on the current military dictatorship of President Musharraf. in countering these processes, the women's movement risks being cast as collaborating with the Americans. The position has produced a stalemate on the issue of women's rights because it is so caught up with the issue of nationalism, national pride and sovereignty, a tension that is reminiscent of the relationship between the British colonial power and the subjugation of the native subject. The emergence of an autonomous women's movement in Pakistan has been critical to the demand for and enactment of legal reforms.

One of the most challenging issues facing the contemporary women's movement is the rise of Islamism and the increasing tensions being produced over the position of women in Islam and women's roles in a modern Islamic state. As discussed elsewhere in this essay, various governments over the years have failed to be progressive in this area and attempted to formalize a specific interpretation of Islamic law. Although the issue of evidence has been a central concern regarding women's legal status, other issues such as mandatory dress codes for women and whether females can compete in international sports competitions have also been sources of agitation. There is a split amongst women's groups in Pakistan regarding the role of religion.

Human rights lawyers in particular are quite insistent that religion has no role in the public sphere and that the laws should be based on purely secular understandings. However, this position appears to have made little headway, given that fact that the role of the Islamists has only increased and there appears to be considerable support for the role of religion in the public arena. The problem with a formal secular stand is that it never engages with the religious domain. Therefore, it does not address the ways in which religion mediates access to women's rights, characterizes or may be integral to their daily lives, and may force women into the position of choosing between their rights to gender equality and the rights to freedom of religion.

Unfortunately, the current period has witnessed the proliferation of militant 'Islamist' politico-religious parties and sectarian groups. The success of the parties in the 2002 elections has made them a significant voice in government at the central as well as the provincial levels. Donors and the women's movement thus face extreme hurdles in Pakistan, partly because of the constant re-emergence of the military in running the affairs of the country and the fact that religion played such an obstructive role in the struggle for gender justice. Despite a very active women's movement, the fact remains that the formal law continues to be highly discriminatory and women are not treated as full citizens in Pakistan. The relationship between gender justice, religion and law may need to be further explored in order to develop more creative ways of securing gender justice in deeply coercive circumstances.

In Bangladesh, the issue of the role of religion in public life has created less controversy than in Pakistan, though more recently, there has been an intensification of the role of the religious fundamentalists in public life. Bangladesh's Constitution is avowedly secular and its civil code is based on laws inherited from the British. Religion is a primary factor in determining women's rights in the private domain. For example, Muslim marriages are regulated by the Muslim Family Ordinance 1961 or the Muslim Marriages and Divorce (Registration) Act 1974. Hindu marriages are regulated by (among others) the Hindu Marriages Disabilities Removal Act 1946 or the Hindu Widow's Remarriage Act 1856. Christian marriages are governed by the Marriage Act 1872.

The existence of separate laws for each community means that the kind of justice meted out to a woman is determined by the religious community to which she belongs. Invariably, this is characterized by inequality and assumptions about women as being weak and inferior. In the political context of Bangladesh, the growing power of religious fundamentalist groups has restricted efforts to increases women's equal rights in the private domain. The government of Bangladesh has implemented specific legal protections for women, including the 1980 Anti-dowry Prohibition Act and the 1983 Cruelty to Women Law.

Bangladesh has also passed laws protecting women from arbitrary divorce and from husbands taking additional wives without the consent of the first wife. But these protections only apply to registered marriages. In rural areas where most Bangladeshis live, few marriages are registered. The Islamic fundamentalists in Bangladesh have been able to exert their influence on government through their participation in democratic processes since 1991. Their influence has ensured that the line between the public and private is further entrenched and that the domestic sphere remains a space of religious control, where the state is not allowed to intervene. However, the increasing participation of women in the economic sphere as a result of the neo-economic liberal regime, plus the greater emphasis placed by donors on incorporating a women and development thinking into the development process, poses a threat to fundamentalist thinking.

Therefore, they have increasingly targeted high profile women, such as the women's rights activist Sufia Kamal, writer Taslima Nasrin, as well as NGO workers or active village women. The case of Taslima Nasrin and the fatwa controversy that emerged around her writing illustrates the conflict. The fatwa was first issued in September 1993, after the publication of her novel *Lajja*, a story of the plight of a Hindu family in

Bangladesh persecuted in the aftermath of the destruction of the Babri Masjid in India in December 1992. The stakes were increased following an interview by Nasrin in an Indian newspaper, where she called for the reform of religious texts that oppressed women. The fatwa was reasserted. Facing increasing protests and calls for Nasreen's death, the Bangladeshi government brought blasphemy charges against her and Nasrin was forced to flee the country.

The fundamentalists were able to shift the controversy from one about women's rights to one about affront to religion and Islam, and the resulting injury inflicted on the religious sentiments of the majority. It was a very powerful indictment. Although many women's organizations were willing to fight for Nasrin's rights to free speech, they carefully distanced themselves from her brand of 'feminist politics' and did not support her views on religion. The caution exercised by women's groups illustrates the tension they experience in taking up women's rights and its conflict with both issues of nationalism and religion and to take sides only serves to cast them as threatening, foreign and unpatriotic.

The tension between religion or culture and women's rights was also illustrated in the 1993 case of Nurjahan, a woman who lived in Chattakchara village in the district of Sylhet, who was threatened with stoning for marrying a second time. Her first husband had left her and the marriage had been annulled. However, the village headman objected to her marriage and a *sailash* (village meeting) was called. It declared Nurjahan should be punished by placing her in a waist-deep hole on the ground and having 101 stones thrown at her. Her parents, who had allowed the marriage, were to be given a hundred whips each which was later reduced to 50 each. Nurjahan committed suicide before the sentence could be carried out.

The incident was taken up by women's and human rights organizations and a case filed against the nine people involved in the *sailash*, who had passed the judgment. They were accused of inciting a person to commit suicide and were subsequently sentenced to seven years imprisonment. This case illustrates the kinds of tensions that are emerging in the conflict between women's rights and attempts to break the stranglehold of the familial or private sphere and customary norms. In Bangladesh, the women's movement also called for a Uniform Civil Code as a way in which to address the inequities and incongruities within the different personal law.

In 1996, two large non-governmental organizations involved in women's rights advocacy, the *Bangladesh Mohila Parishad* and *Ain O Shalish Kendra* produced a draft of a Uniform Family Code that encompasses a wide range of rights for women. For example, under the code, a husband and wife have equal status and responsibility. Men and women are to be treated equally in matters of marriage, divorce, custody and guardianship of children as well as inheritance. All marriages are to be registered under civil law and child marriage abolished. The minimum age for marriage of both men and women was suggested as 18 years. Polygamy is to be abolished, and both spouses are to equally participate in matters of finance. An unemployed spouse (whether husband or wife) is entitled to the maintenance from the employed spouse, and both parents are considered as the natural and legal guardians of children.

Among other things the Code provided equal inheritance rights, the right to adopt by both men and women, and maintenance of children from each parent on the basis of his or her financial capability. The proposal has not been enacted by lawmakers, though it represents an important demand for gender justice by the women's movement. The Bangladesh government has ratified the Convention on the Elimination of all forms of Discrimination Against Women (CEDAW). However, it entered reservations to Article 2, where states undertake to condemn discrimination against women in all its forms. In September 2000, Bangladesh was the first country to ratify the Optional Protocol to CEDAW, which strengthens the enforcement mechanisms available for the rights within the Convention and provides for complaints to be taken directly to the UN.

In light of this ratification, maintaining reservations to Article 2 is contradictory, and groups should lobby for the removal of the restriction. In India, the Constitution gives equal rights to women under Indian civic law. At the same time, Muslims and Hindus can adhere to their personal laws in marriage, divorce and other family matters. Since Independence, the Indian state has aimed at abolishing the various Hindu personal laws in favour of a uniform civil code. For example, the *Special Marriage Act of 1954* provides that any couple can marry, irrespective of community, in a civil ceremony. Yet efforts to enact a uniform civil code have not been successful. Such initiatives are increasingly held in deep suspicion by minority religious communities, in light of the emergence of the Hindu Right and their support for a Uniform Civil Code.

The sati controversy that arose in India shortly after the Shah Bano controversy is an interesting contrast to it. The sati of Roop Kanwar in Deorala, Rajasthan in 1987, gave rise to a campaign against the practice and a demand for further legislation. Roop Kanwar's public sati was immediately followed by a campaign to glorify sati, as the site of immolation became a pilgrimage spot, orchestrated by pro-sati supporters. The issue rapidly became integrally connected to Rajput community identity, and many within the Hindu Right stepped in to protect and uphold Rajput tradition. Sati was defended, yet again, as a cultural tradition, sanctioned by religious scriptures. In opposition, the women's movement organized marches and demonstrations, denouncing the practice and demanding that the government take action. The Rajasthan state government moved quickly and introduced the *Rajasthan Sati (Prevention) Ordinance* in October 1987, and the Central Government soon followed with the *Commission of Sati (Prevention) Act* in January 1988.

The politics of religion is thus an issue that is emerging as a critical site of tension for women's rights advocates and the project of gender justice. The cases illustrate how women's assertion of their rights threatens to disrupt orthodox understandings or interpretations of the appropriate roles of women in society and in the home. The emergence of these orthodox, conservative and fundamentalist voices must be addressed and countered in ways that do not set up women's equality rights claims in opposition to the right to freedom of religion. As the Shah Bano case illustrates, this can only lead to further disempowerment.

The issue of religion needs to be addressed not through oppositional language and divisive strategies, but in ways that appeal to the diverse interpretations and the plurality of cultural practices, exposing the homogeneity of religion as a myth. There needs to be recognition that religion and gender are sutured together in the South Asian context and that any engagement with gender justice must also necessarily entail an engagement with religious identity. An exclusive focus on gender justice simply results in setting up women's equality claims in opposition of their religious identity and claims for religious freedom. As Narayan explains the practice of sati was a traditional practice only in some communities in India; it was exceptional rather than a routine practice.

FUTURE AREAS OF RESEARCH AND ADVOCACY

There is a considerable support for issues of law and a pursuit of gender justice based primarily on securing formal equal rights for women. However, as outlined in this chapter, the achievement of formal equality is not sufficient. There must be greater support to groups for developing more critical perspectives and strategic interventions in the area of law. This is essential both in terms of bringing about a change in the way in which groups engage with law, as well as for the purpose of challenging assumptions about women that inform the law and existing legal strategies. The recommendations made in this section relate to the need to develop a more engaged and dynamic programme in the area of gender justice and law that focuses on the complexity and contradictory potential of pursuing gender justice in and through law.

Future research is needed to prioritize investigations into the ways in which gender and other inequalities inform the law and rights agendas of different groups, including well-intentioned women's groups, human rights groups, as well as state-supported projects and programs. Research on gender justice must re-evaluate the focus on gender violence. Gender violence has been critical to addressing the wrongs that women have experienced, especially in the home. However, this has also led to an inadvertent focus on reforming the criminal law in South Asian countries which addresses harms against the state rather than women's rights violations. It also tends to reinforce the victim image of women in the Third World which denies them their subjectivity and agency. Research needs to focus on how to promote a rights agenda that attends to issues of violence, but empowers women rather than the law or the state.

A related recommendation is to increase research in the area of sexuality and sexual rights, and not focus exclusively on sexual wrongs. The attempt should be to build up greater space for an affirmative understanding of women's sexual autonomy and bodily integrity, and in the process women's subjectivity and decision-making ability.

The objective should be to challenge stagnant images and assumptions of women primarily as victims, and ensure that women are also regarded as active participants in the gender-justice project. Attention needs to be given to how gender justice can be addressed in the context of globalization and a neo-liberal economic agenda. The rise of new non-state actors and the recruitment of women into the informal jobs sector need to be addressed in greater detail, along with strategies for protecting and promoting women's rights in these non-state centred environments.

There should be specific research into how legal interventions can reinforce exclusion and gender discrimination. A related recommendation is the need to conduct further evaluations into how existing laws-which ostensibly have been enacted for the benefit of women in different South Asian countries-can obstruct the gender justice project because of the protectionist, moralistic or sameness approach on which they might be based. This is a critical need, for law-reform movements-even by well-intentioned women's groups-frequently undermines the project of gender justice by failing to address the underlying assumptions about gender on which law is based.

Legal projects need to be envisaged in more complex and contextually specific ways. Breaking down the distinction between law and politics, and locating law within broader political struggles must include moving beyond the narrow focus upon rights discourses. An evaluation of the role of rights claims in social change must also include a consideration of the role of law reform and of legal literacy strategies. A research priority for the region is to focus on how the politics of religion has influenced the gender justice agenda in law. One issue to address is the area of personal family laws and the strength and limitations of the call for a Uniform Civil Code.

Research needs to be conducted on how to develop legal literacy strategies that are compatible with the pursuit of gender justice. Currently, information-giving approaches characterize legal literacy projects in South Asia, that do not address underlying assumptions and structural inequalities on which law is based. Providing women with specific legal information is important, but does not inform them of the normative obstacle they may encounter in the course of pursuing their rights claims. It does not address the strengths and limitations of engaging with the legal arena, as women or as poor women or as women belonging to religious minority communities. There is a need to develop legal literacy strategies that are based on understanding both the strengths and limits of specific laws for women, and how to develop more effective legal interventions.

4

Law and Women Identity

For the last three decades, the concept of "identity" has taken center place in political, social, and cultural debates. Charles Taylor has conceptualized identity as the search for the authentic self. Anthony Appiah has argued that identity involves the playing out of narrative scripts that we have learned from childhood. Whether we root out identity within the essence of the human personality or in the constructions of social life, identity politics has certainly conditioned many of the modern debates about rights, politics, and justice. Identity is not an essential, immutable, permanent status, it has many constituent elements. Future experiences often transform the nature and direction of personal identity. Identity is often composite, made up of multiple selves, often contesting, contradicting, and transforming the other.

Identity therefore reconstitutes itself, reacting to and negotiating ideology and lived experience. This objective experience as it interacts with our everyday life and conditions the way we think about ourselves. Our group-based identity often goes to the core of our sense of self and our desire for dignity. For many women, their sense of identity arises as a result their experience as women, living within groups primarily governed by men. Though their sense of self and dignity comes from how the wider society treats women, they often have to face discrimination within local groups. They may have to submit to discriminatory practices and laws, as well engage in rituals, customs, and habits that re-inscribe the subordinate status of women within the hierarchy of their religious, ethnic, or tribal identity.

Many women acquiesce because they see their group identity as the most important aspect of their lives. Others resist, only to be branded as traitors or "bad women" who bring the group into disrepute. For outsiders, especially women's activists interested in pursuing gender equality, discrimination within minority groups and third world societies poses a profound set of challenges. On the one hand, the feminist movement has always seen itself as an ally of third world societies and minority groups in their fight for equality and struggle against discrimination and prejudice. On the other hand, as a movement for the recognition of personal choice, it has sought to maximize individual freedom and creativity even at the expense of the group.

Fighting prejudice against underprivileged groups while struggling for women's empowerment goes to the heart of the modern dilemma between the universalism of human rights and the particularity of cultural experience. In a world where western imperialism has historically been the champion of third world females in Asia or Africa, the struggle for women's rights acquires another dimension. How does one fight for women's rights without being complicit in the racism and prejudice that characterizes Northern attitudes toward Southern countries or the majority-minority dynamics within particular societies?

THE LEGACY OF COLONIALISM

The historical legacy of colonialism points the third world female as being an important part of the encounter between the West and third world societies. The colonial powers acted as catalysts in the emergence of a new relationship between the sexes. By highlighting the position of women in colonial societies to denigrate the third world "other," the colonial powers served to focus attention on certain cultural practices that discriminated against women. As a result, according to Kumari Jayawardena, the early nationalist movements in many societies sought to improve the position of women in their societies by trying to eliminate the practices that they saw as inimical to their standing. They sought to regain the moral high ground by standing for women's equality and by combating practices harmful to women.

Nowhere is this legacy more visible than in India, where British social reform of the nineteenth century focused entirely on Indian females, especially Indian girls and Indian widows. In 1870, the British Colonial regime enacted the Special Act of 1870, which eradicated the practice of female infanticide in the Northwest provinces. Census data gathered from the 1840s shows startling imbalances in sex ratios, indicating that the practice was widespread. The British government took draconian measures to curtail the practice, including criminalization, surveillance, registering births, monitoring pregnancies, and putting parents in jail. By 1906 they withdrew the law because it had been so effective in the provinces under consideration-Rajasthan, the Punjab, and the Northwest Frontier.

The British made it clear that the British colonial regime had the monopoly on violence, and that it alone could determine issues of life and death. Of-court settlement saved her from what would have been for her a fate worse than death; she went on to become India's first woman doctor. But her case was not in vain. The early Indian nationalists were greatly moved by her agitation. Reformers such as Vidyasagar, Ranade, and Roy took up the cause of preventing child marriage. Indian women of Gandhi's Congress in 1929 managed to get Indian nationalists to push for the Child Marriage Restraint Act without much opposition. Because of women like Rakhmabai, the Indian nationalist movement had a social reform component that stressed elimination of this discriminatory practice.

Stability of the local order and the terms of collaboration with the feudal elite were ignored. The colonial power would insist that they were only respecting local customs and practices. The colonial legacy of western powers championing the cause of third world women conditions the debate on women's equality in many parts of the world. This was also rendered possible by what Partha Chatterjee calls the resolution of the woman question within the nationalist movement of India and probably in many other societies affected by colonialism. Early nationalists influenced by the British social reform movement called for reform from within and for the protection of the rights of women.

Later nationalists moved away from the early focus on social reform to emphasizing the preservation of the Indian identity and tradition. Seizing on the public/private distinction that provided the basis for the colonial common law, these conservative groupings took control of nationalist movements. The private was seen as the space for women who would keep the family insulated from the pressures of the public colonial world. Women then became the custodians of the culture of ethnic, religious, and tribal groups. While men began to don suits and move into the modern public space, women were expected to carry the cultural markers and make the home the traditional space to nurture and pass on ethnicity and symbols of identity to future generations.

Although the British brought women into the public discourse in the nineteenth century, the late nationalists returned women to the home and made them the caretakers of the very culture that often discriminates against them that discriminate against them. In addition, women in many societies believe that their dignity is intricately linked to the identity of the group. They see any attack on that identity as an assault on their own dignity. Although there are exceptional women who have moved away from strong cultural ties to the community of their birth, the vast majority feel a deep connection to group identity. Any attempt to fight for women's rights must keep this symbiosis in mind.

THE INTERNATIONAL FRAMEWORK

The international human rights framework attempts to deal with concepts of culture and cultural relativism through the prism of the rights of minorities. Since World War II, the international community has attempted to come to terms with the issue of minority rights. When the Human Rights Commission was created, the issue of human rights was a central part of its mandate. Furthermore, the Sub-Commission on Minorities was created with independent experts as a means of ensuring its impartiality and objectivity. There have been only a few actual legal developments with regard to minorities since its inception, however, such as the Convention on the Elimination of Racial Discrimination in the 1960s and, in the 1990s, the Declaration on the Rights of Persons Belonging to National or Ethnic, Religious and Linguistic Minorities.

In addition, The Human Rights Commission in Geneva created the Working Group on Minorities in the late nineties to allow for more focused attention on the rights of minorities. The World Conference on Racism, to be held in South Africa, will be another watershed event, however, but there was no agreement on any final course of action. It gives minorities the right to enjoy their own culture, to profess and practice their own religion, and to use their language. The Declaration on the Rights of Minorities (Minorities Declaration) gives minorities the right of survival and the right to promote their identity.

The Minorities Declaration also gives minorities the right to enjoy their own culture, religion, and language and to effectively participate in political decision-making. The State has an affirmative obligation to grant minorities equality and to create conditions that will enable minorities to develop their culture, language, and religion. Against women is a manifestation of historically unequal power relations between men and women, which have led to domination over and discrimination against women by men."

In addition, international human rights standards with regard to women are comprehensive and involve the accountability of state and non-state actors. CEDAW obligates states to remove all forms of discrimination against women by "any person, organization or enterprise." Article 5 of

CEDAW requires state parties to take all appropriate measures to modify the social and cultural patterns of conduct of men and women, with a view to achieving the elimination of prejudices and customary and all other practices which are based on the idea of the inferiority or the superiority of either of the sexes or on stereotyped roles for men and women. International standards recognize the transforming nature of the project at hand.

MANIFESTATIONS OF THE TENSION BETWEEN WOMEN'S RIGHTS, CULTURAL RELATIVISM, AND MINORITY RIGHTS

The tension between the rights of groups to practice their culture and the rights of women under international human rights norms plays itself out in the everyday life of women across the globe. The controversy surrounding female genital mutilation (FGM) provides one example of this tension. In 1990 Fuambai Ahmadu, an African scholar from Sierra Leone spoke these emotional words before the American Anthropological Association.

> It is difficult for me, considering the number of ceremonies I have observed, including my own, to accept that what appear to be expressions of joy and ecstatic celebrations of womanhood in actuality disguise hidden experiences of coercion and subjugation. Indeed, I offer that the bulk of Kono women who uphold these rituals do so because they want to... they embrace the legitimacy of female authority, and particularly, the authority of their mothers and grandmothers.

Joined by western feminists such as Alice Walker and human rights crusaders such as Fran Hosken and Equality Now, they have managed to garner worldwide revulsion against this cultural practice. FGM comes in various forms. The first, pharonic infibulations is the most drastic, involving the removal of the clitoris, labia minora, and the labia majora. The second, an intermediate form, involves the removal of the clitoris and the labia minora. The third contains the removal of only the clitoris. There is a fourth type of symbolic practice that sometimes involves placing a knife on the genitalia, but no cutting.

For some anthropologists, the emphasis on rights and sexuality are misplaced and are part of a legacy of neocolonialism. Some argue that FGM is about "being human the African way;" that it is about the notion of a rite of passage to adulthood, integrally linked to concepts of symbolic birth and African ideas about women and womanhood. FGM is seen as a great moment in the life of women, a celebration, a wedding, and women's space. While earlier feminists and nationalists accepted the western critique and tried to move forward, many of the young African anthropologists question the critique itself. Concepts of right and wrong, good and bad, are thrown up for grabs in a world with no moral anchor and where human rights is seen as the last outreach of the Enlightenment project.

The debate concerning FGM therefore becomes a conversation about colonialism and imposed western values. More importantly African anthropologists react to the way western feminists struggle against FGM, who place much emphasis on morality and self-righteousness. The United States has banned the practice under federal law and has made loans to African states conditional on measures taken to fight FGM. African scholars bristle at this type of intervention. They believe that FGM has become the vehicle for "the arrogant gaze" through which the west looks at and passes judgment on other cultures. Therefore, the legal imperative of rights discourse sometimes gets lost in the larger politics of the post-colonial era.

Fauzia, with the help of her mother and sister, fled the country and came to the United States to seek asylum. After a long struggle and a terrible experience in U.S. asylum centers, she received her vindication. She was given asylum as the United States recognized the imminent threat of FGM as a ground for gender-based persecution. Since her case, Togo has banned FGM and her own patriarch has become a convert in the struggle against FGM. While African anthropologists react to disorder in their symbolic universe, many women activists in Kenya, Senegal, and Egypt have begun door-to-door campaigns to fight FGM at the grassroots level.

Isabelle Gunning captures the majority viewpoint in her article on the best strategy to fight FGM. In it, she warns against the arrogant gaze of imperialism and finds that the best way to fight FGM is through education and health programs supported by the international community. Recognizing that FGM is a violation of a woman's rights and dignity, she suggests the best strategy is teaching the community. For many others, however, such as the feminist pioneers Nawal el Sadaawi, banning the practice and imposing criminal sanctions is an essential element in fighting these practices. A ban imposed by law also represents state recognition that it will not tolerate such practices.

In addition, one of the reasons why women perpetuate the practice is that they feel that their daughters will become unmarriageable unless circumcised. Unless the practice is banned, parents do not have an excuse to prevent their daughters from being subjected to the practice. Many campaigners argue that mothers often tell them that they are relieved when the practice is banned because they then have an excuse not to comply with cruel cultural practices. Its intrinsically violent nature rooted in the sexual subjugation of women, and the fact that it involves a child who cannot exercise choice, many human rights activists around the world feel that there should be a two-pronged attack in fighting the practice of FGM.

The attack would include banning the practice, which would serve a summons on society that such practices are unacceptable, as well as education and health programs involving African women that will try and engage the community in a discussion about why this practice is harmful to their women. But Gunning's caution that all this should be done without the arrogant gaze of the outsider is essential if rights discourse is to win the ideological battle. The full participation and consultation of women and men living in these societies must be the ultimate goal.

FGM is in the genre of violations against women that deserves international attention framed in terms of the rights discourse. It is violent, it causes severe pain and suffering, it is irreversible, and it shocks the conscience of everyone who does not perpetrate the practice. The shocks-the-conscience test of all outsiders (not only the West) is not always negative. It may actually be a reflection of international consensus in the making. Such practices deserve international agitation, international legal sanctions, and international programs and policies to combat the practices so that girls are spared this violence of the most intimate sort, which prevents them from being human in the most wholesome way.

Other cultural practices that fall into this type of genre are, for example, Sati in India or honor crimes practiced in many Arab and Mediterranean societies. The question of Sati in India raised many of the same debates as FGM, but this time between the central government of India and the government of the region where the practice was taking place. The issue came to a head in India when in the late 1980s Roop Kanwar committed Sati on her husband's pyre. The Central government and the Rajasthani government acted swiftly to outlaw the practice and to bring in strong measures against those that aid, abet, or watch such a spectacle. Nevertheless, thousands of Rajasthanis gathered to protest these measures as violating the traditional customs of the Rajputs.

Sati was an aspect of religious mythology, a story of sacrifice and resurrection. Moreover, it was strongly argued that the beliefs of the community should not be brought into question. Women who really wanted to commit Sati should be allowed to do so and what should be prevented are forced *Satis*. More nuances exist, however, when evaluating social and economic data. A political-economic analysis of Sati, devoid of mythological significance, shows that Sati provided a means of dealing with the unwanted widow.

Allowing Sati would result in great pressure being put on women to commit Sati, pressures they may not be able to resist. If "true" Sati was allowed, the ideological pressure on a young woman would compel her to give in to family demands to commit Sati. She would have no bargaining power in such a context, surrounded by her husband's family. To prevent this social pressure, most writers felt that Sati should be banned both at the center and the periphery. A widow who truly loved her husband could find other means through which to express her grief.

As with FGM, little disagreement existed that the modern practice should be discouraged. But people did call into question the arrogance of the central government and feminists in passing judgment on the beliefs and practices of a community. The vernacular press in India demonized the feminist groups that led the attack on the practice. Sati as a practice thrived in the same part of the country where female infanticide thrived during the time of the British. Though the mythology of Sati depicts a poignant story, the actual fact is that it is practiced in the area of the country where a female life is greatly undervalued and where violence against women and girls is widespread.

The practice reflects this misogyny and not an isolated religious belief. Feminist militancy in this regard may therefore be justified. Few further cases of Sati have been recorded in Rajasthan since the government took this strong action with regard to Sati after Roop Kanwar's case. In honor killings, family members kill women or girls for destroying the honor of the family. The type of behavior that can bring on this type of gruesome death could be adultery, falling in love, wanting a divorce, asking to choose one's own marriage partner, or mere allegations of illicit sexual conduct. The manner of death is often horrendous, involving stoning or being ritually stabbed and killed in public.

Despite its gruesome nature, there is general community support for honor killings in the societies where it is practiced. Mothers interviewed after the death of their daughters often shed no tears, saying that their daughters deserved the death. The case of Samia Sarwar in Pakistan brought international attention to the practice of honor killings. Samia was a married woman from a powerful landowning family in Peshawar, Pakistan. She wanted a divorce from her abusive husband who was also a relative.

There were also hints of her being in love with someone else. Finally, after months of disagreement during which Samia had to be hidden in a shelter by women's groups, her family agreed to the divorce. Her mother, uncle, and an unidentified man came to the office of Samia's lawyers to work out the details of her divorce. Before the discussions could proceed, the man who accompanied her family suddenly pulled out a gun and shot Samia dead. The aftermath of the shooting was equally disturbing. The State only reluctantly prosecuted members of Samia's family though there were many witnesses. Attempts to bring legislation against honor killings failed because many of the legislators did not want to take a stand against them.

Feminists analyzing the doctrine of provocation in Brazilian criminal law have argued that provocation essentially equals the honor defense. A man who catches his wife committing adultery is allowed a greater license to commit violence than the average citizen committing an ordinary crime. The reverse is not necessarily true. Provocation is rarely used to defend women who kill their husbands. The notion that men can commit violence against women who shame them in any way serves as an underlying assumption in many legal systems.

Honor in the family, like FGM, is closely linked to the control of female sexuality and movement. Honor is a code that ensures that women will behave in a manner that preserves their chastity and their obedience. If they dare to cross the boundaries, violence will be their fate.

In Brazil, honor was seen as a matter of self defense. To shame a man was to attack his person and property. In addition, masculinity and machismo as they are played out in some societies have an undercurrent of violence, and honor is the excuse for its manifestation.

TORTURE-LIKE PRACTICES

The practices in the area of violence against women outlined above are exceptional human rights practices because they most resemble torture. They involve "severe pain and suffering," and this aspect puts them in a separate category from other human rights abuses. One of the prohibited purposes of torture is discrimination, and one may argue that the above practices constitute an attempt to discriminate. One could also argue that state inaction and complicity in these cases involving violence against women meets the public official and acquiescence requirement of the Torture Convention. Because these cultural practices resemble torture, universal human rights must be seen to easily trump cultural relativist arguments that foster these particular practices.

Minorities or majorities that engage in such practices arguably violate some of the most fundamental principles of international law and international human rights law. In deciding which cultural practices existing in the world require international action and agitation, one must surely consider those practices that most resemble torture. States have taken firm action against FGM, Sati, and honor killings. Foot binding in China provides another similar example. Michel Foucault and others have argued that modern law finds physical violence against the integrity of the body totally unacceptable. The public spectacle killings in ancient societies that were so gruesome as to strike terror in the hearts of the public are no longer tolerated.

Other forms of violence, however, do not receive as much consideration and whatever the criticism, Foucault's argument that, violence against the integrity of the body that causes "severe pain and suffering" is the type of human rights abuse that immediately receives censure must be seen as a reflection of an international consensus. Cultural practices that challenge this norm must therefore receive the maximum degree of international scrutiny. Many groups in the countries in question campaign against these forms of violence. One should enter into partnership with these organizations and assist them in their attempts to fight these practices. These organizations have to win the ideological battle in their own societies to eliminate these practices.

DISCRIMINATORY LAWS

Short of inflicting violence and severe pain and suffering, many other customary and religious laws and practices also violate women's human rights. These usually deal with family law and the relationship between men and women within the family. In this area, a different approach aimed at balancing international women's rights with the rights of minorities may be necessary from a strategic viewpoint. Cultural practices relating to polygamy, inheritance rights, maintenance, consent at the time of marriage, child custody, child marriage, and others are among the issues that women's advocates raise their fight for equality within the family.

CEDAW article 16 is very clear about the nature and structure of marriage: there must be free and full consent of the spouses at the time of marriage and full equality between the partners during the marriage and at its dissolution. Many customary and religious systems around the world contest this recognition of freedom and equality as the principles on which to base marriage. Sandra Lovelace was a Canadian-Indian born in New Brunswick on the Tobique Indian reserve. She married a non-Indian, went out of the reserve, and had a son. The marriage broke up and she came back to the reserve.

The elders informed her that once she married a non-Indian she lost all rights and returns to the reserve as a stranger. As a result, they denied her housing and other benefits allowed on the reserve. Men who marry outsiders, however, retain their status within the reserve. They shall ensure in particular that neither marriage to an alien nor change of nationality by the husband during marriage shall automatically change the nationality of the wife."This type of provision is not peculiar to the Tobique Indians. Though many laws have been changed recently, most systems in the world link the domicile of the wife to the domicile of the husband

and the nationality of the wife and children to the nationality of the husband and father.

Family integrity was the argument usually put forward by these systems that also recognize the father's bloodline as the only legitimate bloodline. Sandra Lovelace took her case to the Canadian courts and then to the Human Rights Committee in Geneva. The Canadian government defended itself by relying on section 4 of the Indian Act, which placed these matters squarely within the jurisdiction of Indian Councils that run the reservations. They argued that this related to Article 27 of the Universal Declaration of Human Rights and the ICCPR that states clearly: "In those States in which ethnic, religious or linguistic minorities exist, persons belonging to such minorities shall not be denied the right, in community with the other members of their group, to enjoy their own culture, to profess and practice their own religion, or to use their own language."

When the case came up before the Human Rights Committee, commentators were eager to see how the Committee balanced the right to equality guaranteed to women in Article 3 of the ICCPR with the right to enjoy one's culture, a central dilemma for those fighting for women's rights internationally. They were sorely disappointed. The Committee disregarded the equality argument and claimed that Article 27 gave Sandra Lovelace the right to enjoy her identity as a Tobique Indian and the present practice prevented her from enjoying that right. They held for her but without dealing with the issues of discrimination or women's equality of land and resources on the Indian reservation provides another reason why the tribal leaders want to limit the numbers and the possibilities.

Therefore, they see outsider men as far more threatening to the tribe as outsider women who would probably not claim resources and benefits from the tribal leaders. In this context the rights of indigenous women to equality has been a question of great debate in Canada. Indigenous women often frame their rights within the discourse of the rights of the Indian people. Their dignity as women requires that others recognize and respect their status as Indians. But they believe that according women equality within that framework would not disrupt tribal realities. Many of them feel that the best strategy is to work with tribal leaders to get them to change their minds and change their laws.

Others, like Lovelace, feel that the Canadian government should intervene and ensure women's rights even at the expense of going against the wishes of the tribal leaders. A similar dilemma emerges when one deals with the Shah Bano case in India. Shah Bano was a seventy-year-old woman whose husband unilaterally divorced her and refused to pay her maintenance. The Muslim personal law in India sanctions both unilateral divorce and non-payment of maintenance. Shah Bano sued her husband under a provision of general criminal law that allowed destitute wives to sue their husbands for maintenance. The Indian Supreme Court held with her, but her case led to a great deal of Muslim unrest in India and the political leaders decided to change the law so that women in her situation would not have the criminal law recourse in the future.

This confrontation made many feel that the only way forward was reform from within the community instead of reform imposed by the Indian Supreme Court or any other outside force. At the international level, the Shah Bano case raises questions of a woman's right to equality but it also raises the dilemma of article 18 of the Universal Declaration of Human Rights and the ICCPR. Article 18 states that everyone shall have the right to freedom of thought, conscience, and religion. The right shall include freedom to have or adopt a religion or belief of his choice, and freedom, either individually or in community with others and in public or private, to manifest his religion or belief of his choice.

This provision arguably gives protection to religious law on personal matters; if people do not agree with the laws, they can change their religion. Others such as Courtney Howland have argued strongly against this position. Howland argues that systematic sex discrimination violates the U.N. Charter. Using the judgment of the International Court of Justice on apartheid, she argues that systematic sex discrimination should receive the same treatment, and that countries that engage in such discrimination should receive the same treatment as apartheid-dominated South Africa.

She points out that the U.N. Charter governs countries joining the United Nations and that Article 55 clearly states that one of the purposes of the United Nations is "universal respect for and observance of Human Rights and Fundamental Freedoms for all without distinction as to race, sex, language or religion." In addition she notes that Article 56 requires all states to pledge themselves to the purposes of the United Nations, including those set out in Article 56. She goes on to point out that the International Court of Justice has held that Article 56 imposes a legal obligation on states. Howland's main argument rests on the premise that when states join the United Nations and sign onto the Charter they are legally obligated to respect the observance of Human Rights and Fundamental Freedoms without distinction as to sex.

The U.N. General Assembly passed a Declaration on the Elimination of Religious Intolerance and Discrimination. The declaration makes it clear that international law protects the manifestations of religious belief related to worship, maintaining places of worship, charitable institutions, articles for rites and customs, publication of materials, teaching the religion, soliciting funds, religious holidays, and communicating with others. It does not include as a protected aspect of religious worship religious laws that discriminate against women. Regardless of the international legal status of the relevant religious law in Shah Bano's case, the practical reality was very different.

The Indian Supreme Court held for her, but ethnic riots and political bargaining got in the way of her remedy. In this political context, the search for solutions other than top-down legal impositions by courts of law, which may be insensitive to minority sentiments, may have to evolve for women to truly receive the benefits of the international rights and remedies articulated in the international human rights instruments. The dilemma between international rights and local realities also manifests itself in customary law and inheritance practices in Africa. Land is the most valuable economic resource in the Third World but, due to inheritance laws in these societies, a great disparity exists between male and female access to land.

Under customary legal regimes in Sub-Saharan Africa, women do not inherit any land, and only enjoy the land through their husbands and sons. Unmarried women and young widows without sons have little access to family resources. Old widows with sons and young widows with young sons have to live at the mercy of their sons or under the guardianship of their husband's brothers. Though a few tribes use a matrilineal system, the vast majority of tribes in Africa greatly restrict women's rights to inherit and use land. Women's lack of inheritance is central to the practices of patriarchy and the belief that the continuity of the family depends only on father and son, that women are only a means by which to continue this line.

Such beliefs often underpin customary law and even immigration law, which automatically gives women the domicile, residence, and nationality of their husbands. In addition, the belief that male labor is bread-winning, while female labor in the home is only supportive, justifies many of these inheritance laws as fruits of the labor of male members of the household. Practically speaking, societies also encourage these inheritance practices to prevent fragmentation of the land into too many parts. Increasingly, development support groups argue for changing these inheritance laws and giving women greater access to land. The current practices flagrantly violate CEDAW, especially Article 13, which states clearly "[s]tate Parties shall take all appropriate measures to eliminate discrimination against women in other areas of economic and social life in order to ensure, on a basis of equality of men and women, the same rights, in particular the right to family benefits."

In addition, women's equality will only come about with women's economic independence and, therefore, access to land rights is imperative with regard to other areas of women's rights. For example, domestic violence might decrease if women have their own plot of land and their own economic resources. Women's access to land will also gives access to credit, information, and technology to work the land. Access to land also provides security against poverty in old age. With access to land, women's status and bargaining power will increase dramatically rethink the concept of head of the household, which once automatically implied the male husband, and to invest more money in women's potential?

Rethinking inheritance rights in Sub-Saharan Africa implies restructuring customary law to ensure greater equality for women. This has become a heated issue, especially in South Africa. Many scholars have resisted any attempt to reform customary law, viewing it as an attempt to westernize and destroy the African family. In 1998, South Africa promulgated a new law called The Recognition of Customary Law Act, which kept provisions of the family law but took away some provisions that accentuated inequality between the sexes. In South Africa, kings and chiefs head a large number of traditional groups, all of which have their own customary law. Despite minor differences, however, they are all premised on certain common practices.

The first is the practice of "lobolo," where the husband's family negotiates with the parents of the bride to be, and an agreement is made regarding a payment by the bride's family to the groom's family. This payment could be in the form of cattle, money, or, in urban areas, other forms of amenities. In all of the systems, the wife leaves to live with the husband's family; she has no right to inheritance or to custody of the children, and her husband can practice polygamy. Widows are at the mercy of the male members of the husband's family and sometimes have to marry another male member in a levirate marriage. Native courts headed by the chiefs and kings of the traditional groups often enforce these customary laws.

The South African Law Commission (SALC) engaged in an interesting process in dealing with this contradiction. The feminists in South Africa were pushing for some form of uniform civil law that would incorporate the provisions of CEDAW as the only family law in the country. The tribal chiefs wanted the courts to recognize customary law. They were ready to agree to allow couples to choose the law that would govern their marriage, but wanted to ensure that all customary marriages, past and future, would be seen as valid. The SALC engaged in an open process to discover the best method to reconcile these opposing viewpoints. It received communication from all manner of sources and advice from individuals and experts around the world.

Ultimately, the SALC decided that all couples should have the option of choosing between having their marriages governed by the customary law or by the general law. In addition, the Recognition of Customary Marriages Act (Marriages Act) provides a minimum core of required provisions that apply to all marriages. These provisions require that all marriages be freely chosen and consensual. Unless a prenuptial contract exists, all property acquired during marriage is community property. This provision strikes at the heart of the inheritance regime that discriminates against women. Under the Marriages Act, married women may also acquire and dispose of assets and enter into contracts. Couples must register marriages and only a civil family law court judge can permit a divorce.

In this context, the judge uses the general law to divide the property, award alimony, and determine the custody of children. In addition, a polygamous marriage is valid if the first wife consents, and a written contract with the first wife divides the property accrued to that point. Levirate marriages may also continue if the widow consents to marrying the brother of her deceased husband. Some may argue that "consent" in this context is a misplaced concept, but the SALC believed that agency is possible and that women may wish to conform to traditional practices. The SALC also focused on the freedom to choose partners as an essential aspect of the minimum core of rights and took steps to protect the economic and material interests of the woman in marriage.

Recognizing the centrality of women's economic independence to equality, the SALC ensured that customary law did not take away their economic rights. The passage by Parliament of the Marriages Act did not please everyone, but it did gain general acceptance. The colonial powers and the apartheid regime always gave communities maximum space and control over family lives. The independent South African government dismantled this system of deference to tradition, keeping in mind the Bill of Rights and the equality of women. They were successful because they engaged in a consultative process and because socio-economic realities of urban South Africa required a reassessment of marriage practices.

TOWARD A RESOLUTION

While the legal paradigm of torture helps us sort out those cultural practices that deserve international attention, the South African experience may assist us in determining those aspects of customary and religious law that require amendment so that the ideal of the universality of human rights retains some significance for women in their every day life. In determining those aspects of cultural practice that do not withstand human rights scrutiny, general principles underlying international human rights law may prove useful.

The Convention on the Rights of the Child (CRC) is the most widely ratified convention in history; only two countries (Somalia and the United States) have not yet signed it. In some sense, Courtney Howland's argument that countries signing international documents are bound by the standards and principles set forth in those documents has special significance in this area. Unlike in the case of the Universal Declaration of Human Rights, state parties to the CRC had all achieved independence when they signed and, therefore, made affirmative decisions to be bound by the CRC. This worldwide consensus, with few reservations on substantive articles, must reflect the fact that countries are ready to accept international scrutiny with regard to the rights of the child.

The CRC precludes those aspects of customary and religious law and practice that violate the rights of the child. This would include provisions relating to child marriage as well as any practice that prevents the education of girls. In addition, those practices that result in health hazards for girls would also open a country to international scrutiny. In all these areas customary and religious law and practice must give way to international standards. Countries or minority groups with their own customary laws must bring these laws and practices into conformity with international norms and principles reflected in the CRC. The welfare of children is of national and international concern and reflects an international consensus. The space for the justification of cultural relativism is, therefore, somewhat limited. The strategies used to implement this concern, however, may differ.

Other principles may also assist us in determining how to resolve issues relating to cultural relativism in family law. For example, unlike the Covenant on Civil and Political Rights, the ICESCR defines its provisions in terms of the progressive realization of rights within available resources. This type of framework allows us to see rights in a more fluid sense, without immediate resolution. General Comment Number Three of the Covenant on Economic Social and Cultural Rights Committee (ICESR Committee) argues that, although these rights are not necessarily immediately realizable, a minimum core of rights should be immediately granted. Immediate rights include the right to primary education or the right to safe childbirth.

In the case of women's rights within a given cultural context, this framework of progressive realization over a period of time may prove the best approach in the long term. Though torture-like practices require immediate action, provisions relating to family law may be more effective if they are modeled on the ICESCR approach. Progressive realization of equality propelled by women's groups working on the ground may actually result in more lasting and effective solutions. Committees such as CEDAW can also push governments to comply with their international obligations. As suggested in General Comment Number Three by the ICESCR Committee, in the short term, governments should ensure that women receive a minimum core of rights within the family and the community.

For this reason, the concept of autonomy is also concerned with economic and social rights of women as a way of ensuring meaningful choice in everyday life. In some ways the SALC that inquired into customary law accepted this principle of autonomy as its guiding principle. It required that women have freedom of choice when it comes to marrying and accepting polygamy, and that women's economic independence be assured through the removal of provisions that prevented them from enjoying the economic resources of the family. The principle of autonomy is integrally linked to concepts of freedom and choice that underpin what is loosely called a western epistemology.

The project of the Enlightenment enshrined these concepts in law and practice. Individual men became the centerpiece of the universe, not God. Many of the struggles of the twentieth century have been to expand the beneficiaries of the Enlightenment project to include women and non-western males. But writers such as Michel Foucault have deconstructed this ideal in its many manifestations and have proven to the world that this framework, with its facade of respectability, masks a cruel and ruthless system of power.

Writers such as Edward Said "land other young post-colonial scholars have shown how this model applied to the colonies and how it operated to subjugate and victimize people of color. Their studies provide convincing portrayals of the Enlightenment project as an arrogant, western system of belief that destroyed everything in its path is no doubt that there is "globalization from below," and that third world groups are active members of this community. These groups dialogue with one another, often at world conferences, and there is an informal consensus has developed to their approach. Central to their consensus is the importance and primacy of the concept of democracy; not democracy in the narrow sense of western representative government, but democracy in a more inchoate sense of the need to include people of all groups and communities in a process of participation and decision-making.

If one were to read the many declarations and resolutions of the United Nations, one would see that democracy and participation by individuals and groups at all levels is a central animating tenet. Except for the documents dealing with peace and security or the economy, the political and civil documents of the United Nations make democracy and participation their central political concept. Therefore, it may be said that democracy as a general principle, even if not in its specific western manifestation, is part of an international consensus and is the underlying principle of organizations like the United Nations. Though it has not been recognized as *jus cogens,* the development of international norms since the end of the Second World War does point to democracy in a general sense as an emerging norm.

For democracy to be meaningful in the lives of individual women, these women must have the opportunity to make choices and decisions. Therefore, those aspects of customary religious law and practice that completely preclude them from making important decisions about their lives should be brought under scrutiny by national and international regimes. Provisions that deny women the right to give their consent to marriage or to leave an abusive relationship must surely be contested. In addition, provisions that deny women economic independence, such as those relating to her right to own property, enter into contracts, or receive inheritance, should also deserve intensive scrutiny.

CEDAW recognizes the right to freely choose the partner and the context of one's marriage. Choosing to deny oneself the rights given by international standards is a different matter than recognizing the fact that such standards do exist and those who prefer such standards should be given the right to be governed by them. Therefore, central to the question of discriminatory laws under custom and tradition is the issue of optionality.

All married couples on the date of their marriage should have the right to choose the system of laws that should govern their marriage. This protects the right of free choice central to international standards and documents of human rights. Some feminists have suggested that there be a "reverse optionality," that everyone is born into the general law but can choose to opt for a customary or religious system of law on their wedding day.

In addition, an approach to cultural practice that takes autonomy as a central guiding principle would require national governments to engage in a process much like the proceedings of the South African Commission. National governments should sift through their family and personal laws and identify a minimum core of provisions common to all legal systems. This minimum core would protect the rights of the child and the basic autonomy of the woman so that she could make decisions about her life. Couples on their wedding day could then choose which system of law should govern their marriage, legal provisions drafted in accordance with CEDAW or legal provisions relating to their own customary or religious law.

LEARNING FROM BELOW

Reformists who try to improve the situation of women always exist within each tradition. Women's groups have become increasingly active and involved. Where such groups exist, leadership on these issues at the national and international level should come from them. Any strategy should be formulated after full consultation and discussion with these groups because they are aware of the ground realities and the cultural and economic sensitivities. Only where such groups do not exist and where there is a situation of terror, such as in Taliban ruled Afghanistan, should one consider direct international action.

Action such as denying aid to governments or imposing penalties on third world states or communities for violation of women's rights should only be considered if the space does not exist for internal change and transformation and if local groups call for such intervention. While being an attempt to record the legal status of a specific group in contemporary India - the categorisation of which will be explained shortly- it is also an attempt to use this as a case study to critically analyse the role of law in social change. Specifically it looks at the strengths and the weaknesses of identity/community based legal lobbying and the nature of the change desired in that process.

When speaking of any queer person in India or in other country of South Asia the oft remembered law is sec. 377 or the colonial sodomy law of 1860. The legal status however, extends way beyond this particular section of the Indian penal code as do the implications for queer people. This particular chapter will review the position of queer women in Indian law and their position in the campaigns/ struggles around the same. Before we begin, it is important to define what we mean by the term 'queer women'. Politically, the word queer is often used among some activists in India to mean any person who questions norms of gender and sexuality. While the strength of this definition lies in its potential inclusivity, the need to state more exclusive identity 'tags' as it were, are important in many contexts such as in this very chapter.

In this chapter we use 'queer' merely as an umbrella term for lesbian, bisexual and female-to-male (FTM) persons and some others unnamed so far. Thus, by queer we are referring to those individuals who are only or are also attracted to people of the same gender as their own. We mean in behaviorial terms- lesbian and bisexual and female-to-male persons. The word queer as an overarching term however, might still remain a useful term in this particular chapter as it is not often lesbian or bisexual sexual acts/behaviour that one is referring to in terms of legal changes but an assertion and acknowledgment of an identity based on the same that is the threat.

The act, though illegal in our country, will still be tolerated if done in silence, in the private sphere and in a way that does not hinder the normative processes in a woman's life such as marriage, child birth etc. the political identity of lesbian/ bisexual or queer are what are the potent threats to hegemonic patriarchal norms that govern all our lives. Further, any behavioural term such as 'lesbian' 'bisexual' and so on will not and can not capture the whole array of sexual practices, gender performance and identities that the women in this chapter exhibit. Thus one is left with the need for an inclusive term.

It is important to describe here who are referring to when we say 'women'. The category being one that can not be taken for granted, it becomes important to explain any limited interpretation and the justifications for the same. As discussed the word queer would also include people who are FTM or MTF. In our own comfortable reading of butler and Greer in a concoction of feminist theory, we believe that gender performativity even if subversive and assertive does not take away from the oppression and hegemony on the genders written on our bodies. Thus in this chapter, we are discussing the stories of vaginas who like other vaginas. Having said that, we cannot underestimate the influence of the performance of transgressive gender as in the case of 'butch' lesbians or FTM persons on the way they inhabit spaces and thus the course of their struggles.

This choice is a conscious political one to also state that a male to female person's experience or the experience of a *hijra* who might identify as a woman are different from the stories we tell in this chapter. The community of *hijras* are a distinct cultural community with a complex set of ritual, Social and economic norms and kinship ties. It would be limiting both to a discussion of the 'queer women' we are referring to as well as the transgender community to club them together in the category of women solely based on their own subjective identification.

We would also like to establish at the very outset that the women referred to in this chapter are not just queer but belong to specific regions, religions, castes and classes. These identities also have a profound impact on their struggles. The exact nature of the impact is unascertainable but it is significant to remember a larger political framework of intersectionality of identities and thus struggles. We will return intermittently to this point. As we know queer men, by virtue of being male often have the freedom of movement and thus access to the public sphere in India and other south Asian countries.

Further, this interaction of men with the public sphere is the norm necessitated by employment for instance, which is a significant aspect of normative masculinity. This access to the public sphere then provides freedom for men to live their lives with their various preferences and identities however deviant they may be for certain periods/moments in their lives. This very access to the public sphere might even be a pressure rather than a privilege for some. The relative lack of access for women to the public sphere and the segregated female space has also meant freedom for some in many ways including to facilitate same sex sexual activity. Segregated spaces of any kind- male or female- both provide the quintessential space for same sex sexual activity which is the fortunate and rare fallout of silence and invisibility.

With regard to women however, the awareness of one's body and of sexual pleasure and even pain are often not allowed. For men there is often allowed a culture of sexual talk and exposure. However limited, factually wrong and sometimes offensive (to some) this exposure might be, it is seen as 'part of growing up' for boys. Women are not attributed any knowledge or the freedom to explore their own bodies, leave alone that of others. It is for this reason that lesbian sexual activity is often a huge threat and is seen as a significant 'aberration' of accepted women's sexuality. But myths such as it is only men who masturbate and women don't and so on are part of this differential status of sexual speech in the lives of men and women.

Given these background lesbian women, like many heterosexual women who choose their own partners (irrespective of caste, class, religion, race, region) and/or choose to engage in sexual activity before or outside of wedlock and so on challenge patriarchal structures in significant ways. While some parts of the struggles of women who assert their own sexual identities- heterosexual, homosexual or bisexual- are shared, lesbian identified women have a significantly different experience. This is often due to a number of reasons. First, they shake the very basis of heteronormativity, which is the need for a man in an intimate, interdependent or sometimes just compulsorily dependant relationship.

Second, the structure of family is challenged significantly as these women then engage in sexual activity which does not and cannot result in procreation. Third, and most significantly, lesbian women engage in activities that give them sexual pleasure. Sexual pleasure a 'luxury' not allowed to women as a whole (illustrated very clearly by the not so popular status of the clitoris internationally) is in many ways the basis of lesbian sexual activity, thus making it a serious threat to heteronormative structures and thus the often violent homophobic reaction to queer women. Yet another argument that can be made based on case law is the fact that women have to face the repercussions of being women, legally and socially in the first place.

The very fact that a woman is wishing to and sometimes demanding that she live outside the natal home and not in the custody of another man, namely the husband and/or his family is in itself a significant threat. The fact that she might want to live with another woman then adds fuel to the fire. In terms of the legal status of queer men and women, there are significant differences as well as some shared struggles. Section 377 is used against queer men and women as a threat. In many cases, police often do not want to make arrests but use it as a threat.

This is common between queer men and women, although queer men face it much more due to their prominence in public spaces as compared to women. Similarly the use of the legal status as a threat within the private sphere is vastly different for queer men and women. sec. 377 is used by parents of queer men as a threat. There are various other laws, however, that are often used either as threats or most often for filing cases against queer women by their own families and others. Apart from section 377, there are a number of laws in the Indian penal code which have had a direct impact on the lives of queer women. These laws include, 340- wrongful confinement, 361- kidnapping and 362- abduction, 366 - inducing woman to compel her marriage, and 368 of the IPC and Habeas Corpus writs are only some examples.

A case which saw an interesting judgment was in Delhi in early 2006. A lesbian couple approached queer rights groups in Delhi. One of them had left home due to which the parents had filed a kidnapping charge against the other woman under section 366 of the IPC. Eventually the charge was nullified based on the statement of the woman who ran away from home that she was not forced, but left home out of her own will and volition. As this was celebrated by all the activists and lawyers involved as a victory we chose almost to momentarily ignore the fact that throughout the case, any reference to the lesbian relationship between the two women was avoided by all those involved.

The line of argument was to prove the woman's adult status while covering up and even denying her lesbian ness in the court room. This is a classic example of the difficulties in even recording cases that might have involved lesbian women. This is one of the many cases when the legal adultness of the women in question has been highlighted to ensure their rights while consciously invisibilising their lesbian identity. In many 'runaway' lesbian cases the two adult women have found themselves charged with the offences of kidnapping and abduction. For example in a 'runaway' lesbian case in Kerala the one of the two women was charged with abduction and the parents also filed a 'man missing case'.

It is interesting to note in this case is that the magistrate heard the case and sent the two adult women back to the custody of their parents only to be treated for mental illness.

In complete contradiction, also in Kerala, in a case where the parents of one of the girls' filed a habeas corpus, the magistrate decreed that the two women could live by themselves or together if they choose to do so as they are adults and cannot be charged under the custody of anybody. Adult hood then always remains a precarious strength.

The writ of habeas corpus is used to secure release of a person who has been detained unlawfully or without legal justification. Habeas corpus may also be issued when a person complains of illegal custody or detention by a private person. When the conflicting claims are made for the custody of an infant, the court can enquire into these claims and award the custody to the proper person. In the context of habeas corpus involving men, where it is filed against the detention in state institutions, it is a grievance redressal mechanism. In the case of women, however, who wish and choose to live with chosen partners who might be men (of an unacceptable nature due to caste, class, religion, character etc) or any woman, it is a repressive mechanism.

It is also significantly ironic to note that the court in the first place would allow parents to file a writ of habeas corpus against their adult daughter's 'lover' and that the court would then hear it and grant custody to the parents when the daughter clearly states that she does not wish to live with them. In some instances when the court has not granted custody to the parents, it has taken the role of the *parens patriae* and placed them in shelters created for women and kept the two women apart. Let us of course remember that in the case of heterosexual couples, it is still easier for the male lover to reunite with the woman. The unacknowledged nature of homosexual relationships makes the case harder for the couple.

In the case of R and N in Kerala, they did receive a positive judgment from court that they can live with each other. The parents of both women were however asked to facilitate this process. The parents intercept the execution of the judgment, separate the women, and physically and emotionally torture them. N after having escaped confinement in her house filed a habeas corpus petition to find R. This petition however is immediately dismissed on the grounds that N has no *locus standi*. This as we know is an erratic dismissal based entirely on notions of first, that women, who are not family members cannot file for custody of another woman and two, a woman cannot file for custody of any human being who is not related to her familiarly.

In another case, two women S and J fought a legal battle to retain their right to live together. This case took place with an open acknowledgement of their relationship as lovers by both women. The gender identity of one of the women- as one who dresses and lives as a man was both a weakness and a strength. In court, the question emerged of whether this person was a man or a woman. This case is significant in the context of this discussion as it was one of the few cases where the exact nature of the relationship between the two women was known to all those involved such as the women, the parents, the lawyers and the court. Given all these circumstances the women were allowed to live with each other on the grounds that they are adults.

On the contrary, Shahzina and Shumail from Lahore are another case in point. In this recent case this couple, one of whom, Shumail, is FTM were charged with purgery and sentenced 3 yrs in jail. The court released the couple saying that there is nothing illegal about two women living together. The judgment although unrelated to the earlier purgery charge, freed the women nevertheless. What is to note here is that Shumail, who had gone through some surgery and also identified as a man in court was not accepted to be one and thus the women could so easily be charged with purgery, although the case was about their relationship and not their gender identities.

The utter confusion in court spaces when it comes to cases involving two women is highlighted in the following case. In Jalgaon, Bombay two women were long-term lovers and neighbors, both of whom were married to men and had children. They decided to approach the local police authority to get married to each other. The police in turn questioned the women and eventually put them in prison along with the husband of one of the women who came looking for them. They were all eventually let off.

The couple in question seemed to have approached the police due to the notion of 'authority' in society where the lack of parental support has often meant seeking support from state structures such as the police. Inspired by the 'partially inspired by real lives'- Bollywood cinema- where we have number of heterosexual couples who are not accepted by their families turning to police structures where their right to marry is upheld. Extending this notion of the rights of these couples the Jalgaon women seem to have also expected a 'right to marry' that the police would uphold. The police on the other hand, completely perplexed by the scenario not only make completely illegal arrests of the women and the husband but also subject the women to medical scrutiny to detect finger prints inside their vagina as proof of sexual activity between the two women.

In another case in Bombay a woman who was involved in a lesbian relationship was collectively threatened by her own mother and brother-in-law with the help of the police with section 377 of the IPC. Although no action was pursued this threat was strong enough to cause substantial emotional harm to the woman in question. This as we may note is one of the few cases where sec. 377 was directly quoted. Here too, the law was not used to file a case but to threaten the woman out of her relationship. As a lesbian activist Shalini from Bombay put it – it was used in the exact manner that it is supposed to- for moral policing'. This process is common to both queer men and women- the threat of 377 as the 'curing mechanism'.

Thus legal lobbying around section 377 within the ambit of sexuality rights is of enormous political and symbolic significance. In terms of ground reality the problem is however a much more complicated legal battle. In the case of women, the struggles and impact are nuanced. Legal changes and its significantly public nature with regard to case law have a very different impact on women than it does on men. In general, positively empowering laws that provide redressal mechanisms for women from violence or within other institutions such as marriage and the workplace have a pronounced impact on women's lives. Comparatively, negatively empowering legal changes such as the decriminalising of adult consensual same sex activity have little impact even symbolically for women.

This is due to a number of reasons. First, at the ground level, the police harassment based on the law is targeted largely on men and the changes in the law have little impact for women. Second, the association of 377 as the sodomy law has often been related to men rather than women. The history of the law in terms of cases and the imagination of this law over time have also largely involved sex between men rather than between women. We can use this analysis also as a ground to take a critical look at the role of law in social change. This can be articulated through a two pronged approach. First the centrality attributed to legal change in processes of social change can be questioned. Second this centrality and visibility to legal battles as they may leave out certain communities/ identities as the law per se has invisibilizes them.

Further the public nature of the law as mentioned earlier, in many ways structure forms of dissent. It thus follows that the struggles of queer women are not often the material for posters for queer struggles in India as they are not part of the public eye of the law and neither do the women have the privilege to identify as queer openly. Having said that, one must clarify that we are not suggesting a blatant inclusion of queer women in the law or in the struggles against the same, but the use of their stories to question both the law and the expressed dissent. We must be conscious that the structures of oppressions that are being questioned in many ways also configure the dissent.

The life of Section 377 will invariably decide who is involved and/or is affected by the protest against it. In other words, if sodomy laws have been associated with men, the protest against it will involve and affect more men than it does women. We must be wary of internalising, in our struggles the exclusions and inclusions necessitated by the structures we oppose. One is also not suggesting that varied forms of dissent and struggle do not thrive. We are however critiquing the popular representation and perception of queer struggles in India around the law which is often "male". This questioning emerges not from a fear of difference within the movements- which in our opinion is nothing but a strength- but as a word of caution from the perspective of long term social change.

The enormous significance of the campaign against sec.377 at this historical moment is beyond doubt. However, from a broader perspective, we must be conscious that struggles that are of real and symbolic significance for one community/ identity, is only a spec in the universe of political struggles based on an alternative world view. Legal battles- a even smaller aspect of social change- can in itself be revisited critiqued and strengthened. In this context the significance of habeas corpus writs, for example, in the lives of queer women is an excellent strategy to establish solidarity with various other struggles of women. This solidarity need not be just a strategic alliance but a broader political dialogue which might or might not mean consensus but it will strengthen the different and yet shared struggles of various women.

With regard to the queer struggles across the south Asia region, there is a need to constantly re-emphasise and cherish the existence of the whole array of diverse forms of struggles. While some are shared, others need to be different. Exclusive spaces for men, women, gay men, *hijras*, lesbian and bisexual women etc are of enormous value. Our shared struggle in many ways can sometimes be strategic alliances on specific instances and/or issues.

At most other times it might mean a larger political articulation of 'queerness' which is the dream of a world where persons and communities have the right to question norms of gender and sexuality and make their choices. The latter we see as a desirable larger politics which includes identity-based articulations only in specific and hopefully short moments as strategy. Rights of identities and communities may seem to be the beginning, middle and end of many social struggles. We must acknowledge and remember that no philosophy of social change is about or for any one group of people.

We are arguing that we need to be critical of a few things we often taken for granted in academic and activist work around issues of gender and sexuality. One, the clubbing of LGBT. We have to remember that the selection of alphabets is not exhaustive and never will be given the vibrancy of human experience. And two, the alphabets are not equals but are hierarchised and sometimes invisibilised etc. second, we need to be critical of addressing sexuality issues from the vantage point of sexual identities alone but try and evolve a language that is complex including various aspects that affects our lives of which sexuality is a part. The ghettoisation of any one kind of politics in both academics and activism, we are arguing has to be countered effectively.

In India while we are still at the initial stages of activism, academic writing and public discourse on the whole gamut of issues of sexuality we are struggling (at least some of us) to highlight the differences and diversity in our struggles as a strength and a formidable force against simplistic arguments couched in the language of rights of specific communities and people, which in the long run might and often ahs in history leave oppressive and hegemonic systems non-shattered if not untouched.

5

Legal and Philosophical Perspectives on Women

Women around the world have been demanding the universal implementation of human rights standards. Nevertheless women's rights can be considered as the most overlooked aspect in the human rights framework. Although the participation of women in the review and reporting of human rights conditions has grown in many ways, it must also be recognised that the cooperation and coordination of principled policies to address international guarantees of the human rights of women in the field remains underdeveloped in the programming of the United Nations.

Thus, despite the improvements that have come with the establishment of the Convention on the Elimination of All Forms of Discrimination Against Women (CEDAW) and in the United Nation's field-based programs in countries where women's rights are still challenged (i.e., Iraq, Afghanistan, China), the tendency to take an easier path – favouring a non-confrontational approach to humanitarian assistance as the Taliban case showed – "may overwhelm the need for direct and insistent action on the enforcement of international human rights guarantees to women".

Consequently, women's groups working at the national level in many Asian and African countries are still facing innumerable obstacles.

As Ackerly rightly recognises, women's human rights activism demonstrates that the challenges of gaining recognition of women's human rights are as much the challenges of changing local social contexts as they are the challenges of promoting universal norms of human rights. This is because international standards of women's rights, which are at the frontier of human rights development "collide with cultural movements at the national level that question the very articulation of women in human rights terms".

Considering such challenges, the main aim of this article will be to examine possible resolutions for internal and local encounters between women's rights claimants and those who condemn women's rights in non-Western contexts.

Here a particular focus will be on Asian/Confucian and Islamic cultural contexts, as it can be argued that these are the most antagonistic challengers to universal human rights of women. The challenges to women's human rights will then be analysed from both culturally relativist and Universalist perspectives.

This analysis will be used to accentuate the inadequacies of both culturally relativist and the (current) Universalist approach in addressing women's human rights issues. Instead, I intend to argue that the 'capabilities approach' as developed by Martha Nussbaum possesses the theoretical preconditions to address the more adequate universalistic establishment of women's human rights and also to offer potential resolutions for some outstanding issues concerning women's rights.

CEDAW

The Convention on the Elimination of All Forms of Discrimination Against Women (CEDAW) was introduced in 1979 (becoming operational in 1981) as the Universal Declaration was considered, particularly by many feminist theorists, as potentially less than universal, particularly in respect to it being in many respects, applicable only to men's rights. One of its most distinctive features is a requirement that States undertake affirmative steps to modify cultural practices that impair the enjoyment of equal rights between men and women. Thus, CEDAW requires signatories to eliminate discrimination against women in civil, political, economic, and cultural fields. The Convention permits ratification subject to reservations, provided that the reservations are not incompatible with its object and purpose.

There have been numerous countries that have filed many formal reservations - perhaps more than to any other major human rights treaty (The UN website for the Division for the Advancement of Women). Some of these limit the obligations undertaken by the signatory in vague and sweeping terms, while others focus on areas of fundamental importance to the achievement of women's equality, such as family law. Consequently some reservations, indeed, appear to be inconsistent with CEDAW's "object and purpose".

In order to explain these inconsistencies, it is worthwhile to consider the example of Egypt inserting the following reservation:

The Arab Republic of Egypt is willing to comply with the content of (Article 2), provided that such compliance does not run counter to the Islamic Shari'a ... This is out of respect for sacrosanct nature of the firm religious beliefs which govern marital relations in Egypt and which may not be called in question and in view of the fact that one of the most important bases of these relations is an equivalency of rights and duties so as to ensure complementary which guarantees true equality between the spouses.

The inconsistency on CEDAW's object and purpose appear obvious, as with this reservation Egypt is not just protecting its religiously sanctioned customs but it appears, in using the language of "balance" between spouses, to take issue with the Convention's assertion that men and women should enjoy identical rights.

The ideology conveyed through this reservation maintains that men and women are not identical and that even though many of their rights may be different, they are complementary and of equal value. Hence, for them, difference is not the same as discrimination or a breach of women's human rights. Nevertheless, it is such culturally particular laws that have been emphasised by many Third World countries in their rejection of, or the reservations placed on, the measures of CEDAW. Thus these Convention standards do not ensure the protection for human rights of all women.

THE ISLAMIC CHALLENGE

The Islamic challenge to women's human rights has been identifiable since the introduction of the Universal Declaration. When the declaration was being drafted in 1947, the Saudi Arabian delegation objected particularly to Article 16, involving the free marriage choice and Article 18 on the freedom of religion. The Saudi delegate's proposal to the committee examining the draft to the Universal Declaration has been reverberating ever since in Islamic encounters with Western human rights. It stated:

> The authors of the draft declaration had, for the most part, taken into consideration only the standards recognized by Western civilization and had ignored more ancient civilizations which were past the experimental stage and the institutions of which, for example marriage, had proved their wisdom through centuries. It was not for the Committee to proclaim the superiority of one civilization over all other[s] or to establish uniform standards for all countries of the world.

This was, as Ignatieff (2001:59) recognises, a defence of Islamic faith and a defence of patriarchal authority at the same time. Consequently, the argument of Saudi delegates emphasised that "the exchange and control of women is the very basis of traditional cultures and that the restriction of female choice in marriage is central to the maintenance of patriarchal property relations". On the basis of these objections to Articles 16 and 18, the Saudi delegation refused to endorse the Declaration.

The antagonism of the situation has been growing since the 1970s. Advocates supporting the Islamic challenge have been emphasising that "the Western separation of a church and state, secular and religious authority is alien to the jurisprudence and political thought of the Islamic tradition". The freedoms articulated in the Universal Declaration make no sense within the theocratic bias of Islamic political thought. In addition, the right to marry and found a family and to freely choose one's partner directly challenges Islamic law that insists on the family choice of spouse, polygamy and the keeping of women in *purdah.*

In Islamic eyes, the universalising rights discourse implies a sovereign and discrete individual, which is offensive from the perspective of the Koran. According to Fatima Mernissi in Islam "the idea of the individual in a state of nature, in the philosophical meaning of the word, is non-existent". Muslims see individual identity, as a disturbance of collective harmony and maintain that traditional Muslims should be submissive to the group. Liberal democracy with majority rule and individual rights cannot coexist with the application of Shari'a, "the expression of the will of God for the betterment of man". Thus, neither universal human right of men nor of women can be implemented under the Shari'a law.

Under such law the needs of the individual can never prevail over community needs. Moreover, whilst the law proscribing individual rights can be damaging to men as well, Shari'a has particular impact on women, because of its patriarchal nature. The Islamic law makes distinctions between men and women; not all rights and privileges available to men are available to women. Shari'a law maintains men as household heads with exclusive rights to allocate property and thus make all decisions in, and on behalf of, all the members of the family.

Furthermore, the current misuse of power under the traditional Shari'a law is evident from the recent Amnesty International findings on women's situation is post-war Iraq. The findings highlight that Iraqi fundamentalists still perform "honour killings" which are justified under Shari'a law. The police are unable or unwilling to act against these crimes (Amnesty International, 2005). The example of Iraq highlights just one example illustrating that certain cultural practices infringe upon basic human right to life.

THE ASIAN CHALLENGE

The universality of women's human rights is challenged currently not only from the side of Islamic values but also from the Asian-Confucian side. Although the modern nation-states in Asia have risen to international economic and political prominence in the last two decades, leaders and individuals within these have reacted to universal human rights discourse with "the brand of outraged cultural relativism referred to as Asian values". The principal agents of this counter trend have been state agencies and political figures from Singapore, the People's Republic of China and Malaysia.

Asian values are understood as an "emphasis on the community and the societal harmony, over the individual, a sense of loyalty and duty toward one's family, self-reliance, thrift, a general tolerance of benign authoritarianism". The concept is believed to have arisen from the patriarchal Confucian ideology, which maintains that harmony is to be maintained by adherence to the social order. In Asian countries upholding Confucian ideology, women are expected to remain at home and play no part in public affairs. They were advised to abide by "The Three Obediences" and "The Four Virtues".

Under these cultural precepts women were absent from the public sphere, and practices such as foot binding and concubinage reinforced their subordinate position in society. Today, although there have been some major cultural transformations in respect to the role of Asian women in general, the unequal position of some Asian women is still prevalent. The majority of the reviewed literature on Asia lists women's rights and women's exploitation among a number of "negative particularities", which are claimed in need of urgent reform.

Although human rights theorists and activists in Asia have been arguing that certain civil and political rights, such as freedom of expression, are claimed necessary to promote the kinds of economic, social and cultural rights that would benefit those fighting against discrimination, there are women in some parts of Asia who are simply not granted human rights.

PROBLEMS WITH CULTURAL RELATIVIST APPROACH

The central obstacle to the achievement of women's human rights is, as the previous analysis underlines, the presence of culturally relativist dogma. Cultural relativists, as the Muslim secularist and human rights theorists Reza Afshari (1994:7) rightly points out, "share the view that human rights do not constitute the cultural ideal adhered by the world's ethical systems, with the exception of West". Afshari (1994:7-8) further identifies, what she calls "the most uncompromising" relativist stance according to which "local cultural traditions (including religious, political and legal practices) properly determine the existence and scope of civil and political rights enjoyed by individuals in a given society".

According to Afshari (1994:8) "this position espouses the view that culture is the supreme ethical value, more important than any other. Human rights, in particular, should not be promoted if their implementation might result in a change in a particular culture". Afshari (1994) shows this approach as the one prominently used in the views of most conservative Islamists. On the basis of their culturally relativist beliefs, some Islamists, as Afshari (1994) illustrates, reject, explicitly or implicitly the universal applicability of the Universal Declaration of Human Rights.

Thus, the states that reject universal human rights justify this on the basis of cultural relativism, arguing that all cultures are particular and there is no such thing as a universality of principles. According to this relativist view, as Li (1995:410) indicates in the Chinese case, "any attempt to produce cross-cultural notions of human well-being is bound to protect certain understandings of the human good and to dismiss others". Thus these non-Western countries reserve their right to implement universal human rights arguing that because this is a Western concept it is bound to bring about Western understandings of human good, and dismiss non-Western ones.

Here it is important to note that the governments rejecting a universality of standards as Western, on the basis of cultural relativism, do not posses the ground for such claims. In other words, those that reject universal human rights standards because they claim that these are in reality Western, are not, despite their claims to the contrary, arguing along relativist lines but rather in an absolutist fashion. This practice of absolutism is evident as non-Western governments, whilst refusing the universal human rights, actually promote the local and traditional laws in an enforced, absolutist way, as the only principles legitimate for the non-Western countries. In other words, non-Western governments in this ratifying process use the rhetoric of relativism but the practice of absolutism.

Nevertheless, Islamic and Asian countries further justify their resistance to the universal human rights standards arguing that these are inapplicable because they are not only a Western construct, but are also of Western imperialistic nature. The basis for rejecting the principles on the basis of this "Western imperialism" argument, as Li (1995) recognises, resides in the fear of non-Western governments that dominant social prejudices about the understanding of human value would be imposed on women by the stronger foreign culture, in this case Western culture. In respect to women's rights, considering that societies are often patriarchally structured and controlled by dominant groups, cultural relativists do have a point for suspicion: the dominant comprehension of human rights are more than likely to put females at a disadvantage.

However, the same difficulty besets cultural relativism itself for two reasons. Firstly, the countries that reject universal standards for women do so out of patriarchal reasons, amongst others. Secondly, adopting a culturally relativist approach precludes the possibility for the establishment of universal standards for all people. And yet the situation without universal norms begs the question of who will evaluate and arbitrate on human rights and attend to the claims of all the rights claimants: should it be the local government (i.e. state), the traditional philosophical or religious doctrines, or women's own perceptions of their interest?

As the analysis of Islamic and Asian contexts makes clear, the cultural laws, such as Shari'a and Confucian laws, have shown to represent the patriarchal status quo and put females at a disadvantage. Nevertheless, the justifications shielded under the umbrella of culturally relativist discourse hinder the universal standards with the notion that these, as Western constructs are culturally insensitive and neglecting of historical and cultural differences. Thus, the universality of human rights standards for women is inapplicable as different cultural traditions and communities diverge in their understanding of human values as well as of women's status and roles in society.

For this reason, the argument goes, cultural law should determine what kind of rights women would have. So, if Shari'a states that men should be the head of the family that make decisions on behalf of his entire family, then that should be so in practice. If this means that a woman in that family will not have equal rights to participate in decision-making processes, because this is culturally appropriate, then this is also justified under cultural relativism.

Consequently, this leads to the conclusion that the argument of such cultural relativists, according to which we cannot arbitrate between the cultural practices that a certain culture upholds and proposes, allows for the persistence of gender inequality. The case of East Asia where the plights of 'comfort women' are largely ignored, as these women had no power or language to articulate their claims, can be used to support this argument. The long-term problem with the adoption of the culturally relativist approach is that it results in what Li (1995) calls a "false consciousness" that further aids to maintaining the status quo. Li's (1995) study on women in China highlights this argument.

The study showed that the results of maintaining the patriarchal status quo and long-term subordination results in "false consciousness", which further influences, the willingness for change for many women in China. Women in China are still captive to their long-standing patriarchal society propaganda. Li (1995) has argued that "growing up in Chinese sexist morality, women have deposited within them a 'psychological complex': the inferior morality". This attitude highlights the argument that women in China "have not transcended the male domination and have taken it so much for granted that they even inflict the repression on themselves".

Martha Nussbaum, a women's rights theorist whose approach will be discussed to a greater detail in the following paragraphs, warns us of this, arguing that implementation of universal standards is necessary as "one must not assume that the statements of the people who have long been subordinated are reliable indicators of what is really essential." For this reason, we cannot rely on the unreflective and uncritical self-expressions serving as a justification for and highlighting the cultural relativist cause, as these are misleading.

Instead, the implementation of universal human rights for women is crucial as this will provide education, raise consciousness, and make sure that women have "adequate information about alternative ways of life and real freedom to form a conception of the good without fear". Nevertheless, for this to take place, even the universal framework needs further reconstruction, as one of the main problems with the lack of implementation of women's rights in both Asian and Islamic countries resides even within the problematic nature of the universal framework.

PROBLEMS WITH THE UNIVERSALIST APPROACH

The problematic nature with the Universalist approach resides primarily in the universal model being restricted only to men's rights, and not being realised as such. Agosin (2001) rightly recognises that most governments that propose universal human rights, as well as non-governmental organisations (NGOs), still define universality of human rights in terms of male models and patterns of thinking. Consequently, this is still causing women's rights abuses to be so pervasive and systematic that they are regarded as part of the natural order of things.

In other words, because the universal human rights are defined in terms of male models and patterns of thinking, some Universalists tend to justify some of the women's rights violations under the notion of patriarchy. For instance, the fact that women are being denied their civil and political rights as equal citizens in China, might be justified by patriarchal universalists who might argue that these civil and political rights are important for men, and not so much for women. Such patterns of thinking will obviously lead to ignorance of the importance of all universal human rights to be applied to women equally.

The further problems with such a universalising approach are evident from the fact that the Declaration of Human Rights with its prioritising of civil and political rights has left the responsibility and protection of social and economic rights (reduced to a notion of basic needs) to national governments and international development agencies. The problem is that such responsibility was not, however, accompanied with any binding guarantee that civil and political rights for women actually exist in these states.

Thus, relying on national governments to deliver civil and political human rights can be an uncertain and controversial process. In Islamic countries, the governments do deliver human rights within the Shari'a context. However as discussed above, this law does not ensure the equality of human rights to both men and women and it is particularly damaging to women. In Asia, some governments that advocate Asian-values propose that political and civil rights should be deferred until other, more pressing, economic rights are dealt with.

For example, in a 1993 statement Singapore's then Minister for Foreign Affairs Wong Kan Seng declared that, if political and civil human rights are an obstacle to economic progress, they would not be accepted, and an overemphasis on individual rights would retard the process of development. The consequences arising out of this lack of attention to human rights results in the absence of legal intervention to protect women in the community and in the home. This further keeps devaluing women's roles and keeps even the traditional male-dominated hierarchy of the family intact.

Consequently, the fact that civil and political rights focus on protecting the individual against the state in the public sphere, rather than addressing the private sphere of family and home, has meant that issues such as violence against women, including rape, are generally not considered human rights violations. Even today, although the recognition that the focus on civil and political rights ignored women's concerns has helped broaden the international human rights agenda, we still witness the gender-based violations that cut across cultural, social and political lines.

Many of these abuses discriminate against status as equal partners and citizens. Widow burning (*sati*) and honour killings are just two of the most extreme examples. Thus, one of the main issues within the universal framework is that in many ways it resembles male models and patterns of thinking, signifying a man, "endowed with reason, unfettered and equal to other men". However, it is also the fact that, regardless of its many flaws, a universal approach is essential and justified on the basis that women's rights would not have gained any ascendancy in the world today if there had not been a universal discourse.

Consequently, an approach for addressing women's rights issues could best be achieved by improving on the areas within the universal human rights framework. Thus, while not abandoning that framework, what seems essential is a possible reconstruction of a current model of universal human rights. One model that can be considered as a philosophical precondition that would allow for a defence of universal women's rights is Martha Nussbaum's capabilities approach.

PROPOSING NUSSBAUM'S "CAPABILITIES APPROACH"

Martha Nussbaum (1995) is a women's rights theorist, whose approach is particularly appropriate for our analysis for two reasons. Firstly, Nussbaum (1995) recognises, like many non-Western feminists, that women's rights do not constitute a "part of the Western human rights talk" but are nonetheless universal and are in need of serious consideration. And secondly, in her "capabilities approach" Nussbaum advances resolutions for women's rights issues.

The competence of the "capabilities approach" resides in its aim to provide the basis for the conception of minimal constitutional principles that should be respected and implemented by the governments of all nations. The basis for these constitutional principles would include "a minimum of what respect for human dignity requires". Thus the achievement of such social minimum would be provided by the approach that focuses on human capabilities with what people are able to do and to be. Nussbaum (2000:5) sees this approach as the "best solution for the women's rights issues".

In order for the approach to deliver women's human rights, Nussbaum (1995:88) firstly emphasises the necessity for the universalisation of human rights standards. Human rights standards need to be universally adopted for all people because, as Nussbaum (1995) highlights, human beings (irrespective of the cultural contexts they live in), once provided with the rights to education and material support, can become fully capable of their "self-actualising" development.

In other words, the capabilities exist in the metaphysical realm and this existence makes the reference to their functioning. If they are deprived of these capabilities, these human beings are nothing "but a shadow of themselves". If the functioning of these capabilities ceases to appear, these human beings will not realise their full potential. Nussbaum (1995:88) does recognise the philosophical nature of this argument, but argues "that certain basic and central human endowments have a claim to be assisted in developing and exercise that claim onto others, especially on governments".

Furthermore and most importantly for women's rights, these human capabilities need to be pursued for each and every person, "treating each as an end and none as a mere tool of the ends of others". This is particularly relevant in the context of this article since, as Nussbaum (2000:2) recognises, women have rarely been "treated as the ends in their own, persons with dignity that deserves respect from laws and institutions". Instead, women "are treated as mere instruments of the ends of others - [as] reproducers, care givers, sexual outlets, agents of a family's general prosperity".

An additional positive aspect of Nussbaum's (2000:5) approach for universal applicability resides in her argument that these human capabilities can be the object of the "overlapping consensus among people who otherwise have very different comprehensive conceptions of good". This can be achieved by considering the experiences and sense of important functions from women as well as from men.

NUSSBAUM'S RESOLUTION FOR THE ISSUES JUSTIFIED IN THE NAME OF CULTURAL RELATIVISM

The conception of universal women's human rights standards is achievable by grounding these in a cross-cultural assessment of women's well being. Such cross-cultural assessment is feasible by applying a "conception of the good" that encompasses "the shape of the human form of life" and a good human life, which "abstract[s] from traditional gender distinctions". The traditional gender distinctions are, as Nussbaum rightly recognises (1995:75), socially constructed and dependent on the local contexts that reinforced them.

Consequently, the usefulness of Nussbaum's (1995:75) approach resides in its thorough deconstruction of social constructions of gender roles, on the basis of which Nussbaum conceives her analysis from the intuitive idea of human being as "capable and needy". In this process, she suggests that:

> ...a life, if it is constituted by certain traits such as the fact of mortality (a fear of and aversion of death); the bodily needs for food and drink, shelter, sex, and mobility; the capacity for pleasure and pain; the cognitive capabilities; early childhood development; practical reason, affiliation and concern for other

human beings; relatedness to other species and to nature; humour and play; and separateness... is characteristically human, no matter within what culture it is lived".

Whilst treating all of the capabilities or traits mentioned above as good and essential Nussbaum (1995:84) does attribute "a special role" to two of the capabilities, practical reason and affiliation. Practical reason is the capability that allows human being to be able "to form a conception of good and to engage in critical reflection about the planning of one's own life. According to Nussbaum (1995:78), the capability of practical reason can be expressed in different forms and as such it is linked to the "other capabilities, emotional, imaginative and intellectual.

A being that altogether lacks any one of these capabilities would not be likely to be regarded as fully human in any society". The capability of affiliation consists of an idea that all human beings "recognise and feel some sense of affiliation and concern for other human beings. We live with and in relation to others, and regard a life not lived in affiliation with others to be a life not worth living". Nussbaum (1995:82) emphasises both of these capabilities as she considers them to be "architectonic, holding the whole enterprise together and making it human".

Whilst the other capabilities make human beings equal, these two distinguish them from other creatures. "What is distinctive and distinctively valuable to us, about the human way of doing all this is that each and every one of these [capability] functions is, first of all, planned and organized by practical reason and second, done with and to others". Here, Nussbaum (1995:82) argues that the development of the capability to evaluate, choose, plan and execute plans of life or conceptions of the good, and the capability to live to and with others, are said to need "special attention" because "none of the others will be truly human without them". These two capabilities of practical reason and affiliation are particularly relevant in respect to the attainment of women's rights in the practical context. Their practical implications will be addressed in the following discussion.

APPLYING NUSSBAUM'S APPROACH

The capability of "practical reason" is highlighted in the findings of Li's (1995) study on women in China. In this study Li (1995) emphasises Nussbaum's (1995) "capability approach" as adequate to take precedence over what she calls the "local tradition cultural relativism". "Local tradition cultural relativism" is essentially a form of cultural relativism, which emphasises that because we cannot judge one culture by the standards of another, the local traditional approach should be considered as the only relevant one for addressing women's rights issues in China.

This type of cultural relativism arises from a fear that the universalism might take up the form of dominant ideology and thus impose its principles "upon the disadvantaged female in a society tormented by gender discrimination" (Li, 1995:422). As Li (1995:422) highlights, her study illustrated that:

The cultural relativism's rejection of any universal or cross-cultural conception, and its proposal to assess women's conditions by "local traditional" norms, has not been able to avoid this danger in the case of China. Instead, such an approach has contributed to [as the Chinese case demonstrates] perpetuating the status quo.

The perpetuation of status quo in China has meant, according to Li (1995), the perpetuation of long-term subordination under the patriarchal ideology, which has been influential in maintaining that women are not capable of practical reason. Li's (1995) analysis of women's status in China shows that "growing up in Chinese sexist morality women has deposited within them a "psychological complex": the inferior morality. As a result they feel comfortable with the idea that women are not expected to the same as men, which further gives way to women distancing themselves from political processes.

Considering such a scenario, Nussbaum's (1995) approach, according to which we need to call attention to the consent and nourishment of the capability to conduct practical reasoning, appears to consist of very adequate grounds for the promotion of universal women's rights. This is because the application of Nussbaum's (1995) approach would mean the encouragement by the Chinese government for Chinese women to decide and form a version of good and at the same time to engage in critical reflection about their lives would provide Chinese women with power to reflect and criticize the pervasive social norms and to claim their rights.

Thus, the "local tradition cultural relativism", upholding the status quo, can be challenged if, as Nussbaum (1995) proposes, the voices of both women and men are heard particularly in regard to functions that both men and women consider important.

The result of the consensus should produce the emergence of new perspectives on the conception of human (and women's) good that had not emerged as so important on patriarchal agenda. This step will offset the institutionalised projection of male preferences in local culture.

Consequently, in the Asian case, if both sets of voices are considered, women and men can both agree to uphold the Confucian virtues while still allowing women to have their human rights. The example of such a process would include the preference for goodness of excellence in professional careers in the list of Confucian female virtues (instead of their "obedience to father, brother and husband") to become important now, as it has been regarded by recent female reflections.

These female reflections highlight that, for example, in respect to professional career, the majority of Chinese women make it clear that they do not want to leave work (just before the birth of their children), but rather, that it is the pressures of new social reforms that are pushing them in that direction. Thus, if such perspectives from women were considered this would add to the conception of human (and women's) good that had not been considered before, and most importantly such reflections would highlight the need for women's rights standards, such as gender equality to be implemented.

FOR THE RESOLUTION OF WOMEN'S RIGHTS ISSUES IN THE ISLAMIC CONTEXT

Nussbaum's approach can also be argued as a very relevant theoretical precondition supporting some of the efforts of Islamic feminists to accentuate that gender equality is gaining more and more importance. Particularly Nussbaum's capability for 'practical reasoning' becomes accentuated in the arguments of numerous Islamic feminists who are urging for a social reform emphasising that the Koran actually proposes equality for both men and women. In the Koran there are many *ayaat* (verses) that seem to declare male/ female equality. One is Al- Hujurat:

> Oh humankind. We have created you from a single pair of a male and a female and made you into tribes and nations that you may know each other [not that you may despise one another]. The most honored of you in the sight of God is the most righteous of you [the one practicing the most taqwa].

Recognising this, Islamic feminists have been campaigning for their rights, emphasizing that, according to the Koran, all human beings are equal and they are only distinguished among themselves on the basis of their rightful practice or implementation of the fundamental Koranic principle to be "moral" [meaning to be genuine and sincere] towards others. Thus, in order for a just and righteous society, as the Koran exhorts, both the voices of men and women need to hear. If this is achieved, and if the both women and men in Islamic context are fair towards one another, then gender inequality will be shown as unjust and as a result it will not be further reinforced.

Here the adequacy of Nussbaum's (2000) approach is accentuated as she argues that one of the ways to overcome gender inequality would be to focus on similarities between women and men rather than differences. Consequently, such proposals and the others discussed in the previous paragraphs, underline that Nussbaum's (2000) approach possesses the basis to challenge the various forms of cultural or traditional relativism, which have been used to justify the rejections of the implementation of women's rights conventions. However Nussbaum (2000) emphasises that for the approach to deliver human (and women's) rights, it needs to be politically legitimised.

POLITICALLY LEGITIMISING THE "CAPABILITY APPROACH"

For universal women's human rights to be recognised as such, the standards need to be acknowledged in the public political spheres worldwide. Recognising this Nussbaum (1995) argues for the political legitimisation of the "capabilites approach" implying that the established norms from the cross-cultural consensus need to politically bind every government to propose and uphold human rights for all. This is necessary because as Sen rightly uno women's human rights would have to be politically legitimised. An additional advantage of the "capabilities approach" resides in the notion that, while Nussbaum (1995) argues that universal human rights should be available to everyone, she also notes that governments are not supposed to push their citizens into developing a certain, more culturally valued, capabilities over others.

Instead it is essential that governments provide all the necessary resources and conditions for a full development of all human capabilities in every individual (such as education, health care) and once these individuals are provided with these resources they have a choice whether to use or deprive themselves of these resources. Thus, by making the opportunities available, government enhances and does not remove choices. Providing choice is one of the most important reasons why the "capabilities approach" carries enormous significance for attainment of universal women's human rights.

Nussbaum (1995:95) argues for the consideration of the capability approach, highlighting that "its own comprehensive concern with flourishing across all areas of life is a better way of promoting choice than is the liberal narrower concern with spontaneity alone". Here the liberal approach to human rights is disregarded as inadequate, for its tolerance of situations in which individuals are in other ways deprived of the fully human use of their faculties. Proclaiming that the "capabilities approach" improves on these flawed areas of the Universalist framework of human rights, Nussbaum urges its implementation in the practical domain.

The capabilities approach does, in fact, seem plausible to deliver universal human (and women's) rights as it: Aspires to deal with issues raised by local tradition relativism, by advancing a conception of women's well-being that attends fully to the rich culture and tradition of local communities, while opening up for cross-cultural examination.

This gives it a universal perspective and embodies hope to divulge "false consciousness". Such Universalist approach to women's human rights is possible and can be realised, according to Nussbaum (2000:7) through a framework that relies on the notion of consent: women (and men) being given the right to choose which law should govern their private lives. This notion of choice is, as both Nussbaum (1995) and Coomaraswamy (1999) recognise, such integral to a human rights understanding of the issue of cultural pluralism, because as Coomaraswamy (1999) highlights, many feel that our attitude toward cultural diversity should be conditioned by this choice.

In other words, "cultural diversity should be celebrated only if those enjoying their cultural attributes are doing so voluntarily". By protecting choice, voluntariness, and the integrity of female decision-making, we may be able, as Coomaraswamy (1996:181) argues, to reconcile the conflicts between cultural diversity and the need for the protection of women's human rights universally.

Feminism is an intellectual, philosophical and political discourse aimed at equal rights and legal protection for women. It involves various movements, theories, and philosophies, all concerned with issues of gender difference; that advocate equality for women; and that campaign for women's rights and interests. According to Maggie Humm and Rebecca Walker, the history of feminism can be divided into three waves. The first wave was in the nineteenth and early twentieth centuries, the second was in the 1960s and 1970s, and the third extends from the 1990s to the present. Feminist theory emerged from these feminist movements. It is manifest in a variety of disciplines such as feminist geography, feminist history and feminist literary criticism.

Feminism has altered predominant perspectives in a wide range of areas within Western society, ranging from culture to law. Feminist activists have campaigned for women's legal rights (rights of contract, property rights, voting rights); for women's right to bodily integrity and autonomy, for abortion rights, and for reproductive rights (including access to contraception and quality prenatal care); for protection of women and girls from domestic violence, sexual harassment and rape; for workplace rights, including maternity leave and equal pay; and against other forms of discrimination.

During much of its history, most feminist movements and theories had leaders who were predominantly middle-class white women from Western Europe and North America. However, at least since Sojourner Truth's 1851 speech to American feminists, women of other races have proposed alternative feminisms. This trend accelerated in the 1960s with the Civil Rights movement in the United States and the collapse of European colonialism in Africa, the Caribbean, parts of Latin America and Southeast Asia. Since that time, women in former European colonies and the Third World have proposed "Post-colonial" and "Third World" feminisms.

Some Postcolonial Feminists, such as Chandra Talpade Mohanty, are critical of Western feminism for being ethnocentric. Black feminists, such as Angela Davis and Alice Walker, share this view. Since the 1980s, standpoint feminists have argued that feminism should examine how women's experience of inequality relates to that of racism, homophobia, classism and colonization. In the late 1980s and 1990s postmodern feminists argued that gender roles are socially constructed, and that it is impossible to generalize women's experiences across cultures and histories.

Feminists and scholars have divided the movement's history into three "waves". The first wave refers mainly to women's suffrage movements of the nineteenth and early twentieth centuries (mainly concerned with women's right to vote). The second wave refers to the ideas and actions associated with the women's liberation movement beginning in the 1960s (which campaigned for legal and social equality for women). The third wave refers to a continuation of, and a reaction to the perceived failures of, second-wave feminism, beginning in the 1990s.

FIRST WAVE

First-wave feminism refers to an extended period of feminist activity during the nineteenth century and early twentieth century in the United Kingdom and the United States. Originally it focused on the promotion of equal contract and property rights for women and the opposition to chattel marriage and ownership of married women (and their children) by their husbands. However, by the end of the nineteenth century, activism focused primarily on gaining political power, particularly the right of women's suffrage. Yet, feminists such as Voltairine de Cleyre and Margaret Sanger were still active in campaigning for women's sexual, reproductive, and economic rights at this time.

In Britain the Suffragettes and, possibly more effectively, the Suffragists campaigned for the women's vote. In 1918 the Representation of the People Act 1918 was passed granting the vote to women over the age of 30 who owned houses. In 1928 this was extended to all women over twenty-one. In the United States, leaders of this movement included Lucretia Mott, Lucy Stone, Elizabeth Cady Stanton, and Susan B. Anthony, who each campaigned for the abolition of slavery prior to championing women's right to vote; all were strongly influenced by Quaker thought.

American first-wave feminism involved a wide range of women. Some, such as Frances Willard, belonged to conservative Christian groups such as the Woman's Christian

Temperance Union. Others, such as Matilda Joslyn Gage, were more radical, and expressed themselves within the National Woman Suffrage Association or individually. American first-wave feminism is considered to have ended with the passage of the Nineteenth Amendment to the United States Constitution (1919), granting women the right to vote in all states. The term 'first wave' was coined retrospectively after the term 'second-wave feminism' began to be used to describe a newer feminist movement that focused as much on fighting social and cultural inequalities as political inequalities.

The first wave of feminists, in contrast to the second wave, focused very little on the subject of abortion. In general, they were against the concept. Though she never married, Anthony published her views about marriage, holding that a woman should be allowed to refuse sex with her husband; the American woman had no legal recourse at that time against rape by her husband. Of primary importance to Anthony was granting to woman the right to her own body which she saw as an essential element for the prevention of unwanted pregnancies, using abstinence as the method. In her newspaper, *The Revolution*, she wrote in 1869 about the subject, arguing that instead of merely attempting to pass a law against abortion, the root cause must also be addressed. Simply passing an anti-abortion law would, she wrote, "be only mowing off the top of the noxious weed, while the root remains."

SECOND WAVE

'Second-wave feminism'refers to a period of feminist activity beginning in the early 1960s and lasting through the late 1980s. The scholar Imelda Whelehan suggests that the second wave was a continuation of the earlier phase of feminism involving the suffragettes in the UK and USA. Second-wave feminism has continued to exist since that time and coexists with what is termed 'third-wave feminism'. The scholar Estelle Freedman compares first and second-wave feminism saying that the first wave focused on rights such as suffrage, whereas the second wave was largely concerned with other issues of equality, such as ending discrimination.

The feminist activist and author Carol Hanisch coined the slogan "The Personal is Political" which became synonymous with the second wave. Second-wave feminists saw women's cultural and political inequalities as inextricably linked and encouraged women to understand aspects of their personal lives as deeply politicized and as reflecting sexist power structures.

THE FEMININE MYSTIQUE

Betty Friedan's *The Feminine Mystique* (1963) criticized the idea that women could only find fulfillment through childrearing and homemaking. According to Friedan's obituary in the *The New York Times, The Feminine Mystique* "ignited the contemporary women's movement in 1963 and as a result permanently transformed the social fabric of the United States and countries around the world" and "is widely regarded as one of the most influential nonfiction books of the 20th century."

In the book Friedan hypothesizes that women are victims of a false belief system that requires them to find identity and meaning in their lives through their husbands and children. Such a system causes women to completely lose their identity in that of their family. Friedan specifically locates this system among post-World War II middle-class suburban communities. At the same time, America's post-war economic boom had led to the development of new technologies that were supposed to make household work less difficult, but that often had the result of making women's work less meaningful and valuable.

THIRD WAVE

Third-wave feminism began in the early 1990s, arising as a response to perceived failures of the second wave and also as a response to the backlash against initiatives and movements created by the second wave. Third-wave feminism seeks to challenge or avoid what it deems the second wave's essentialist definitions of femininity, which (according to them) over-emphasize the experiences of upper middle-class white women.

A post-structuralist interpretation of gender and sexuality is central to much of the third wave's ideology. Third-wave feminists often focus on "micro-politics" and challenge the second wave's paradigm as to what is, or is not, good for females. The third wave has its origins in the mid-1980s. Feminist leaders rooted in the second wave like Gloria Anzaldua, bell hooks, Chela Sandoval, Cherrie Moraga, Audre Lorde, Maxine Hong Kingston, and many other black feminists, sought to negotiate a space within feminist thought for consideration of race-related subjectivities.

Third-wave feminism also contains internal debates between difference feminists such as the psychologist Carol Gilligan (who believes that there are important differences between the sexes) and those who believe that there are no inherent differences between the sexes and contend that gender roles are due to social conditioning.

POST-FEMINISM

'Post-feminism' describes a range of viewpoints reacting to feminism. While not being "anti-feminist," post-feminists believe that women have achieved second wave goals while being critical of third wave feminist goals. The term was first used in the 1980s to describe a backlash against second-wave feminism. It is now a label for a wide range of theories that take critical approaches to previous feminist discourses and includes challenges to the second wave's ideas. Other post-feminists say that feminism is no longer relevant to today's society.

Amelia Jones wrote that the post-feminist texts which emerged in the 1980s and 1990s portrayed second-wave feminism as a monolithic entity and criticized it using generalizations. One of the earliest uses of the term was in Susan Bolotin's 1982 article "Voices of the Post-Feminist Generation," published in *New York Times Magazine*. This chapter was based on a number of interviews with women who largely agreed with the goals of feminism, but did not identify as feminists. Some contemporary feminists, such as Katha

Pollitt or Nadine Strossen, consider feminism to hold simply that "women are people". Views that separate the sexes rather than unite them are considered by these writers to be sexist rather than feminist.

In her book *Backlash: The Undeclared War Against American Women*, Susan Faludi argues that a backlash against second wave feminism in the 1980s has successfully re-defined feminism through its terms. She argues that it constructed the women's liberation movement as the source of many of the problems alleged to be plaguing women in the late 1980s. She also argues that many of these problems are illusory, constructed by the media without reliable evidence. According to her, this type of backlash is a historical trend, recurring when it appears that women have made substantial gains in their efforts to obtain equal rights.

Angela McRobbie argues that adding the prefix post to feminism undermines the strides that feminism has made in achieving equality for everyone, including women. Post-feminism gives the impression that equality has been achieved and that feminists can now focus on something else entirely. McRobbie believes that post-feminism is most clearly seen on so-called feminist media products, such as Bridget Jones's Diary, Sex and the City, and Ally McBeal. Female characters like Bridget Jones and Carrie Bradshaw claim to be liberated and clearly enjoy their sexuality, but what they are constantly searching for is the one man who will make everything worthwhile.

FRENCH FEMINISM

French feminism refers to a branch of feminist thought from a group of feminists in France from the 1970s to the 1990s. French feminism, compared to Anglophone feminism, is distinguished by an approach which is more philosophical and literary. Its writings tend to be effusive and metaphorical, being less concerned with political doctrine and generally focused on theories of "the body." The term includes writers who are not French, but who have worked substantially in

France and the French tradition such as Julia Kristeva and Bracha Ettinger. The French author and philosopher Simone de Beauvoir wrote novels; monographs on philosophy, politics, and social issues; essays; biographies; and an autobiography.

She is now best known for her metaphysical novels, including *She Came to Stay* and *The Mandarins,* and for her 1949 treatise *The Second Sex,* a detailed analysis of women's oppression and a foundational tract of contemporary feminism. It sets out a feminist existentialism which prescribes a moral revolution. As an existentialist, she accepted Jean-Paul Sartre's precept *existence precedes essence*; hence "one is not born a woman, but becomes one." Her analysis focuses on the social construction of Woman as the Other. This de Beauvoir identifies as fundamental to women's oppression. She argues women have historically been considered deviant and abnormal and contends that even Mary Wollstonecraft considered men to be the ideal toward which women should aspire. De Beauvoir argues that for feminism to move forward, this attitude must be set aside.

In the 1970s French feminists approached feminism with the concept of écriture féminine, which translates as female, or feminine writing. Helene Cixous argues that writing and philosophy are phallocentric and along with other French feminists such as Luce Irigaray emphasizes "writing from the body" as a subversive exercise. The work of the feminist psychoanalyst and philosopher, Julia Kristeva, has influenced feminist theory in general and feminist literary criticism in particular. From the 1980s onwards the work of artist and psychoanalyst Bracha Ettinger has influenced literary criticism, art history and film theory. However, as the scholar Elizabeth Wright pointed out, "none of these French feminists align themselves with the feminist movement as it appeared in the Anglophone world."

THEORETICAL SCHOOLS

Feminist theory is an extension of feminism into theoretical or philosophical fields. It encompasses work in a variety of disciplines, including anthropology, sociology, economics, women's studies, literary criticism, art history, psychoanalysis and philosophy. Feminist theory aims to understand gender inequality and focuses on gender politics, power relations and sexuality. While providing a critique of these social and political relations, much of feminist theory focuses on the promotion of women's rights and interests. Themes explored in feminist theory include discrimination, stereotyping, objectification (especially sexual objectification), oppression and patriarchy.

The American literary critic and feminist Elaine Showalter describe the phased development of feminist theory. The first she calls "feminist critique," in which the feminist reader examines the ideologies behind literary phenomena. The second Showalter calls "gynocriticism," in which the "woman is producer of textual meaning" including "the psychodynamics of female creativity; linguistics and the problem of a female language; the trajectory of the individual or collective female literary career and literary history." The last phase she calls "gender theory," in which the "ideological inscription and the literary effects of the sex/gender system" are explored. The scholar Toril Moi criticized this model, seeing it as an essentialist and deterministic model for female subjectivity that fails to account for the situation of women outside the West.

MOVEMENTS AND IDEOLOGIES

Several sub movements of feminist ideology have developed over the years; some of the major subtypes are listed below. These movements often overlap, and some feminists identify themselves with several types of feminist thought.

SOCIALIST AND MARXIST FEMINISMS

Socialist feminism connects the oppression of women to Marxist ideas about exploitation, oppression and labor. Socialist feminists think unequal standing in both the workplace and the domestic sphere holds women down. Socialist feminists see prostitution, domestic work, childcare and marriage as ways in which women are exploited by a patriarchal system that devalues women and the substantial work they do. Socialist feminists focus their energies on broad change that affects society as a whole, rather than on an individual basis. They see the need to work alongside not just men, but all other groups, as they see the oppression of women as a part of a larger pattern that affects everyone involved in the capitalist system.

Marx felt when class oppression was overcome; gender oppression would vanish as well. According to some socialist feminists, this view of gender oppression as a sub-class of class oppression is naive and much of the work of socialist feminists has gone towards separating gender phenomena from class phenomena. Some contributors to socialist feminism have criticized these traditional Marxist ideas for being largely silent on gender oppression except to subsume it underneath broader class oppression.

Other socialist feminists many of whom belong to Radical Women and the Freedom Socialist Party, two long-lived American organizations, point to the classic Marxist writings of Frederick Engels and August Bebel as a powerful explanation of the link between gender oppression and class exploitation. In the late nineteenth century and early twentieth century both Clara Zetkin and Eleanor Marx were against the demonization of men and supported a proletarian revolution that would overcome as many male-female inequalities as possible. As their movement already had the most radical demands of women's equality, most Marxist leaders, including Clara Zetkin and Alexandra Kollontai, counterposed Marxism against feminism, rather than trying to combine them?

RADICAL FEMINISM

Radical feminism considers the male controlled capitalist hierarchy, which it describes as sexist, as the defining feature of women's oppression. Radical feminists believe that women can free themselves only when they have done away with what they consider an inherently oppressive and dominating patriarchal system. Radical feminists feel that there is a male-based authority and power structure and that it is responsible for oppression and inequality, and that as long as the system and its values are in place, society will not be able to be reformed in any significant way. Some radical feminists see no alternatives other than the total uprooting and reconstruction of society in order to achieve their goals.

Over time a number of sub-types of Radical feminism have emerged, such as Cultural feminism, Separatist feminism and Anti-pornography feminism. Cultural feminism is the ideology of a "female nature" or "female essence" that attempts to revalidate what they consider undervalued female attributes. It emphasizes the difference between women and men but considers that difference to be psychological, and to be culturally constructed rather than biologically innate. Its critics assert that because it is based on an essentialist view of the differences between women and men and advocates independence and institution building, it has led feminists to retreat from politics to "life-style".

Once such critic Alice Echols (a feminist historian and cultural theorist) credits Redstockings member Brooke Williams introducing the term cultural feminism in 1975 to describe the depoliticisation of radical feminism. Separatist feminism is a form of radical feminism that does not support heterosexual relationships. Its proponents argue that the sexual disparities between men and women are unresolvable. Separatist feminists generally do not feel that men can make positive contributions to the feminist movement and that even well-intentioned men replicate patriarchal dynamics. Author Marilyn Frye describes separatist feminism as "separation of various sorts or modes from men and from institutions, relationships, roles and activities that are male-defined, male-dominated, and operating for the benefit of males and the maintenance of male privilege– this separation being initiated or maintained, at will, by women".

LIBERAL FEMINISM

Liberal feminism asserts the equality of men and women through political and legal reform. It is an individualistic form of feminism, which focuses on women's ability to show and maintain their equality through their own actions and choices. Liberal feminism uses the personal interactions between men and women as the place from which to transform society. According to liberal feminists, all women are capable of asserting their ability to achieve equality; therefore it is possible for change to happen without altering the structure of society. Issues important to liberal feminists include reproductive and abortion rights, sexual harassment, voting, education, "equal pay for equal work", affordable childcare, affordable health care, and bringing to light the frequency of sexual and domestic violence against women.

BLACK FEMINISM

Black feminism argues that sexism, class oppression, and racism are inextricably bound together. Forms of feminism that strive to overcome sexism and class oppression but ignore race can discriminate against many people, including women, through racial bias. The Combahee River Collective argued in 1974 that the liberation of black women entails freedom for all people, since it would require the end of racism, sexism, and class oppression. One of the theories that evolved out of this movement was Alice Walker's Womanism.

It emerged after the early feminist movements that were led specifically by white women who advocated social changes such as woman's suffrage. These movements were largely white middle-class movements and had generally ignored oppression based on racism and classism. Alice Walker and other Womanists pointed out those black women experienced a different and more intense kind of oppression from that of white women. Angela Davis was one of the first people who articulated an argument centered on the intersection of race, gender, and class in her book, *Women, Race, and Class*. Kimberle Crenshaw, a prominent feminist law theorist, gave the idea the name Intersectionality while discussing identity politics in her essay, "Mapping the Margins: Intersectionality, Identity Politics and Violence Against Women of Color".

POSTCOLONIAL FEMINISM AND THIRD-WORLD FEMINISM

Postcolonial feminists argue that oppression relating to the colonial experience, particularly racial, class, and ethnic oppression, has marginalized women in postcolonial societies. They challenge the assumption that gender oppression is the primary force of patriarchy. Postcolonial feminists object to portrayals of women of non-Western societies as passive and voiceless victims and the portrayal of Western women as modern, educated and empowered. Postcolonial feminism emerged from the gendered history of colonialism: colonial powers often imposed Western norms on colonized regions.

In the 1940s and 1950s, after the formation of the United Nations, former colonies were monitored by the West for what was considered "social progress". The status of women in the developing world has been monitored by organizations such as the United Nations and as a result traditional practices and roles taken up by women-sometimes seen as distasteful by Western standards-could be considered a form of rebellion against colonial oppression. Post-colonial feminists today struggle to fight gender oppression within their own cultural models of society rather than those imposed by the Western colonizers.

Post-colonial feminism is critical of Western forms of feminism, notably radical feminism and liberal feminism and their universalization of female experience. Postcolonial feminists argue that cultures impacted by colonialism are often vastly different and should be treated as such. Colonial oppression may result in the glorification of pre-colonial culture, which, in cultures with traditions of power stratification along gender lines, could mean the acceptance of, or refusal to deal with, inherent issues of gender inequality. Postcolonial feminists can be described as feminists who have reacted against both universalizing tendencies in Western feminist thought and a lack of attention to gender issues in mainstream postcolonial thought.

Third-world feminism has been described as a group of feminist theories developed by feminists who acquired their views and took part in feminist politics in so-called third-world countries. Although women from the third world have been engaged in the feminist movement, Chandra Talpade Mohanty and Sarojini Sahoo criticize Western feminism on the grounds that it is ethnocentric and does not take into account the unique experiences of women from third-world countries or the existence of feminisms indigenous to third-world countries.

According to Chandra Talpade Mohanty, women in the third world feel that Western feminism bases its understanding of women on "internal racism, classism and homophobia". This discourse is strongly related to African feminism and postcolonial feminism. Its development is also associated with concepts such as black feminism, womanism, "Africana womanism", "motherism", "Stiwanism", "negofeminism", chicana feminism, and "femalism".

MULTIRACIAL FEMINISM

Multiracial feminism (also known as "women of color" feminism) offers a standpoint theory and analysis of the lives and experiences of women of color. The theory emerged in the 1990s and was developed by Dr. Maxine Baca Zinn, a Chicana feminist and Dr. Bonnie Thornton Dill, a sociology expert on African American women and family.

LIBERTARIAN FEMINISM

According to the Stanford Encyclopedia of Philosophy, "Classical liberal or libertarian feminism conceives of freedom as freedom from coercive interference. It holds that women, as well as men, have a right to such freedom due to their status as self-owners." There are several categories under the theory of libertarian feminism, or kinds of feminism that are linked to libertarian ideologies. Anarcha-feminism (also called *anarchist feminism* or *anarcho-feminism*) combines feminist and anarchist beliefs, embodying classical libertarianism rather than contemporary conservative libertarianism. Anarcha-feminists view patriarchy as a manifestation of hierarchy, believing that the fight against patriarchy is an essential part of the class struggle and the anarchist struggle against the state.

Anarcha-feminists such as Susan Brown see the anarchist struggle as a necessary component of the feminist struggle. In Brown's words, "anarchism is a political philosophy that opposes all relationships of power, it is inherently feminist". Recently, Wendy McElroy has defined a position (which she labels "ifeminism" or "individualist feminism") that combines feminism with anarcho-capitalism or contemporary conservative libertarianism, arguing that a pro-capitalist, anti-state position is compatible with an emphasis on equal rights and empowerment for women. Individualist anarchist-feminism has grown from the US-based individualist anarchism movement.

Individualist feminism is typically defined as a feminism in opposition to what writers such as Wendy McElroy and Christina Hoff Sommers term, *political* or *gender feminism*. However, there are some differences within the discussion of individualist feminism. While some individualist feminists like McElroy oppose government interference into the choices women make with their bodies because such interference creates a coercive hierarchy (such as patriarchy), other feminists such as Christina Hoff Sommers hold that feminism's political role is simply to ensure that everyone's, including women's, right against coercive interference is respected. Sommers are described as a "socially conservative equity feminist" by the *Stanford Encyclopedia of Philosophy*. Critics have called her an anti-feminist.

POST-STRUCTURAL AND POSTMODERN FEMINISM

Post-structural feminism, also referred to as French feminism, uses the insights of various epistemological movements, including psychoanalysis, linguistics, political theory (Marxist and post-Marxist theory), race theory, literary theory, and other intellectual currents for feminist concerns.

Many post-structural feminists maintain that difference is one of the most powerful tools that females possess in their struggle with patriarchal domination, and that to equate the feminist movement only with equality is to deny women a plethora of options because equality is still defined from the masculine or patriarchal perspective.

Postmodern feminism is an approach to feminist theory that incorporates postmodern and post-structuralist theory. The largest departure from other branches of feminism is the argument that gender is constructed through language. The most notable proponent of this argument is Judith Butler. In her 1990 book, *Gender Trouble*, she draws on and critiques the work of Simone de Beauvoir, Michel Foucault and Jacques Lacan. Butler criticizes the distinction drawn by previous feminisms between biological sex and socially constructed gender. She says that this does not allow for a sufficient criticism of essentialism. For Butler "woman" is a debatable category, complicated by class, ethnicity, sexuality, and other facets of identity. She states that gender is performative. This argument leads to the conclusion that there is no single cause for women's subordination and no single approach towards dealing with the issue.

In *A Cyborg Manifesto* Donna Haraway criticizes traditional notions of feminism, particularly its emphasis on identity, rather than affinity. She uses the metaphor of a cyborg in order to construct a postmodern feminism that moves beyond dualisms and the limitations of traditional gender, feminism, and politics. Haraway's cyborg is an attempt to break away from oedipal narratives and Christian origin-myths like Genesis. She writes: "The cyborg does not dream of community on the model of the organic family, this time without the oedipal project. The cyborg would not recognize the Garden of Eden; it is not made of mud and cannot dream of returning to dust."

A major branch in postmodern feminist thought has emerged from the contemporary psychoanalytic French feminism. Other postmodern feminist works highlight stereotypical gender roles, only to portray them as parodies of the original beliefs. The history of feminism is not important in these writings-only what is going to be done about it. The history is dismissed and used to depict how ridiculous past beliefs were. Modern feminist theory has been extensively criticized as being predominantly, though not exclusively, associated with Western middle class academia. Mary Joe Frug, a postmodernist feminist, criticized mainstream feminism as being too narrowly focused and inattentive to related issues of race and class.

ECOFEMINISM

Ecofeminism links ecology with feminism. Ecofeminists see the domination of women as stemming from the same ideologies that bring about the domination of the environment. Patriarchal systems, where men own and control the land are seen as responsible for the oppression of women and destruction of the natural environment. Ecofeminists argue that the men in power control the land, and therefore they are able to exploit it for their own profit and success. Ecofeminists argue that in this situation, women are exploited by men in power for their own profit, success, and pleasure. Ecofeminists argue that women and the environment are both exploited as passive pawns in the race to domination.

Ecofeminists argue that those people in power are able to take advantage of them distinctly because they are seen as passive and rather helpless. Ecofeminism connects the exploitation and domination of women with that of the environment. As a way of repairing social and ecological injustices, ecofeminists feel that women must work towards creating a healthy environment and ending the destruction of the lands that most women rely on to provide for their families. Ecofeminism argues that there is a connection between women and nature that comes from their shared history of oppression by a patriarchal Western society.

Vandana Shiva claims that women have a special connection to the environment through their daily interactions with it that has been ignored. She says that "women in subsistence economies, producing and reproducing wealth in partnership with nature, have been experts in their own right of holistic and ecological knowledge of nature's processes. But these alternative modes of knowing, which are oriented to the social benefits and sustenance needs are not recognized by the capitalist reductionist paradigm, because it fails to perceive the interconnectedness of nature, or the connection of women's lives, work and knowledge with the creation of wealth." However, feminist and social ecologist Janet Biehl has criticized ecofeminism for focusing too much on a mystical connection between women and nature and not enough on the actual conditions of women.

Society

The feminist movement has effected change in Western society, including women's suffrage; greater access to education; more nearly equitable pay with men; the right to initiate divorce proceedings and "no fault" divorce; and the right of women to make individual decisions regarding pregnancy (including access to contraceptives and abortion); and the right to own property.

Civil Rights

From the 1960s on the women's liberation movement campaigned for women's rights, including the same pay as men, equal rights in law, and the freedom to plan their families. Their efforts were met with mixed results. Issues commonly associated with notions of women's rights include, though are not limited to: the right to bodily integrity and autonomy; to vote (universal suffrage); to hold public office; to work; to fair wages or equal pay; to own property; to education; to serve in the military; to enter into legal contracts; and to have marital, parental and religious rights.

In the UK a public groundswell of opinion in favour of legal equality gained pace, partly through the extensive employment of women in men's traditional roles during both world wars. By the 1960s the legislative process was being readied, tracing through MP Willie Hamilton's select committee report, his Equal Pay For Equal Work Bill, the creation of a Sex Discrimination Board, Lady Sear's draft sex anti-discrimination bill, a government Green Paper of 1973, until 1975 when the first British Sex Discrimination Act, an Equal Pay Act, and an Equal Opportunities Commission came into force.

With encouragement from the UK government, the other countries of the EEC soon followed suit with an agreement to ensure that discrimination laws would be phased out across the European Community. In the USA, the US National Organization for Women (NOW) was created in 1966 with the purpose of bringing about equality for all women. NOW was one important group that fought for the Equal Rights Amendment (ERA). This amendment stated that "equality of rights under the law shall not be denied or abridged by the United States or any state on account of sex." But there was disagreement on how the proposed amendment would be understood. Supporters believed it would guarantee women equal treatment. But critics feared it might deny women the right be financially supported by their husbands.

The amendment died in 1982 because not enough states had ratified it. ERAs have been included in subsequent Congresses, but have still failed to be ratified. In the final three decades of the 20th century, Western women knew a new freedom through birth control, which enabled women to plan their adult lives, often making way for both career and family. The movement had been started in the 1910s by US pioneering social reformer Margaret Sanger and in the UK and internationally by Marie Stopes.

The *United Nations Human Development Report 2004* estimated that when both paid employment and unpaid household tasks are accounted for, on average women work more than men. In rural areas of selected developing countries women performed an average of 20% more work than men, or an additional 102 minutes per day. In the OECD countries surveyed, on average women performed 5% more work than men, or 20 minutes per day. At the UN's Pan Pacific Southeast

Asia Women's Association 21st International Conference in 2001 it was stated that "in the world as a whole, women comprise 51% of the population, do 66% of the work, receive 10% of the income and own less than one percent of the property".

Language

Gender-neutral language is a description of language usages which are aimed at minimizing assumptions regarding the biological sex of human referents. The advocacy of gender-neutral language reflects, at least, two different agendas: one aims to clarify the inclusion of both sexes or genders (gender-inclusive language); the other proposes that gender, as a category, is rarely worth marking in language (gender-neutral language). Gender-neutral language is sometimes described as non-sexist language by advocates and politically-correct language by opponents.

Heterosexual Relationships

The increased entry of women into the workplace beginning in the twentieth century has affected gender roles and the division of labor within households. Sociologist Arlie Russell Hochschild in *The Second Shift* and *The Time Bind* presents evidence that in two-career couples, men and women, on average, spend about equal amounts of time working, but women still spend more time on housework. Feminist writer Cathy Young responds to Hochschild's assertions by arguing that in some cases, women may prevent the equal participation of men in housework and parenting.

Feminist criticisms of men's contributions to child care and domestic labor in the Western middle class are typically centered on the idea that it is unfair for women to be expected to perform more than half of a household's domestic work and child care when both members of the relationship also work outside the home. Several studies provide statistical evidence that the financial income of married men does not affect their rate of attending to household duties. In *Dubious Conceptions*, Kristin Luker discusses the effect of feminism on teenage women's choices to bear children, both in and out of wedlock.

She says that as childbearing out of wedlock has become more socially acceptable, young women, especially poor young women, while not bearing children at a higher rate than in the 1950s, now see less of a reason to get married before having a child. Her explanation for this is that the economic prospects for poor men are slim; hence poor women have a low chance of finding a husband who will be able to provide reliable financial support. Although research suggests that to an extent, both women and men perceive feminism to be in conflict with romance, studies of undergraduates and older adults have shown that feminism has positive impacts on relationship health for women and sexual satisfaction for men, and found no support for negative stereotypes of feminists.

Religion

Feminist theology is a movement that reconsiders the traditions, practices, scriptures, and theologies of religions from a feminist perspective. Some of the goals of feminist theology include increasing the role of women among the clergy and religious authorities, reinterpreting male-dominated imagery and language about God, determining women's place in relation to career and motherhood, and studying images of women in the religion's sacred texts. Christian feminism is a branch of feminist theology which seeks to interpret and understand Christianity in light of the equality of women and men. Because this equality has been historically ignored, Christian feminists believe their contributions are necessary for a complete understanding of Christianity.

While there is no standard set of beliefs among Christian feminists, most agree that God does not discriminate on the basis of biologically-determined characteristics such as sex. Their major issues are the ordination of women, male dominance in Christian marriage, and claims of moral deficiency and inferiority of abilities of women compared to men. They also are concerned with the balance of parenting between mothers and fathers and the overall treatment of women in the church. Islamic feminism is concerned with the role of women in Islam and aims for the full equality of all Muslims, regardless of gender, in public and private life.

Islamic feminists advocate women's rights, gender equality, and social justice grounded in an Islamic framework. Although rooted in Islam, the movement's pioneers have also utilized secular and Western feminist discourses and recognize the role of Islamic feminism as part of an integrated global feminist movement. Advocates of the movement seek to highlight the deeply rooted teachings of equality in the Quran and encourage a questioning of the patriarchal interpretation of Islamic teaching through the Quran, *hadith* (sayings of Muhammad), and *sharia* (law) towards the creation of a more equal and just society.

Jewish feminism is a movement that seeks to improve the religious, legal, and social status of women within Judaism and to open up new opportunities for religious experience and leadership for Jewish women. Feminist movements, with varying approaches and successes, have opened up within all major branches of Judaism. In its modern form, the movement can be traced to the early 1970s in the United States.

According to Judith Plaskow, who has focused on feminism in Reform Judaism, the main issues for early Jewish feminists in these movements were the exclusion from the all-male prayer group or *minyan*, the exemption from positive time-bound *mitzvot*, and women's inability to function as witnesses and to initiate divorce. The Dianic Wicca or Wiccan feminism is a female focused, Goddess-centered Wiccan sect; also known as a feminist religion that teaches witchcraft as every woman's right. It is also one sect of the many practiced in Wicca.

FEMINIST THEOLOGY

Feminist theology is a movement found in several religions to reconsider the traditions, practices, scriptures, and theologies of those religions from a feminist perspective. Some of the goals of feminist theology include increasing the role of women among the clergy and religious authorities, reinterpreting male-dominated imagery and language about God, determining women's place in relation to career and motherhood, and studying images of women in the religion's sacred texts.

In Wicca "the Goddess" is a deity of prime importance, along with her consorts the Horned God. In the earliest Wiccan publications she is described as a tribal goddess of the witch community, neither omnipotent nor universal, and it was recognised that there was a greater "Prime Mover", although the witches did not concern themselves much with this being.

Architecture

Gender-based inquiries and conceptualization of architecture have also come about in the past fifteen years or so. Piyush Mathur coined the term "archigenderic" in his 1998 article in the British journal Women's Writing. Claiming that "architectural planning has an inextricable link with the defining and regulation of gender roles, responsibilities, rights, and limitations," Mathur came up with that term "to explore...the meaning of 'architecture" in terms of gender" and "to explore the meaning of "gender" in terms of architecture".

WOMEN'S WRITING

Women's writing came to exist as a separate category of scholarly interest relatively recently. In the West, second-wave feminism prompted a general reevaluation of women's historical contributions, and various academic sub-disciplines, such as Women's history (or her story) and women's writing, developed in response to the belief that women's lives and contributions have been underrepresented as areas of scholarly interest. Virginia Balisn et al. characterize the growth in interest since 1970 in women's writing as "powerful". Much of this early period of feminist literary scholarship was given over to the rediscovery and reclamation of texts written by women.

Studies such as Dale Spender's *Mothers of the Novel* (1986) and Jane Spencer's *The Rise of the Woman Novelist* (1986) were ground-breaking in their insistence that women have always been writing. Commensurate with this growth in scholarly interest, various presses began the task of reissuing long-out-of-print texts. Virago Press began to publish its large list of nineteenth and early-twentieth-century novels in 1975 and became one of the first commercial presses to join in the project of reclamation. In the 1980s Pandora Press, responsible for publishing Spender's study, issued a companion line of eighteenth-century novels written by women.

More recently, Broadview Press has begun to issue eighteenth- and nineteenth-century works, many hitherto out of print and the University of Kentucky has a series of republications of early women's novels. There has been commensurate growth in the area of biographical dictionaries of women writers due to a perception, according to one editor, that "most of our women are not represented in the 'standard' reference books in the field". Another early pioneer of Feminist writing is Charlotte Perkins Gilman, whose most notable work was *The Yellow Wallpaper.*

Feminist Science Fiction

In the 1960s the genre of science fiction combined its sensationalism with political and technological critiques of society. With the advent of feminism, questioning women's roles became fair game to this "subversive, mind expanding genre". Two early texts are Ursula K. Le Guin's *The Left Hand of Darkness* (1969) and Joanna Russ' *The Female Man* (1970). They serve to highlight the socially constructed nature of gender roles by creating utopias that do away with gender. Both authors were also pioneers in feminist criticism of science fiction in the 1960s and 70s, in essays collected in *The Language of the Night* (Le Guin, 1979) and *How To Suppress Women's Writing*. Another major work of feminist science fiction has been *Kindred* by Octavia Butler.

Riot Grrrl Movement

Riot grrrl (or riot grrl) is an underground feminist punk movement that started in the 1990s and is often associated with third-wave feminism (it is sometimes seen as its starting point). It was grounded in the DIY philosophy of punk values. Riot grrls took an anti-corporate stance of self-sufficiency and self-reliance. Riot grrrl's emphasis on universal female identity and separatism often appears more closely allied with second-wave feminism than with the third wave.

Riot grrrl bands often address issues such as rape, domestic abuse, sexuality, and female empowerment. Some bands associated with the movement are: Bikini Kill, Bratmobile, Excuse 17, Free Kitten, Heavens To Betsy, Huggy Bear, L7, and Team Dresch. In addition to a music scene, riot grrrl is also a subculture; zines, the DIY ethic, art, political action, and activism are part of the movement. Riot grrrls hold meetings, start chapters, and support and organize women in music.

The riot grrrl movement sprang out of Olympia, Washington and Washington, D.C. in the early 1990s. It sought to give women the power to control their voices and artistic expressions. Riot grrrls took a growling double or triple r, placing it in the word *girl* as a way to take back the derogatory use of the term.

The Riot Grrrl's links to social and political issues are where the beginnings of third-wave feminism can be seen. The music and zine writings are strong examples of "cultural politics in action, with strong women giving voice to important social issues though an empowered, a female oriented community, many people link the emergence of the third-wave feminism to this time". The movement encouraged and made "adolescent girls' standpoints central," allowing them to express themselves fully.

Pornography

The "Feminist Sex Wars" is a term for the acrimonious debates within the feminist movement in the late 1970s through the 1980s around the issues of feminism, sexuality, sexual representation, pornography, sadomasochism, the role of transwomen in the lesbian community, and other sexual issues. The debate pitted anti-pornography feminism against sex-positive feminism, and parts of the feminist movement were deeply divided by these debates.

Anti-pornography Movement

Anti-pornography feminists, such as Catharine MacKinnon, Andrea Dworkin, Robin Morgan and Dorchen Leidholdt, put pornography at the center of a feminist explanation of women's oppression. Some feminists, such as Diana Russell, Andrea Dworkin, Catharine MacKinnon, Susan Brownmiller, Dorchen Leidholdt, Ariel Levy, and Robin Morgan, argue that pornography is degrading to women, and complicit in violence against women both in its production (where, they charge, abuse and exploitation of women performing in pornography is rampant) and in its consumption (where, they charge, pornography eroticizes the domination, humiliation, and coercion of women, and reinforces sexual and cultural attitudes that are complicit in rape and sexual harassment).

Beginning in the late 1970s, anti-pornography radical feminists formed organizations such as Women Against Pornography that provided educational events, including slide-shows, speeches, and guided tours of the sex industry in Times Square, in order to raise awareness of the content of pornography and the sexual subculture in pornography shops and live sex shows. Andrea Dworkin and Robin Morgan began articulating a vehemently anti-porn stance based in radical feminism beginning in 1974, and anti-porn feminist groups, such as Women Against Pornography and similar organizations, became highly active in various US cities during the late 1970s.

Sex-positive Movement

Sex-positive feminism is a movement that was formed in order to address issues of women's sexual pleasure, freedom of expression, sex work, and inclusive gender identities. Ellen Willis' 1981 essay, "Lust Horizons: Is the Women's Movement Pro-Sex?" is the origin of the term, "pro-sex feminism"; the more commonly-used variant, "sex positive feminism" arose soon after. Although some sex-positive feminists, such as Betty Dodson, were active in the early 1970s, much of sex-positive feminism largely began in the late 1970s and 1980s as a response to the increasing emphasis in radical feminism on anti-pornography activism.

Sex-positive feminists are also strongly opposed to radical feminist calls for legislation against pornography, a strategy they decried as censorship, and something that could, they argued, be used by social conservatives to censor the sexual expression of women, gay people, and other sexual minorities. The initial period of intense debate and acrimony between sex-positive and anti-pornography feminists during the early 1980s is often referred to as the Feminist Sex Wars. Other sex-positive feminists became involved not in opposition to other feminists, but in direct response to what they saw as patriarchal control of sexuality.

Since the 1990s, other feminists such as Patricia Petersen have argued that pornography may serve an important function for women in that it may reduce the likelihood that they will be raped or become victims of other forms of sex crimes. She has also argued that governments should not determine what individual women do with their bodies.

Socialism

Since the early twentieth century some feminists have allied with socialism. In 1907 there was an International Conference of Socialist Women in Stuttgart where suffrage was described as a tool of class struggle. Clara Zetkin of the Social Democratic Party of Germany called for women's suffrage to build a "*socialist order, the only one that allows for a radical solution to the women's question*". In Britain, the women's movement was allied with the Labour party. In America, Betty Friedan emerged from a radical background to take command of the organized movement. Radical Women, founded in 1967 in Seattle is the oldest (and still active) socialist feminist organization in the U.S.

During the Spanish Civil War, Dolores Ibárruri (*La Pasionaria*) led the Communist Party of Spain. Although she supported equal rights for women, she opposed women fighting on the front and clashed with the anarcho-feminist Mujeres Libres. Revolutions in Latin America brought changes in women's status in countries such as Nicaragua where Feminist ideology during the Sandinista Revolution was largely responsible for improvements in the quality of life for women but fell short of achieving a social and ideological change.

Fascism

Scholars have argued that Nazi Germany and the other fascist states of the 1930s and 1940s illustrate the disastrous consequences for society of a state ideology that, in glorifying women, becomes anti-feminist. In Germany after the rise of Nazism in 1933, there was a rapid dissolution of the political rights and economic opportunities that feminists had fought for during the prewar period and to some extent during the 1920s. In Franco's Spain, the right wing Catholic conservatives undid the work of feminists during the Republic. Fascist society was hierarchical with an emphasis and idealization of virility, with women maintaining a largely subordinate position to men.

Scientific Discourse

Some feminists are critical of traditional scientific discourse, arguing that the field has historically been biased towards a masculine perspective. Evelyn Fox Keller argues that the rhetoric of science reflects a masculine perspective, and she questions the idea of scientific objectivity. Many feminist scholars rely on qualitative research methods that emphasize women's subjective, individual experiences. According to communication scholars Thomas R. Lindlof and Bryan C. Taylor, incorporating a feminist approach to qualitative research involves treating research participants as equals who are just as much an authority as the researcher. Objectivity is eschewed in favor of open self-reflexivity and the agenda of helping women.

Also part of the feminist research agenda is uncovering ways that power inequities are created and/or reinforced in society and/or in scientific and academic institutions. Lindlof and Taylor also explain that a feminist approach to research often involves nontraditional forms of presentation. Primatologist Sarah Blaffer Hrdy notes the prevalence of masculine-coined stereotypes and theories, such as the non-sexual female, despite "the accumulation of abundant openly available evidence contradicting it". Some natural and social scientists have examined feminist ideas using scientific methods.

Biology of Gender

Modern feminist science is based on the view that many differences between the sexes are based on socially constructed gender identities rather than on biological sex differences. For example, Anne Fausto-Sterling's book *Myths of Gender* explores the assumptions embodied in scientific research that purports to support a biologically essentialist view of gender. Her second book, *Sexing the Body* discussed the alleged possibility of more than two *true* biological sexes. This possibility only exists in yet-unknown extraterrestrial biospheres, as no ratios of true gametes to polar cells other than 4:0 and 1:3 (male and female, respectively) are produced on Earth.

However, in *The Female Brain*, Louann Brizendine argues that brain differences between the sexes are a biological reality with significant implications for sex-specific functional differences. Steven Rhoads' book *Taking Sex Differences Seriously* illustrates sex-dependent differences across a wide scope. Carol Tavris, in *The Mismeasure of Woman*, uses psychology and sociology to critique theories that use biological reductionism to explain differences between men and women. She argues rather than using evidence of innate gender difference there is an over-changing hypothesis to justify inequality and perpetuate stereotypes.

Evolutionary Biology

Sarah Kember-drawing from numerous areas such as evolutionary biology, sociobiology, artificial intelligence, and cybernetics in development with a new evolutionism-discusses the biologization of technology. She notes how feminists and sociologists have become suspect of evolutionary psychology, particularly inasmuch as sociobiology is subjected to complexity in order to strengthen sexual difference as immutable through pre-existing cultural value judgments about human nature and natural selection. Where feminist theory is criticized for its "false beliefs about human nature," Kember then argues in conclusion that "feminism is in the interesting position of needing to do more biology and evolutionary theory in order not to simply oppose their renewed hegemony, but in order to understand the conditions that make this possible, and to have a say in the construction of new ideas and artefacts."

Men and Feminism

The relationship between men and feminism has been complex. Men have taken part in significant responses to feminism in each 'wave' of the movement. There have been positive and negative reactions and responses, depending on the individual man and the social context of the time. These responses have varied from pro-feminism to masculism to anti-feminism. In the twenty-first century new reactions to feminist ideologies have emerged including a generation of male scholars involved in gender studies, and also men's rights activists who promote male equality (including equal treatment in family, divorce and anti-discrimination law).

Historically a number of men have engaged with feminism. Philosopher Jeremy Bentham demanded equal rights for women in the eighteenth century. In 1866, philosopher John Stuart Mill (author of "The Subjection of Women") presented a women's petition to the British parliament; and supported an amendment to the 1867 Reform Bill. Others have lobbied and campaigned against feminism. Today, academics like Michael Flood, Michael Messner and Michael Kimmel are involved with men's studies and pro-feminism.

A number of feminist writers maintain that identifying as a feminist is the strongest stand men can take in the struggle against sexism. They have argued that men should be allowed, or even be encouraged, to participate in the feminist movement.

Other female feminists argue that men cannot be feminists simply because they are not women. They maintain that men are granted inherent privileges that prevent them from identifying with feminist struggles, thus making it impossible for them to identify with feminists. Fidelma Ashe has approached the issue of male feminism by arguing that traditional feminist views of male experience and of "men doing feminism" have been monolithic. She explores the multiple political discourses and practices of pro-feminist politics, and evaluates each strand through an interrogation based upon its effect on feminist politics.

A more recent examination of the subject is presented by author and academic Shira Tarrant. In *Men and Feminism*, the California State University, Long Beach professor highlights critical debates about masculinity and gender, the history of men in feminism, and men's roles in preventing violence and sexual assault. Through critical analysis and first-person stories by feminist men, Tarrant addresses the question of why men should care about feminism in the first place and lays the foundation for a larger discussion about feminism as an all-encompassing, human issue. Tarrant touches on similar topics in *Men Speak Out: Views on Gender, Sex, and Power*.

Pro-feminism

Pro-feminism is the support of feminism without implying that the supporter is a member of the feminist movement. The term is most often used in reference to men who are actively supportive of feminism and of efforts to bring about gender equality. The activities of pro-feminist men's groups include anti-violence work with boys and young men in schools, offering sexual harassment workshops in workplaces, running community education campaigns, and counseling male perpetrators of violence. Pro-feminist men also are involved in men's health, activism against pornography including anti-pornography legislation, men's studies, and the development of gender equity curricula in schools. This work is sometimes in collaboration with feminists and women's services, such as domestic violence and rape crisis centers. Some activists of both genders will not refer to men as "feminists" at all, and will refer to all pro-feminist men as "pro-feminists".

Anti-feminism

Anti-feminism is opposition to feminism in some or all of its forms. Writers such as Camille Paglia, Christina Hoff Sommers, Jean Bethke Elshtain and Elizabeth Fox-Genovese have been labeled "anti-feminists" by feminists. Daphne Patai and Noretta Koertge argue that in this way the term "anti-feminist" is used to silence academic debate about feminism. Paul Nathanson and Katherine K. Young's books *Spreading Misandry* and *Legalizing Misandry* explore what they argue is feminist-inspired misandry. Christina Hoff-Sommers argues feminist misandry leads directly to misogyny by what she calls "establishment feminists" against (the majority of) women who love men in *Who Stole Feminism: How Women Have Betrayed Women*. "Marriage rights" advocates criticize feminists like Sheila Cronan who take the view that marriage constitutes slavery for women, and that freedom for women cannot be won without the abolition of marriage.

6

Violence against Women and the Legal Systems of some Asian Countries

Violence affects the lives of millions of women worldwide, in all socio-economic and educational classes. It cuts across cultural and religious barriers, impeding the right of women to participate fully in society.

Violence against women takes a dismaying variety of forms, from domestic abuse and rape to child marriages and female circumcision. All are violations of the most fundamental human rights. In a statement to the Fourth World Conference on Women in Beijing in September 1995, the United Nations Secretary-General, Boutros Boutros-Ghali, said that violence against women is a universal problem that must be universally condemned. But he said that the problem continues to grow.

The Secretary-General noted that domestic violence alone is on the increase. Studies in 10 countries, he said, have found that between 17 per cent and 38 per cent of women have suffered physical assaults by a partner. In the Platform for Action, the core document of the Beijing Conference, Governments declared that "violence against women constitutes a violation of basic human rights and is an obstacle to the achievement of the objectives of equality, development and peace".

THE WORK OF THE SPECIAL RAPPORTEUR

The issue of the advancement of women's rights has concerned the United Nations since the Organization's founding. Yet the alarming global dimensions of female-targeted violence were not explicitly acknowledged by the international community until December 1993, when the United Nations General Assembly adopted the Declaration on the Elimination of Violence against Women.

Until that point, most Governments tended to regard violence against women largely as a private matter between individuals, and not as a pervasive human rights problem requiring State intervention.

In view of the alarming growth in the number of cases of violence against women throughout the world, the Commission on Human Rights adopted resolution 1994/45 of 4 March 1994, in which it decided to appoint the Special Rapporteur on violence against women, including its causes and consequences. As a result of these steps, the problem of violence against women has been drawing increasing political attention.

The Special Rapporteur has a mandate to collect and analyse comprehensive data and to recommend measures aimed at eliminating violence at the international, national and regional levels. The mandate is threefold:

- To collect information on violence against women and its causes and consequences from sources such as Governments, treaty bodies, specialized agencies and intergovernmental and non-governmental organizations, and to respond effectively to such information;
- To recommend measures and ways and means, at the national, regional and international levels, to eliminate violence against women and its causes, and to remedy its consequences;
- To work closely with other special rapporteurs, special representatives, working groups and independent experts of the Commission on Human Rights.

INCEST, RAPE AND DOMESTIC VIOLENCE

Some females fall prey to violence before they are born, when expectant parents abort their unborn daughters, hoping for sons instead. In other societies, girls are subjected to such traditional practices as circumcision, which leave them maimed and traumatized. In others, they are compelled to marry at an early age, before they are physically, mentally or emotionally mature. Women are victims of incest, rape and domestic violence that often lead to trauma, physical handicap or death.

And rape is still being used as a weapon of war, a strategy used to subjugate and terrify entire communities. Soldiers deliberately impregnate women of different ethnic groups and abandon them when it is too late to get an abortion. The Platform for Action adopted at the Fourth World Conference on Women declared that rape in armed conflict is a war crime - and could, under certain circumstances, be considered genocide. Secretary-General Boutros-Ghali told the Beijing Conference that more women today were suffering directly from the effects of war and conflict than ever before in history.

"There is a deplorable trend towards the organized humiliation of women, including the crime of mass rape", the Secretary-General said. "We will press for international legal action against those who perpetrate organized violence against women in time of conflict." A preliminary report in 1994 by the Special Rapporteur, Ms. Radhika Coomaraswamy, focused on three areas of concern where women are particularly vulnerable: in the family (including domestic violence, traditional practices, infanticide); in the community (including rape, sexual assault, commercialized violence such as trafficking in women, labour exploitation, female migrant workers etc.); and by the State (including violence against women in detention as well as violence against women in situations of armed conflict and against refugee women). In the Platform for Action adopted at the Beijing Conference, violence against women and the human rights of women are 2 of the 12 critical areas of concern identified as the main obstacles to the advancement of women.

Commitments by Governments

Governments agreed to adopt and implement national legislation to end violence against women and to work actively to ratify all international agreements that relate to violence against women. They agreed that there should be shelters, legal aid and other services for girls and women at risk, and counselling and rehabilitation for perpetrators. Governments also pledged to adopt appropriate measures in the field of education to modify the social and cultural patterns of conduct of men and women. And the Platform called on media professionals to develop self-regulatory guidelines to address violent, degrading and pornographic materials while encouraging non-stereotyped, balanced and diverse images of women.

Defining Gender-based Abuse

The Declaration on the Elimination of Violence against Women is the first international human rights instrument to exclusively and explicitly address the issue of violence against women. It affirms that the phenomenon violates, impairs or nullifies women's human rights and their exercise of fundamental freedoms. The Declaration provides a definition of gender-based abuse, calling it "any act of gender-based violence that results in, or is likely to result in, physical, sexual or psychological harm or suffering to women, including threats of such acts, coercion or arbitrary deprivation of liberty, whether occurring in public or in private life".

The definition is amplified in article 2 of the Declaration, which identifies three areas in which violence commonly takes place:

- Physical, sexual and psychological violence that occurs in the family, including battering; sexual abuse of female children in the household; dowry-related violence; marital rape; female genital mutilation and other traditional practices harmful to women; non-spousal violence; and violence related to exploitation;
- Physical, sexual and psychological violence that occurs within the general community, including rape; sexual

abuse; sexual harassment and intimidation at work, in educational institutions and elsewhere; trafficking in women; and forced prostitution;

- Physical, sexual and psychological violence perpetrated or condoned by the State, wherever it occurs.

Groundwork Laid in Vienna

The importance of the question of violence against women was emphasized over the last decade through the holding of several expert group meetings sponsored by the United Nations to draw attention to the extent and severity of the problem. In September 1992, the United Nations Commission on the Status of Women established a special Working Group and gave it a mandate to draw up a draft declaration on violence against women.

The following year, the United Nations Commission for Human Rights, in resolution 1993/46 of 3 March condemned all forms of violence and violations of human rights directed specifically against women.

The World Conference on Human Rights, held in Vienna in June 1993, laid extensive groundwork for eliminating violence against women. In the Vienna Declaration and Programme of Action, Governments declared that the United Nations system and Member States should work towards the elimination of violence against women in public and private life; of all forms of sexual harassment, exploitation and trafficking in women; of gender bias in the administration of justice; and of any conflicts arising between the rights of women and the harmful effects of certain traditional or customary practices, cultural prejudices and religious extremism.

The document also declared that "violations of the human rights of women in situations of armed conflicts are violations of the fundamental principles of international human rights and humanitarian law", and that all violations of this kind - including murder, systematic rape, sexual slavery and forced pregnancy - "require a particularly effective response".

KINDS OF VIOLENCE AGAINST WOMEN

DOMESTIC VIOLENCE

Violence against women in the family occurs in developed and developing countries alike. It has long been considered a private matter by bystanders - including neighbours, the community and government. But such private matters have a tendency to become public tragedies. In the United States, a woman is beaten every 18 minutes. Indeed, domestic violence is the leading cause of injury among women of reproductive age in the United States. Between 22 and 35 per cent of women who visit emergency rooms are there for that reason.

The highly publicized trial of O. J. Simpson, the retired United States football player acquitted of the murder of his former wife and a male friend of hers, helped focus international media attention on the issue of domestic violence and spousal abuse. In Peru, 70 per cent of all crimes reported to the police involve women beaten by their husbands. In Pakistan, Prime Minister Benazir Bhutto strongly defended a 35-year-old mother of two who was severely burned by her husband in a domestic dispute.

"There is no excuse for such a behaviour", the Prime Minister declared after visiting the hospitalized victim. "My presence here is to send a message to all those who violate Islamic teachings and defy laws of the land with their inhuman treatment of women. This will not be tolerated." According to the Human Rights Commission of Pakistan in the 400 cases of domestic violence reported in 1993 in the province of Punjab, nearly half ended with the death of the wife.

According to the Special Rapporteur's report, many Governments now recognize the importance of protecting victims of domestic abuse and taking action to punish perpetrators. The establishment of structures allowing officials to deal with cases of domestic violence and its consequences is a significant step towards the elimination of violence against women in the family. The Special Rapporteur's report highlights the importance of adopting legislation that provides for prosecution of the offender. It also stresses the importance of specialized training for law enforcement authorities as well as medical and legal professionals, and of the establishment of community support services for victims, including access to information and shelters.

Traditional Practices

In many countries, women fall victim to traditional practices that violate their human rights. The persistence of the problem has much to do with the fact that most of these physically and psychologically harmful customs are deeply rooted in the tradition and culture of society.

Female Genital Mutilation

According to the World Health Organization, 85 million to 115 million girls and women in the population have undergone some form of female genital mutilation and suffer from its adverse health effects. Every year an estimated 2 million young girls undergo this procedure. Most live in Africa and Asia - but an increasing number can be found among immigrant and refugee families in Western Europe and North America. Indeed, the practice has been outlawed in some European countries.

In France, a Malian was convicted in a criminal court after his baby girl died of a female circumcision-related infection. The procedure had been performed on the infant at home. In Canada, fear of being forced to undergo circumcision can be grounds for asylum.

A Nigerian woman was granted refugee status since she felt that she might be persecuted in her home country because of her refusal to inflict genital mutilation on her baby daughter. There is a growing consensus that the best way to eliminate these practices is through educational campaigns that emphasize their dangerous health consequences. Several Governments have been actively promoting such campaigns in their countries.

Son Preference

Son preference affects women in many countries, particularly in Asia. Its consequences can be anything from foetal or female infanticide to neglect of the girl child over her brother in terms of such essential needs as nutrition, basic health care and education. In China and India, some women choose to terminate their pregnancies when expecting daughters but carry their pregnancies to term when expecting sons. According to reports from India, genetic testing for sex selection has become a booming business, especially in the country's northern regions. Indian gender-detection clinics drew protests from women's groups after the appearance of advertisements suggesting that it was better to spend $38 now to terminate a female foetus than $3,800 later on her dowry.

A study of amniocentesis procedures conducted in a large Bombay hospital found that 95.5 per cent of foetuses identified as female were aborted compared with a far smaller percentage of male foetuses. The problem of son preference is present in many other countries as well. Asked how many children he had fathered, the former United States boxing champion Muhammad Ali told an interviewer: "One boy and seven mistakes."

Dowry-related violence and early marriage

In some countries, weddings are preceded by the payment of an agreed-upon dowry by the bride's family. Failure to pay the dowry can lead to violence. In Bangladesh, a bride whose dowry was deemed too small was disfigured after her husband threw acid on her face. In India, an average of five women a day is burned in dowry-related disputes - and many more cases are never reported.

Early marriage, especially without the consent of the girl, is another form of human rights violation. Early marriage followed by multiple pregnancies can affect the health of women for life. The report of the Special Rapporteur has documented the destructive effects of marriage of female children under 18 and has urged Governments to adopt relevant legislation.

VIOLENCE IN THE COMMUNITY

RAPE

Rape can occur anywhere, even in the family, where it can take the form of marital rape or incest. It occurs in the community, where a woman can fall prey to any abuser. It also occurs in situations of armed conflict and in refugee camps. In the United States, national statistics indicate that a woman is raped every six minutes. In 1995, the case of a Brazilian jogger raped and murdered in New York City's Central Park drew international attention once again to the problem. The incident occurred only a few years after an earlier sensational jogger-assault case in which the victim - an American assaulted in the same general area of the park - barely survived after her assailants left her for dead.

Relations between residents of the Japanese island of Okinawa and American GIs were thrown into turmoil in 1995 after two marines and a sailor allegedly kidnapped and raped a 12-year-old girl. The Special Rapporteur's report underlines the importance of education to sensitize the public about the special horrors of rape, and of sensitivity training for the police and hospital staff who work with victims.

SEXUAL ASSAULT WITHIN MARRIAGE

In many countries sexual assault by a husband on his wife is not considered to be a crime: a wife is expected to submit. It is thus very difficult in practice for a woman to prove that sexual assault has occurred unless she can demonstrate serious injury. The report of the Special Rapporteur noted that light sentences in sexual assault cases send the wrong message to perpetrators and to the public at large: that female sexual victimization is unimportant.

SEXUAL HARASSMENT

Sexual harassment in the workplace is a growing concern for women. Employers abuse their authority to seek sexual favours from their female co-workers or subordinates, sometimes promising promotions or other forms of career advancement or simply creating an untenable and hostile work environment. Women who refuse to give in to such unwanted sexual advances often run the risk of anything from demotion to dismissal. But in recent years more women have been coming forward to report such practices - some taking their cases to court.

In her report, the Special Rapporteur stressed that sexual harassment constitutes a form of sex discrimination. "It not only degrades the woman", the report noted, "but reinforces and reflects the idea of non-professionalism on the part of women workers, who are consequently regarded as less able to perform their duties than their male colleagues."

PROSTITUTION AND TRAFFICKING

Many women are forced into prostitution either by their parents, husbands or boyfriends - or as a result of the difficult economic and social conditions in which they find themselves. They are also lured into prostitution, sometimes by "mail-order bride" agencies that promise to find them a husband or a job in a foreign country.

As a result, they very often find themselves illegally confined in brothels in slavery-like conditions where they are physically abused and their passports withheld. Most women initially victimized by sexual traffickers have little inkling of what awaits them.

They generally get a very small percentage of what the customer pays to the pimp or the brothel owner.

Once they are caught up in the system there is practically no way out, and they find themselves in a very vulnerable situation. Since prostitution is illegal in many countries, it is difficult for prostitutes to come forward and ask for protection if they become victims of rape or want to escape from brothels. Customers, on the other hand, are rarely the object of penal laws. In Thailand, prostitutes who complain to the police are often arrested and sent back to the brothels upon payment of a fine.

The extent of trafficking in women and girl children has reached alarming proportions, especially in Asian countries. Many women and girl children are trafficked across borders, often with the complicity of border guards. In one incident, five young prostitutes burned to death in a brothel fire because they had been chained to their beds. At the same time, sex tours of developing countries are a well-organized industry in several European and other industrialized countries. The Special Rapporteur has called on Governments to take action to protect young girls from being recruited as prostitutes and to closely monitor recruiting agencies.

VIOLENCE AGAINST WOMEN MIGRANT WORKERS

Female migrant workers typically leave their countries for better living conditions and better pay - but the real benefits accrue to both the host countries and the countries of origin. For home countries, money sent home by migrant workers is an important source of hard currency, while receiving countries are able to find workers for low-paying jobs that might otherwise go unfilled. But migrant workers themselves fare badly, and sometimes tragically. Many become virtual slaves, subject to abuse and rape by their employers.

In the Middle East and Persian Gulf region, there are an estimated 1.2 million women, mainly Asians, who are employed as domestic servants. According to the independent human rights group Middle East Watch; female migrant workers in Kuwait often suffer beatings and sexual assaults at the hands of their employers. The police are often of little help. In many cases, women who report being raped by their employers are sent back to the employer - or are even assaulted at the police station.

Working conditions are often appalling, and employers prevent women from escaping by seizing their passports or identity papers. The report of the Special Rapporteur draws attention to the fact that there are many international instruments that can be used to prevent abuse against migrant women and suggests some measures to protect the human rights of migrant women.

Pornography

Another concern highlighted in the Special Rapporteur's report is pornography, which represents a form of violence against women that "glamorizes the degradation and maltreatment of women and asserts their subordinate function as mere receptacles for male lust".

VIOLENCE PERPETRATED OR CONDONED BY STATES

Custodial Violence against Women

Violence against women by the very people who are supposed to protect them - members of the law enforcement and criminal justice systems - is widespread. Women are physically or verbally abused; they also suffer sexual and physical torture. According to Amnesty International, thousands of women held in custody are routinely raped in police detention centres worldwide. The report of the Special Rapporteur underlines the necessity for States to prosecute those accused of abusing women while in detention and to hold them accountable for their actions.

Violence against Women in Situations of armed Conflict

Rape has been widely used as a weapon of war whenever armed conflicts arise between different parties. It has been used all over the world: in Chiapas, Mexico, in Rwanda, in Kuwait, in Haiti, in Colombia. Women and girl children are frequently victims of gang rape committed by soldiers from all sides of a conflict. Such acts are done mainly to trample the dignity of the victims. Rape has been used to reinforce the policy of ethnic cleansing in the war that has been tearing apart the former Yugoslavia.

The so-called "comfort women" - young girls of colonized or occupied countries who became sexual slaves to Japanese soldiers during the Second World War - have dramatized the problem in a historical context. Many of these women are now coming forward and demanding compensation for their suffering from Japanese authorities. "Such rape is the symbolic rape of the community, the destruction of the fundamental elements of a society and culture - the ultimate humiliation of the male enemy", the report by the Special Rapporteur noted. It stressed the need to hold the perpetrators of such crimes fully accountable.

Violence against refugee and Displaced Women

Women and children form the great majority of refugee populations all over the world and are especially vulnerable to violence and exploitation. In refugee camps, they are raped and abused by military and immigration personnel, bandit groups, male refugees and rival ethnic groups. They are also forced into prostitution. In her report, the Special Rapporteur proposes the following measures to be taken for the protection of women and girls in refugee camps: improvement of security, deployment of trained female officers at all points of the refugees' journey, participation of women in organizational structures of the camps and prosecution of government and military personnel responsible for abuse against refugee women.

LEGAL STEPS TO CRIMINALIZE VIOLENCE AGAINST WOMEN

In recent years some countries have taken significant steps towards improving laws relating to violence against women. For example:

- In July 1991, Mexico revised its rape law in several important ways. A provision was eliminated that allowed a man who rapes a minor to avoid prosecution if he agrees to marry her. Now judges are required to hand down a decision regarding access to an abortion within five working days.
- On 9 June 1994, the Organization of American States adopted the Inter-American Convention to Prevent, Punish and Eradicate Violence against Women (also called Convention of Belém do Parà), a new international

instrument that recognizes all gender-based violence as an abuse of human rights. This Convention provides an individual right of petition and a right for non-governmental organizations to lodge complaints with the Inter-American Commission of Human Rights.

- In Australia, a National Committee on Violence against Women was established to coordinate the development of policy, legislation and law enforcement at the national level as well as community education on violence against women.
- In 1991, the Government of Canada announced a new four-year Family Violence Initiative intended to mobilize community action, strengthen Canada's legal framework, establish services on Indian reserves and in Inuit communities, develop resources to help victims and stop offenders, and provide housing for abused women and children.
- In Turkey, a Ministry of State for Women was established whose main goals are, among others, to promote women's rights and strengthen their role in economic, social, political and cultural life. Legal measures are being adopted towards the elimination of violence against women. The establishment of special courts to deal with violence is envisaged. Psychological treatment for abused women is also planned, along with the establishment of women's shelters around the country. Specially trained female police officers could provide assistance to victims of violence.
- In Burkina Faso, a strong advertising campaign by the Government as well as television and radio programmes on the unhealthy practice of genital mutilation was launched to educate and raise public awareness about the dangerous consequences of such an "operation". A National Anti-Excision Committee was established in 1990 by the present head of State. Today, the practice of genital mutilation has been eliminated in some villages of Burkina Faso. In others, there has been an incredible drop in the number of girls excised: only 10 per cent of the girls are excised compared to 100 per cent 10 years ago.

- Some countries have introduced police units specially trained for dealing with spousal assault. In Brazil, specific police stations have been designated to deal with women's issues, including domestic violence. These police stations are staffed entirely by women.

ENSURING THAT LAWS ARE OBEYED

These examples illustrate some steps taken at the national level towards the eradication of violence against women. Combating and eradicating this scourge require enhanced and concerted efforts to protect women at the local, national and international levels. States have tended to adopt a passive attitude when confronted by cases of violations of women's rights by private actors. Most laws fail to protect victims or to punish perpetrators. Passing laws to criminalize violence against women is an important way to redefine the limits of acceptable behaviour.

States should ensure that national legislation, once adopted, does not go unenforced. State responsibility is clearly underlined in article 4 of the Declaration on the Elimination of Violence against Women, which stipulates that "States should exercise due diligence to prevent, investigate and, in accordance with national legislation, punish acts of violence against women, whether those acts are perpetrated by the State or by private persons". Any approach designed to combat violence must be twofold, addressing the root causes of the problem and treating its manifestations. Society at large, including judges and police officers, must be educated to change the social attitudes and beliefs that encourage male violence.

CHALLENGING TRADITIONAL ATTITUDES

The meaning of gender and sexuality and the balance of power between women and men at all levels of society must be reviewed. Combating violence against women requires challenging the way that gender roles and power relations are articulated in society. In many countries women have a low status. They are considered as inferior and there is a strong belief that men are superior to them and even own them. Changing people's attitude and mentality towards women will take a long time - at least a generation, many believe, and perhaps longer.

Nevertheless, raising awareness of the issue of violence against women, and educating boys and men to view women as valuable partners in life, in the development of a society and in the attainment of peace are just as important as taking legal steps to protect women's human rights. It is also important in order to prevent violence that non-violent means be used to resolve conflict between all members of society. Breaking the cycle of abuse will require concerted collaboration and action between governmental and non-governmental actors, including educators, health-care authorities, legislators, the judiciary and the mass media.

Violence against women is a universal reality but at the same time it is invisible. Reports from all parts of the world point to the fact that violence against women is a "manifestation of the unequal power relationship" between men and women and exists in all societies. Yet such violence is underreported if not "normalized" as acceptable social behaviour. South Asia has been classified as the worst region in terms of indicators with the highest rates of different forms of violence against women.

Until the late 1980s and the 1990s, violence against women was a taboo subject of discussion even in international fora analyzing the question of women's rights. There were in fact two phases with regard to the articulation of the international human rights of women. The first phase, which culminated in the drafting of the Convention on the Elimination of Discrimination Against Women, involved discussion of the issues relating to "discrimination" against women in political and civil life as well as in economic, social and cultural life.

Except for the question of trafficking, issues relating to violence against women were not included in the Convention. With a focus on discrimination in the workplace, access to state services, and discrimination in family law, the Convention was a major landmark for the international articulation of the rights of women. It was only in the 1980s that violence against women became a focal point of international mobilization. In 1991, the CEDAW Committee, responding to pressure from women's groups formulated recommendation 19, that articulated violence against women as gender based discrimination covered by CEDAW.

Women from the grassroots from all over the world came together and mounted an international campaign to make violence against women an important issue of human rights. These activities culminated at the United Nations World Conference on Human Rights that took place in 1993 in Vienna. At the conference women demanded that there be a UN Declaration on the Elimination of Violence Against Women and secondly that the United Nations Human Rights Commission create the post of UN Special Rapporteur on Violence Against Women.

Within six months the United Nations General Assembly passed the United Nation Declaration of the Elimination of Violence against Women and within a year the United Nations Human Rights Commission created the post of UN Special Rapporteur. The violence against women movement is perhaps the greatest success story of international mobilization around a specific human rights issue, leading to the articulation of international norms and standards and the formulation of international programmes and policies.

The World Conference on Human Rights that highlighted the issue of violence against women as a human rights issue brought activists from around the world who were working on issues relating to violence against women. The first group of activists was those working with women victims of sexual violence during wartime and refugee women who were concerned with violence against women during armed conflict. The second group of women was from Asia and Europe working with women victims of trafficking and forced prostitution.

The third group of women was from North and South America as well as Europe working on issues relating to domestic violence, rape, and sexual harassment. The fourth group of women from Asia and Africa were women fighting against cultural and religious practices that were violent toward women and harmful to their health, all these women united around the theme of violence against women as a human rights issue and managed to persuade nation states to accept their formulation. Thus the United Nations Declaration on the Elimination of Violence Against Women was passed unanimously and with a standing ovation by the United Nations General Assembly.

After 1993, in Cairo at the International Conference on Population and Development (1994) and at Beijing at the Fourth World Conference on Women (1995) these principles were taken forward and elaborated on my state parties as well as NGOs. The international standards set out in the international documents that were a result of the violence against women movement, call on states to act decisively on issues relating to violence against women.

It calls on them to pass national legislation, to formulate national plans of action, to sensitise and train their criminal justice machinery, to collect data and to provide social services of support to women victims of violence. They also stated clearly that custom, religion and tradition should not be used to justify acts of violence against women. The importance of government action and government sanctions must be emphasized.

Researchers point out that the societies with the lowest levels of partner violence were those that had community sanctions against partner violence and where abused women had access to sanctuary and support. The catalytical role played by international standards and programmes in generating awareness and policies at the national level, especially in the South Asian region, cannot be understated. The dynamic interaction between the international and the local have created space for imaginative intervention and a plethora of strategies to confront what is now accepted as an endemic problem of the region.

THE NATURE OF THE PROBLEM IN SOUTH ASIA

South Asia continues to have the worst indicators with regard to violence against women in the world. In addition to the common problems of violence against women, South Asia has particular cultural and religious practices that also accentuate the problem of VAW in the region. The general low status of women in the region and the entrenched nature of discriminatory structures have led to what is seen as a lifecycle of VAW.

Even before birth women suffer from sex selective abortion, at infancy they may face female infanticide, as young children they will have to put up with incest and son preference, as adolescents they may be sexually abused or trafficked, as young women they may suffer rape, sexual harassment, acid attacks as wives they may experience domestic violence, dowry related violence, marital rape or honour killings, as widows they may be required to self immolate or be deprived of property and dignity.

The vulnerability to violence at every stage of the life cycle makes VAW a terrible South Asian legacy that requires concerted regional, national and local level action.

ARMED CONFLICT

Rani lives in the east coast of Sri Lanka. Rani is a Sri Lankan Tam. Rani's husband was taken away by the Sri Lankan army about fifteen years ago and she has not heard from him since. Her son, who was still a child of 12, was taken by the Liberation Tigers of Sri Lanka. She has lost touch with him and does not know whether he is dead or alive. Rani and her daughter eke out a living doing handicrafts with the help of a local NGO. They barely have enough to survive. Her daughter suffers from nightmares and depression since she was attached to both the father and the brother. Rani doesn't like to speak much- speech is dangerous in the east coast with so many young men with guns. Tears well in her eyes when she speaks and for solace she goes to the nearby oracle to find out about her husband and her son. The oracle tells her that they are alive so she lives in hope.

Armed conflict has been an important part of the post independence legacy of South Asia. Whether on the Afghan Border with Pakistan, in Kashmir, in the Chittagong Hill Tracts, among Maoist rebels or in the north and east of Sri Lanka, armed conflict is a terrible reality that many women in South Asia have to face. Women are affected by armed conflict in different ways. First, they are often the victims of direct violence especially sexual violence by armed soldiers or militants. Rape during wartime is one of the oldest war crimes and is now clearly prohibited by the Statute of the International Criminal Court. However none of the countries of South Asia have become parties to the ICC.

There have been some prosecutions for custodial violence in South Asia. In Sri Lanka in the famous case of Krishanthy Kumaraswamy, the court handed the death penalty to the perpetrators. However, in most of the cases there is no prosecution and the perpetrators are unpunished. Sexual violence during war time continues in all parts of South Asia and there is a sense of impunity on the part of the perpetrators. Another way in which women are affected during war time is as internally displaced persons. 80% of the IDPs are women and children.

As IDPs they live in terrible circumstances. They are given meager rations; they live in large communal halls without any privacy often only separated by a sari. Women are often sexually harassed in these camps by officials and inmates and there are minimal sanitation facilities. They are also subject to restrictions on their freedom of movement. They often dream of returning home but are in these camps for a very long period of time. When the armed conflict is over, resettlement is an even longer process. They often find their lands and homes occupied or destroyed. They usually do not have the communal infrastructure to begin a new life and they are subject to a great deal of bureaucratic regulation.

Women and children in these camps continue to have psycho social problems and long term adjustment problems. Women are also affected by war in that they become war widows, often losing their husbands. In very patriarchal societies that oppress and discriminate against women, these young widows have special problems and concerns. They become among the poorest and most vulnerable communities in the country. They find survival a difficult problem and have to face constant harassment in the community. They are deprived of all socials benefits as widows and live a life of isolation and restriction. Research suggests that they survive because of the future they envision for their children.

In some wars women actually become combatants such as in Sri Lanka. Here the ambiguity of the Geneva Convention on the protection of women combatants raises a whole host of issues. Moreover, in the post conflict situation, other parts of the world such as Colombia, point to obstacles in the reintegration of female cadres into civilian life especially in patriarchal societies. Women as warriors, though exciting because of the transgressing of gender roles, raise other issues relating to the realization of women's rights within the framework of military imperatives and war.

TRAFFICKING

Chamoli was sixteen years old and living with her father and step mother. Her step mother did not like her very much and used to beat her often. One day a young man cam from outside to the village. Chamoli fell in love with him and he promised to marry her. She eloped with him to India. He then took her to a big house and he saw money exchange between her new lover and the madam of the house. After that her lover disappeared and she found she was in a brothel. She was literally tortured into submission. She had to service about ten customers a day and was living in a cubicle the size of a bed. Finally Maiti Nepal a Nepalese NGO came to her brothel and "rescued her" She then spent seven months in an Indian "protection home" before she was sent back to Nepal When she got there doctors as Maiti Nepal discovered that she was suffering from AIDS. Chamoli refuses to return to her family because of the shame and because of her fear of her step mother.

Trafficking of women and girls, especially into the big cities of India, remains a serious problem in the South Asian region. Increasingly young girls between the ages of ten and fourteen are trafficked to different parts of India from within India as well as Nepal and Bangladesh. In other countries there are smaller trafficking enterprises taking place. It is estimated that about 200,000 young girls from Nepal in India of which 45,000 are in Bombay alone.

Women are often trafficked by close friends and family. Sometimes trafficking is linked to traditional contexts and practices. In Nepal, the exploitative experience of the Badi caste, who provided entertainment services to feudal elites and who now must respond to market forces has led to the trafficking of their daughters and wives who leave Nepal in search of a better future. Traditional temple dancers such as *Devadasis, Jogin, Matammas* and *Deukis* were once children pledged by their parents to the temple and who become sex workers associated with the temple. These women also become vulnerable to further trafficking once they become older.

Trafficking is also complicated by the legal regimes that are in place for the regulation of prostitution. Some countries in South Asia have "moralistic" legal regime that criminalize everything associated with prostitution- the sex worker, the client, the middlemen etc...This is true especially in Islamic countries of South Asia. Sri Lanka and India have the "Abolitionist Model" contained in the 1949 Convention, the women is seen as a victim and is not criminalized but those who exploit her prostitution are criminalised.

Though on the books, it is rarely implemented. In both these frameworks the criminal justice system is an integral part of the regime and abuse and corruption in the system often ends up victimizes the trafficked women. This has led to many people in South Asia asking for more liberal legal regimes for prostitution to allow the sex worker a certain social legitimacy and more social and economic rights. This struggle for recognition of prostitution as sex work and prostitutes as sex workers with trade union rights is especially strong in Calcutta and Bombay. However, trafficking is perhaps most complicated by its link to migration.

Research clearly shows that most of the women who are trafficked have a strong desire to migrate and are thereby abused in the process. In the past women may have been kidnapped or abducted but today trafficking is really abuse of the desire to migrate. Women desire to migrate often because there is abuse in the home, in the community or because of dire poverty. To counter trafficking by preventing women's migration is to lock them into domestic systems of oppression. Measures taken to prevent women from migrating such as requiring permission of male members of the family or government sanction may actually compound the problem.

What is needed is an effective system that prevents women from being abused during the process of migration and this can only take place if the approach to trafficking is designed within a human rights framework. The human rights framework would also require a different approach to the women survivor once she leaves sex work. Instead of the metaphor of "rescue", "rehabilitation" and "repatriation" which has conditioned the mainstream approach to trafficking, there is now an emphasis on consulting the women on what she really wants to do. Does she want to remain in sex work? Does she wish to return home? Does she wish to stay in her host country? Does she wish to go back to her parents?

These approaches then require a partnership between the police, immigration officials and women's support groups who can counsel the women survivor. These approaches are not present in South Asia where the approach to trafficking is very much rescue, rehabilitation (or protection) and repatriation.

DOMESTIC VIOLENCE

Asha Rani was a young bride. Her poor family gave her a small dowry but after marriage her in laws wanted another Rs.5, 000 or an auto rickshaw. Her father who had seven daughters could not provide the amount. When he refused, the in laws beat his daughter in front of his eyes. A few weeks later Asha Rani was dead "burnt while making tea". According to her in laws, her synthetic sari caught fire on the stove. But the post mortem revealed otherwise. The Supreme Court finally ruled that she did not die of accident nor did she commit suicide. She was murdered.

Pages of the newspapers in South Asia are full of tales of domestic violence. In 2002, 450 honour killings were reported in Pakistan, 15,000 young brides are burnt to death every year in India, and ten women a week are subject to acid attacks in Bangladesh. Violence by intimate family members is one of South Asia's darkest legacies. 40% of all sexual abuse cases in India are about incest. In a survey on violence against women in India, 94% of the cases involved an offender who was a member of the family.

The violence against women in South Asia often begins before birth. It is estimated the 50 million women are missing in India either through sex selective abortions, female infanticide or female neglect so much so that the sex ratio in certain states of India is very disturbing. There are 79.3 girls for every 100 males in the Punjab and 87.8 girls for every 100 males in Gujarat. Domestic violence rates in South Asia do vary from community to community and depends on the questions asked.

A survey of 1842 women in Uttar Pradesh and Tamil Nadu in India presented a rate of 40% of women interviewed stating they were victims of wife beating. In Pakistan a survey of 1000 indicated that 55% in the urban areas and 35% in the rural areas stated that they were victims of domestic violence, In Sri Lanka, one survey put the figure at 60%, another at 32%. Research on indicators for domestic violence in the region highlight issues such as the fact that children who, themselves are abused or who have witnessed violence in the family are far more likely to beat their wives than other children, In South Asia there is alcohol and drug use that also accentuate domestic violence.

Patriarchal societies where men control all decisions result in greater violence when women seem to question or go outside the framework of such decisions. If a society resolves conflict through the use of violence then violence in the home is also on the increase. The lack of economic independence on the part of women and their inability to move out of a violent situation and state inaction against perpetrators of violence perpetuate an ideological belief that violence may even be justified and if it is not, it is not a terrible matter that requires concerted action.

The insensitivity of the criminal justice system has also been highlighted in many studies. Police stations rarely respond though with the new police women desks this situation is marginally better. A survey of judges in the region pointed to the fact that 48% of judges agreed that it was justifiable for men to beat their wives. 74% endorsed the view that even in cases of violence the preservation of the family should be the primary concern Response to domestic violence requires a concerted national effort. According to the UN standards it requires domestic violence legislation that combines civil and criminal remedies.

This requires ensuring certain civil rights of the woman such as the right to live in the matrimonial home, the right to be protected from an abusive husband and live separately from him and the right to compensation and maintenance. In addition the law should provide for prosecution of punishment for cruelty, grievous hurt and wrongful confinement. In addition the legislation should provide for social support for women survivors while they negotiate their future. India's recent legislation on domestic violence, written in consultation with NGOs has many of these necessary provisions as does the Sri Lankan draft domestic violence Act.

The international standard also call on states to draft national plans of action, ensure a trained and sensitive criminal justice system, support systems for victims, sensitive health professionals and it requires data collection and analysis about the incidents of domestic violence. Some countries in South Asia have begun to respond to these standards in a progressive manner.

RAPE AND SEXUAL HARASSMENT

Mathura was a young girl from the Dalit community. She ran away from home and married her boyfriend. Her family threatened her and her husband. When she went to the police station to make a complaint, she was gang raped by the policemen. Her case so scandalized India, that Parliament passed an amendment to the Penal Code making special provisions to protect the rights of victims who are subject to rape in state custodial institutions.

Rape and sexual harassment continue to be important issues in the South Asian context. In 1998 the Human Rights Commission of Pakistan reported that one person is raped every 354 minutes in Pakistan. In India for the same period there were over 15,000 reported cases while so many go unreported. Such cases are often compounded in the rural areas of gang rape of *Dalit* women by upper caste men as an act of political violence. A CNN survey in New Delhi pointed to the fact that 50% of all working women claimed that they were sexually harassed in the workplace.

In Pakistan, the Alliance Against Sexual Harassment in the Workplace claimed that 93% of women working in the public and private sector had experienced some form of harassment in the workplace. Marital rape and sexual violence as a means of initiation are also reported in some of these surveys, a factor that will influence the marriage relationship for years to come. This is the case even though marital rape is not a crime in all the countries of South Asia. The issue of rape was what first galvanised the women's movement in India and to come extent in the other South Asian countries.

The rape of the *Dalit* girl Mathura in a custodial setting led to a national campaign for the reform of the Rape laws. The Law commission set up to look into this matter decided in cases of custodial rape the onus of proving consent would shift to the accused. In Sri Lanka penal reforms of 1995 gave more serious punishment for custodial violence but like its Indian counterpart called for mandatory enhanced punishments.

Feminists have been challenging the rape laws of their countries for over a generation now.

The need to take away language like "against her will" that requires physical bruises, the need to define rape broadly as sexual assault and not only as penis penetration, the need to make sure that a woman's past history is not introduced into the evidence and the need to get rid of evidentiary procedure that requires corroboration. The National Commission for Women in India presented a draft amendment to the Penal Code on the issues relating to rape is very much along these lines. In the context of these crimes again there is need for effective legislation, a sensitive and trained criminal justice system, support services to the victims and trained health professionals. There is also the need for public campaigns and awareness rising.

The countries of South Asia have responded in amending their legislation and in attempting to train their police and judges. However, the problem still persists and statistics do not indicate that the crimes are getting less or that there is a significant increase in the prosecution of offenders. In this context, given the terrible nature of the crimes against women many young legal scholars are questioning whether the legal system can be effective in dealing with crimes against women and whether other alternatives to prosecution and punishment should be explored.

Statistics for a given period if Bombay show that of the 504 cases that were registered, only 469 were charge sheeted, of which there were 13 convictions, and 10 acquittals, the vast majority were pending trial or never getting to trial. Furthermore, feminists fear that the rape trial often becomes a "pornographic spectacle" Even when judgments convict, the rape survivor emerges brutalized and sometimes scandalized in a very patriarchal society. For this reason most women continue to be silent when they are victims of sexual violence.

The inability of the legal systems to deliver justice in the case of women and the reliance on the prosecution arm of the state has created unease among some women's rights activists.

They argue that reliance on the legal strategy alone is not enough and that a more broad based approach aimed at transforming attitudes and social structures is necessary. It must also be noted that none of the countries of South Asia criminalise marital rape. In Sri Lanka, marital rape is recognized only if the couples are judicially separated.

The notion that the home is a private sphere and that the criminal law of the state should not interfere to prevent men from exercising their traditional rights is very strong in South Asia. In Sri Lanka during recent parliamentary debates on the Domestic Violence Bill, parliamentarian after parliamentarian argued that the law must be carefully crafted to prevent families from breaking up. The notion that the sanctity of the family must be upheld even if there is violence between husband and wife is still remains a strong perception in many South Asian countries.

CUSTOMARY PRACTICES

Samia was married to an abusive husband. One day she ran away from home stating that she wanted a divorce. There were rumours that she had found someone else. Finally her family said they were granting her wish. Her mother, her uncle and a stranger came to the lawyers chambers to discuss the case. Suddenly the stranger pulled a gun out and shot Samia and aimed over the head of the lawyer. The security in the office shot the stranger but the mother and the uncle escaped taking one of the members of the law firm as hostage. She was finally released. The police have not prosecuted the case since they felt it was an "honour" killing.

The failure of the law is particularly relevant when it comes to customary practices in the region that are violent toward women. South Asia is perhaps the region with the largest number of customary practices that are violent toward women. In response to the international critique of our practices, we have had mixed local responses.

One is to say that this is an internal issue and not a concern to the rest of the world; that some of the practices can be justified by the internal logic of our cultural systems and that any attempt to critique and eradicate such customs is part of the arrogant legacy of colonialism and westernization. However, women's groups within these societies have also taken up these issues and highlighted them as evidence of the low status of women in South Asian societies.

These customary practices are in conflict with the international obligations that South Asian states have voluntarily taken upon themselves. The charge of westernization is also disingenuous since many of these societies are rapidly globalizing and the question of culture seems primarily relevant only to the subordinate position of women. The duality between public and private has a special meaning in South Asia where scholars have claimed that the private is also seen as "eastern", "spiritual" and the domain of the women.

To change customary practices would be a necessary transformation of the private and therefore threaten the "eastern" and "spiritual" nature of South Asian societies. As a result, attempts to eradicate customary practices that are violent toward women meet with local level resistance and require both a political as well as a legal approach. The South Asian customary practice that has received the most amount of international attention has been the practice of honor killings.

The case of Samia Sarwar from Peshawar who was allegedly shot to death in her lawyer's office by a hired gunman with her father and mother's complicity for leaving her husband made international headlines. The refusal of the police and other authorities to pursue the case in its initial stages and the reluctance of the Pakistani parliament to pass legislation caused an international furor. In honor killings that take place in many parts of Asia, women are killed by their family members if they commit adultery, if they are the victims of rape, if they fall in love with the wrong person, in short if their sexual and emotional behaviour disturbs the male power hierarchy in the family.

This acceptance of the male patriarch's right to kill the women in his family to protect the family honour is a deep rooted tradition which according to reports even has the full endorsement of women in the family. As a result it is a practice that still remains strong and police prosecution in these cases is weak. Another customary practice that is associated with South Asia is the practice of bride burning. Bride burning reached its height in the early 1990s. Dowry related deaths increased from 437 deaths in 1983 to 4,856 in 1991 and to 5,582 in 1993.

These are the reported cases. In Delhi, in the early 1980s, the frequency of unnatural deaths of housewives was one every twelve hours. While dowry in certain communities was linked to land and immovable property, giving women some sense of security, it has in the modern world become a morbid symptom of a customary practice. Today a dowry consists of first, gifts to the bride in terms of clothes, jewelry and household gifts. Second dowry consists of luxury items for the husband clothes wristwatch, gold chain; thirdly it may include immovable property written in the husband's name and finally modern electronic items such as televisions, fridges, video cassette players etc... Material gifts and cash are paid to the bridegroom, who if widowed and marries again gets the dowry a second time.

Women are burned as brides either because of dowry, incompatibility between husband and wife, the rigidity of the divorce laws, or a desire to have a son.. In recent times the Indian penal code was amended to deal specifically with dowry deaths. Since 1986 the law has provided for punishment not less than seven years and up to life imprisonment for a husband or family member if a woman's death occurs due to burns, injuries or other unnatural circumstances and she was subjected to cruelty or harassment in connection with dowry.

The number of dowry deaths has decreased in recent years due to the penal sanction but they do still occur in many parts of South Asia. In some parts of South Asia, women are victims of acid attacks. This was prevalent in Bangladesh in the late

1990s and still occurs today. In 1998, there were over 200 cases of acid attacks. Acid attacks are often directed at women who reject the advances of men or by family members in the protection of honour. These attacks have received recent attention in Bangladesh but still continue in certain parts.

Linked to the concept of honour it is difficult to eradicate as long as women's emotional and sexual behaviour are seen as reflecting on the honor of the men who are intimately connected to them. Another South Asian practice that has received international attention is the practice of Sati or widow burning in certain parts of India. The case of Roop Kanwar, who in the late eighties committed Sati on her husband's pyre in a public spectacle created major national and international furor.

Some scholars argue that Sati is an act of sacrifice of a wife for her husband and should not be decried since it is a form of heroic death. But scholars such as Kum Kum Sangari and others have argued that given the fact that women's lives are undervalued and restrained, Sati is often always committed under coercive circumstances and a tolerance of Sati will make many families urge their young widows to commit Sati to prevent having to take care of them. For this reason women's groups have not only argued against Sati as a practice but also the ideology of Sati. Luckily the Indian state responded firmly.

Parliament enacted comprehensive anti-sati legislation outlawing Sati and its glorification. Since the law was passed, there have been few reported cases of Sati which points to the importance of criminal sanctions. However, Roop Kanwar's family was acquitted by the jury of their peers pointing to the fact that communities will rarely punish individuals for customary forms of violence against women. The practice of Sati reminds us that violence and discrimination against widows is a common cultural practice in South Asia.

Besides Sati, this often manifests itself in witch killings. In Bihar an average of 200 women are killed every year as witches. In many of these cases there is some dispute over land with her husband's family. The lack of economic independence and security for a widow makes her particularly vulnerable. Supposed to be inauspicious, she is socially secluded and discriminated against. If her presence drains the family of its resources, in some cases there is a cultural form of killing or exclusion that allows families to deal with unwanted widows.

Against the criminal justice system rarely prosecutes families for killing their widows. Another type of violation that takes place in South Asia is around customary practices of marriage. In some South Asian communities, it is expected that a man pursue a young girl, rape her and then marry her. The Veddas community in Sri Lanka and some tribal groups such as the Bhils in India claim that this is their traditional practice. The Attorney General of Sri Lanka made a statement that he would not be prosecuting a young Veddas for rape even though the young girl had complained.

The marriage via rape creates an ideology that one who sexually initiates a woman has the duty to marry her. This is present in mainstream society in situations of rape where pressure is brought on the boy and the girl to marry. International standards and national constitutions require that such customary practices that go to the heart of a woman's dignity and rights have to be reigned in and that the normal criminal process take its course.

The criminal sanction in cases such as these does work in certain contexts and may act as a catalyst to transform behaviour. Another customary practice of marriage in South Asia that is violence toward women is the practice of child marriage. In Nepal 40% of marriages involve girls under the age of fifteen. In Pakistan the Watta Satta marriage is another form of marriage that violates the rights of women. Women become part of barter between men. A woman is given in marriage to a man in return for another woman.

The case of 12 year old Reshma who was given in a watta satta marriage but the marriage took place after a terrible dispute between the two families. On her wedding night her husband shot her dead claiming she had committed adultery. These traditional forms of marriage held together by the concept of honour and community deeply oppress women but are so firmly embedded in South Asia that unless there is concerted action with the State taking the lead, such practices will never change. At the root of much of the violence against women in customary practices relate to son preference in South Asian societies.

Amartya Sen has chronicled how with regard to food, hospitals and schooling there is terrible discrimination against the girl child. Young girls are taken to hospital if they are very ill, young girls are more malnourished than young boys and in schooling- only 15% of girls in rural primary schools go beyond the fifth grade. The gender gap in school enrolment is 14% in India, 19% in Nepal and 24% in Pakistan This son preference and the discrimination against the girl child lasts a lifetime leading to a lifecycle of violence and discrimination.

Customary practices such as those outlined above require the state to create a normative framework that frowns on such practices and criminalizes those who engage in such practices. However, for the most part, because of the political unpopularity, states shy away from insisting on international standards on the protection of women from violence. As a result, there is a sense that the violence is "normal", or "usual" and that severe action should not be taken against the perpetrators.

This normalization of violence shows the inter linkage between ideology and violence against women, In Bangladesh in a recent survey the majority of men argued that violence against their wives was alright in certain circumstances as corrective punishment. The normalization of violence against women is one of the darker elements in South Asian societies. This normalization prevents men from seeing the violence as wrong, prevents women from asserting that the violence is wrong and paralyses the criminal justice system in trying to attain justice.

Another linkage that is often made is that women's lack of economic independence and empowerment has a great deal to do with the levels of violence in South Asian societies.

Women's lack of economic security forces them to put up with extreme acts of violence for the sake of survival. Inheritance laws and practices, the lack of access to land, the lack of education and the denial of mobility contribute to keeping women locked into situations from which there is no escape. David Levinson in an eighty country study found that the lack of economic independence is one of the main reasons for violence against women.

Models of masculinity in the South Asian region also contribute to violence against women. In certain communities, violence is closely linked to honour and the assertion of masculine status. Women who act in a manner that challenges patriarchal rules and expectations are therefore subject to violence. If violence is closely linked to "being a man", then violence against women is also normalized and seen as part of the customs and practices of the society. If being a man means controlling and domesticating your wife, then behaviour patterns emerge accordingly.

Given the deeply held values and time honored "masculine" traditions, changing these models and expectations may only take place over generations. For this, there have to be other masculine non-violent traditions that capture the imagination of young men. In modern times, some of these traditions are merging in South Asia but they are in a nascent phase. Linked to notions of masculinity is also a belief in the proper emotional and sexual behaviour of women. A great part of violence against women has to deal with female sexuality.

Rape is about sexual violence, trafficking is often about sex work, sexual harassment is about discrimination in the workplace, domestic violence is often about a woman's refusal to have sex with her husband and many so called customary practices such as honor killings or female genital mutilation are linked to the control of female sexuality. For this reason many believe that the protection of women from violence must be accompanied by the recognition of the reproductive rights and freedoms of women. This linkage is extremely important if we are to create conditions for women to be free from the fear of violence.

Violence against women is also an aspect of the global phenomenon of HIV AIDS. South Asia accounts for 4.2 million of the total number of people living with HIV worldwide. India has the second largest population of those who are infected by HIV. According to the statistics prepared by UNAIDS there are 3.86 million people living with HIV Aids infection in India, 74,000 in Pakistan, 7500 in Sri Lanka, 34,000 in Nepal, 13,000 in Bangladesh. Women are vulnerable to AIDS infection in the Asian region for a variety of reasons.

Widespread poverty forces young women and even boys into sex work as there are large sex markets in the cities and many clients refuse to use condoms. Because of poverty millions of girls are forced into child labour and are often subject to sexual abuse and exploitation. Lack of development forces many young men to migrate to the cities and live in urban slums without their families. This loneliness drives them into seeking comfort in unsafe sex. Lack of clean sanitary facilities allows for the easy transmission of diseases including STD and HIV.

Because of the lack of access to health care, people are unable to detect and treat STDs as they cannot get the proper tests and treatment. Large numbers of people are unaware of the disease and do not have access to information on STD and HIV aids. Wives and partners of men with HIV Aids do not have the power to refuse unsafe sex and are often victimized as a result. Without sex education and a frank environment for the discussion of sexuality and sex related diseases, unsafe sex continues as a way of life for many young people.

In urban areas with high drug use, HIV is spread through the use of contaminated needles. Women are also subject to discrimination and violence once they are diagnosed as HIV positive. Discrimination occurs because of ignorance about HIV/AIDS. Individuals are subject to extreme quarantine procedures and are discriminated against in their workplace and other public places. There is also very limited understanding of the rights of HIV positive women and the problem of mother child transmissions.

Though there is little legislation covering people with HIV in the South Asian region, the Indian Supreme Court has made a few decisions protecting the rights of the HIV infected people from discrimination. Some of the governments have also developed national level policies to deal with AIDS such as the Indian government's National AIDS Prevention and Control Policy. However, except for India which has a large HIV infected population, the other countries of South Asia have not really developed national legislation or comprehensive programmes.

The WHO in a recent study outlined the enormous costs of violence against women to a society. These include hospital and other costs related to the treatment of injury and the rehabilitation of the victim. It also includes long term costs such as the effect on children for research shows that children who witness violence in the home are more likely to be perpetrators than those who come from a homes where there is no violence. Perhaps the most important cost for women is "fear".

Women are relegated to the home because of the fear of violence and as a result they cannot fully participate in the development goals of the society or in public life. This chilling aspect of violence at the psychological level is one of the factors that have led to women being treated as second class citizens in need of protection and without empowerment.

THE RESPONSE OF GOVERNMENTS

All the governments of the SAARC region have responded positively to the challenges posed by violence against women in their region. In the last decades, there has been a great deal of advances, especially in the area of standard setting and the enactment of policies and programmes. Though a great deal may not have changed at the local level, the policy framework has been developed in most of the countries of the region Bangladesh has responded to the challenges posed by violence against women in the region by declaring openly in its National strategy for Economic Growth, Poverty Reduction and Social Development that it plans to substantially reduce or eliminate violence against women and children by 2015.

In 2000, Bangladesh adopted the Prevention of Oppression Against Women and Children Act which deals comprehensively with crimes of violence against women. In the cases of rape for example, though it did not change the archaic definition of rape, The POAWC Act prescribes severe punishment for perpetrators. Though the standard case of rape carries life imprisonment and a fine, in some aggravated cases, it carries the death penalty. Attempted rape also carries a punishment of 5-10 years imprisonment.

Those arrested for crimes under the Act are not eligible for bail during an initial investigation period of 90 days. The Act also provides for compensation for the victim. Bangladesh does not have specific legislation on domestic violence. However under the POAWC Act a husband or any relative or person acting on behalf of the husband who causes or attempts to cause his wife's death in connection with a demand for dowry is subject to life imprisonment and a fine.

The POAWC Act also prescribes punishments for the "sexual oppression of women", defined as touching the sexual organs of a woman without consent or the sexual organs of a child or indecent gestures. Such acts carry a punishment of two years imprisonment as a minimum and ten years imprisonment as a maximum. Bangladesh continues to have the abolitionist approach to the regulation of sex work. In 2000, over a hundred sex workers brought an action against the police for closing down the brothels. The High Court ruled that sex work is not illegal provided that sex workers obtain a license. One conditions for obtaining such a license is that they prove that they have no other means of earning a livelihood. However, POAWC contains a strong prohibition against trafficking.

The punishment for trafficking is ten years minimum imprisonment and the maximum punishment is the death penalty. Bangladesh has also taken action against the customary practice of acid throwing. POAWC prescribes capital punishment or life imprisonment for causing or attempting to cause death to a woman or child by means of a corrosive or similar substance.

Though these strong laws have been enacted, the number of cases prosecuted under the Act remains small and conviction rates even lower. However, Bangladesh does have a large number of NGOs working in this field providing awareness raising programmes, legal aid, safe shelters, counseling and health care services and special programmes for women victims to develop skills and to reintegrate with the rest of society.

Bangladesh has also set up a National Advisory Council for the Prevention of Violence Against Women with committees to prevent VAW in every district. There are also four investigative cells in police station and a multi-sectoral programme which was adopted in 2000 that tries to combine the efforts of the health services, the police, access to justice and public awareness. India too has taken positive measures with regard to violence against women.

With regard to sex selective abortions, in 1994, India adopted the Pre-Conception and Pre- Natal Diagnostic Techniques Act and this has been amended twice as recently as 2003. The Act prohibits the use of prenatal diagnostic tests for the purpose of sex selection. Certain conditions have been placed for taking of such tests. In addition, the Act prohibits disclosing the sex of a fetus to a pregnant mother or her relatives. The Act also prohibits advertisement for sex selection testing.

Violating the Act can result in imprisonment and a fine. In 2003, the Supreme Court of India also called on the national and state governments to enforce the ban as part of the protection of the girl child from discrimination. India is still in the process of finalizing domestic violence legislation that is quite comprehensive. The law was drafted in partnership with women's NGOs especially the Lawyers Collective. In contains many provisions combining civil and criminal remedies and providing support for women survivors of violence.

The law defines domestic violence comprehensively, provides for protection orders and special provisions for the economic security of the woman concerned. It was scheduled to be debated just before the last parliament was dissolved. It is now again being introduced for debate in the next parliament. India is also in the process of adopting other legislation with relevance for fighting violence against women. Though the 1983 amendments to the Penal Code brought in important provisions with regard to the prosecution of rape, in 2003, the Ministry of Law and Justice put forward Sexual Offenses (Special Courts) Bill which aims at the speedy disposal of cases relating to rape and sexual offenses.

This Bill was challenged by human rights activists as a dangerous precedent. The law seeks to establish special courts throughout the country to try these offenses and the evidence ordinance and the Code of Criminal Procedure was also to be amended before these courts. In 2004, another bill Sexual Harassment of Women in the Workplace (Prevention) Bill was also put forward by the government. The Bill is an attempt to give parliamentary sanction to the decision by the Indian Supreme Court in *Visakha vs. State of Rajasthan*, that the lack of sexual harassment legislation violates the equality provisions of the Constitution.

Quoting CEDAW extensively, the Court defined sexual harassment and stated that both public and private employers have a duty to include the prohibition against sexual harassment in their service rules and that a permanent committee should be set up to deal with these complaints and that the committee must have a majority of women. The government is also considering the possibility of introducing legislation on trafficking. At the moment the main legislation to tackle the problem of trafficking is Immoral Traffic (Prevention) Act.

Though the Act does not criminalize sex work, it criminalizes related activities including soliciting, procuring, maintaining a brothel, etc.. The National Commission for Women has been entrusted with the task of formulating legal reform in this area. The Government has introduced a range of policies to combat trafficking. A Plan of Action to Combat Trafficking and Commercial Sexual Exploitation of Women and Children has been formulated In Nepal in the last decade, a great deal has been done in the area of trafficking, The Ministry of Women, Children and Social Welfare has proposed a new bill to replace the Traffic in Human Beings (Control) Act.

The bill broadens the definition of trafficking and has strong provisions with regard to punishment and evidentiary procedure. In the late nineties, the Ministry also adopted a national anti-trafficking policy and a rehabilitation home for victims of trafficking. The Human Rights Commission of Nepal also created a National Rapporteur on Trafficking. There is also a Task Force for anti trafficking activities with task forces at the district and village levels. There is also a special cell in the police to work on issues of women and child trafficking.

As in other countries NGOs have worked closely with government on issues relating to trafficking. In Pakistan, though many crimes of violence against women are dealt with under the Offence of *Zina* (Enforcement of *Hudood*) Ordinance, which g has difficult evidentiary provisions with regard to the women victim, The National commission on the Status of Women has been requested to review all laws, rules and regulations affecting the status of women. The Commission also set up a Committee of Experts to review the *Hudood* and *Zina* Ordinances.

In 2004, the Parliament adopted legislation criminalizing honour killings with strong punishments for the perpetrators. The law treats honor killings as an aggravated form of murder. The Pakistan Supreme Court has also stated that honor killings are murder and violate a woman's fundamental right. Crisis centres have been established for women in distress in Islamabad, Vehari, Lahore and Sahiwal. In Sri Lanka, the decade witnessed the drafting of the Penal Code Amendments in 1995 which was a major step forward with regard to meeting the challenge of violence against women. Rape is defined without the limiting words "against her will" and special provisions exist for judicially separated couples and statutory rape.

There is enhanced punishment for custodial rape, rape of a pregnant woman, rape of someone under 18, rape of a mentally disabled person and gang rape. There are also provisions for mandatory sentencing. In Sri Lanka a draft law on domestic violence is also pending. The draft law defines domestic violence broadly and provides for a broad range of remedies including interim and permanent protection orders, emergency monetary relief and compensation.

The law was recently debated with conservative MPs voicing opposition to the bill stating that it calls into question the sanctity of the family. The debate is due to continue in a few weeks time. After Beijing, Sri Lanka did adopt a national plan of action but there was no follow up on its implementation. The countries of South Asia have all ratified CEDAW though some of them have done so with reservations. The countries of South Asia have also signed the SAARC Convention on Preventing and Combating the Trafficking in Women and Children for prostitution. The Trafficking Convention defines trafficking narrowly and it is not in conformity with the international definition.

It provides for co-operation among member states, repatriation and rehabilitation of women survivors, and has certain measures to ensure prevention The CEDAW indicators for the region point to the fact that all the countries of South Asia recognize gender equality in their constitutions, though the Indian supreme court has been particularly active in protecting the rights of women under the constitution. With regard to law reform and violence against women, many of the countries of South Asia have taken anti-trafficking initiatives and have begun to reform their rape laws to ensure stricter punishment.

The countries have yet to adopt domestic violence legislation with some countries showing resistance to change. The countries have national policies, projects and programmes on violence against women such as training of the police forces and the setting up of support services for victims. However, the real initiatives in the area of violence against women still comes from non-state groupings who continue to be active in promoting measures to prevent violence against women. However, there is a fear that much of the activity on violence against women is donor driven and that much of the society has been unaffected by the need for change and reform.

The above survey points to the fact that all the states in the South Asian region have responded to some of the challenges posed by violence against women in the region. Many have passed laws or are entertaining draft laws to deal with some of the important questions. Ten years after Beijing, it is still a concern that except for India none of the countries of the region have adopted domestic violence legislation or made the necessary changes to anti -trafficking legislation.

However programmes and policies are in place and a great deal of activity has been conducted by women's ministries, national commissions and individual government departments. There have been many training programmes also for senior level policy officers and other members of the criminal justice system. The changes in South Asia have also made possible by the activism of civil society and the foresight of many women's NGOs. They have conducted research, suggested legal reform and put in place constructive programmes that actually assist women victims of violence.

They have trained police men, they have lobbied politicians and judges and they have put together shelters and crisis centres. They have taken cases to court, demonstrated for women's rights and in some countries mobilized people at the risk to their own lives. They have counseled and cared for many victims of violence breaking their silence and allowing them to regain their dignity. Research from around the world point to the fact that violence against women can only be combated if there is a healthy partnership between women's groups and the state apparatus.

While women's groups must protect their independence, on certain issues they have to work effectively with the criminal justice system, joining forces to protect the rights of women victims. However, this also poses a major dilemma. The decade ends with the triumph of a certain "law and order feminism" which aims at punishing the perpetrator, using draconian provisions in the law.

Whether in trafficking, rape or sexual harassment, there is a punishment rhetoric that belies a complex reality. South Asia is particularly receptive to this excess of law enforcement. Provisions in trafficking legislation, in sexual offenses legislation, in preventing women from migrating procedures, are so draconian that they raise questions about the human rights of the perpetrators and an over reliance on the criminal justice system to solve complex social questions.

Though they provide an immediate sense of something being done, in the long run they pose serious dilemmas. In the end judges and juries just do not convict if they feel that the law is too harsh or unreasonable. Fighting violence against women will only succeed if it is done through the lens of human rights, protecting the rights and dignity of the woman survivor while ensuring a fair trial for the perpetrator.

Any other course of action will not stand the test of time and important legislation will fall into disuse. Fairness must be a central concern for women even when they are dealing with abusers. Moreover, law is an important tool but it is one of the many strategies available to us.

While fighting for justice through the legal system, we should also try and put in place education policies, health strategies and community level programmes that promote equality between men and women and teach non violent methods of resolving conflict. A multipronged approach to violence against women will result in far reaching changes, transforming attitudes and practices so that men and women can live in equality and dignity.

Bibliography

Andrews, B., Brewin, C. R., Rose, S., et al. 2000. "Predicting PTSD Symptoms in Victims of Violent Crime: The Role of Shame, Anger, and Childhood Abuse." *Journal of abnormal psychology* 109: 69-73.

Baldinger, B. G., and Nelson, D. T. 1995. "Crime Victims and Psychological Injuries." *Trial* 31: 56.

Bisson, J. I., and Shepherd, J. P. 1995. "Psychological reactions of victims of violent crime." *The British journal of psychiatry* 167: 718.

Bjerregaard, B. 2000. "An Empirical Study of Stalking Victimization." Violence and Victims 15: 389-406.

Black, J. 1995. "Rethinking the naming of sex crime victims." *Newspaper Research Journal* 16: 96.

Blackburn, S. 1999. "Gender Violence and the Indonesian Political Transition." *Asian Studies Review* 23: 433-448.

Breault, K. D., and Kposowa, A. J. 1997. "The Effects of Marital Status on Adult Female Homicides in the United States." *Journal of Quantitative Criminology* 13: 217-230.

Bubar, Roe, and Pamela Jumper Thurman. 2004. "Violence Against Native Women." *Social justice: a journal of crime, conflict & world order*. 31(4): 70 (17 pages).

Chilton, R., and Jarvis, J. 1999. "Victims and Offenders in Two Crime Statistics Programs: A Comparison of the National Incident-Based Reporting System (NIBRS) and the National Crime Victimization Survey (NCVS)." *Journal of Quantitative Criminology* 15: 193-205.

Cling, B. J., *Sexualized Violence against Women and Children: A Psychology and Law Perspective*. The Guilford Press: 2004.

Davis, K. E., and Frieze, I. H. 2000. "Research on Stalking: What Do We Know and Where Do We Go?" *Violence and Victims* 15: 473-487.

Denkers, A. J .M., and Winkel., F. W. 1998. "Crime victims well being and fear in a prospective and longitudinal study." *Sage Urban Studies Abstracts* 26.

Dunn, J. L. 2001. "Innocence Lost: Accomplishing Victimization in Intimate Stalking Cases." *Symbolic Interaction* 24: 285-313.

Dwyer, D. C. 1995. "Response to the Victims of Domestic Violence: Analysis and Implications of the British Experience." *Crime and Delinquency* 41: 527-541.

Epstein, J. N., Saunders, B. E., and Kilpatrick, D. G. 1997. "Predicting PTSD in Women with a History of Childhood Rape." *Journal of Traumatic Stress* 10: 573-588.

Erez, E., Laster, K. 1999. "Neutralizing Victim Reform: Legal Professionals' Perspectives on Victims and Impact Statements." *Crime & Delinquency* 45: 530-553.

Fenwick, H. 1996. "The rights of victims of crime: Protection from harassment and intimidation?" *The Journal of criminal law* 60: 84-93.

Gartner, R., Dawson, M., and Crawford, M. 1998/1999. "Woman Killing: Intimate Femicide in Ontario, 19741994." *Resources for Feminist Research* 26: 151-173.

Gaumer, C. P. 1995. "Protecting the Innocent: Victim-Witness Rights in Illinois." *Illinois bar journal* 83: 568.

Hart, B. In: Eds. 1996. *Battered Women and the Criminal Justice System*. Thousand Oaks, CA: Sage Publications, pp 98-114.

Herman, S., and Wasserman, C. 2001. "A Role for Victims in Offender Reentry." *Crime & Delinquency* 47:428-445.

Johnson, K. W. 1997. "Professional Help and Crime Victims." *The Social service review* 71: 89-109.

Kalaher, K. 1997. "The Proposed Victim's Rights Amendment: Taking a Bite Out of Crime or a Dog With No Teeth?" *Seton Hall legislative journal* 22: 317.

Kamphuis, J. H., and Emmelkamp, P. M. G. 1998. "Crime-Related Trauma: Psychological Distress in Victims of Bankrobbery." *Journal of anxiety disorders* 12: 199-208.

Katz, J. 1997. "Staying Alive: Women Who Saved Their Own Lives." *Cosmopolitan* 222: 188.

Kenney, J. S. 2002. "Victims of Crime and Labeling Theory: A Parallel Process?" *Deviant behavior* 23: 235-266.

Kumar, G. S. J. 1997. "Victimization of Women: Coping with Violence." *International Journal of Sociology of the Family* 27: 139-155.

Kury , H. Ferdinand., T. 1998. "The Victim's Experience and Fear of Crime." *Sage Urban Studies Abstracts* 26.

Lowenstein, L. F. 2000. "Victims of Violent Crime Leading to Post-Traumatic Stress Disorders." *The Police journal* 73: 256-262.

Lurigio, A. J. 2000. "Are all victims alike? The adverse, generalized and differential impact of crime." *Violence and Abuse Abstracts* 6.

Madriz, E. I. 1997. "Images of Criminals and Victims: A Study on Women's Fear and Social Control." *Gender & Society* 11: 342-356.

Marietta, J. D., and Rowe, G. S. 1999. "Violent Crime, Victims, and Society in Pennsylvania, 1682-1800." *Pennsylvania history* 66.

Martens, P. L. 2002. "Immigrants as victims of crime." *Violence & Abuse Abstracts* 8: 3-84.

McPhail, Beverly A. 2002. "Gender-Bias Hate Crimes: A Review." *Trauma, Violence, & Abuse: A Review Journal* 3: 125-143.

Mesch, G. S. 2000. "Women's Fear of Crime: The Role of Fear for the Well-Being of Significant Others." *Violence and Victims* 15: 323-336.

Nettleton, H., Walklate, S., and Williams, B. 1997. "Three Models of Probation Involvement with Victims of Crime." *The Liverpool law review* 19: 203.

Peltzer, K. 2000. "Risk for traumatization among violent crime victims in an urban community sample in South Africa." *Curationis* 23: 22-27.

Petersilia, J. R. 2001. "Crime Victims With Develo-pmental Disabilities: A Review Essay." *Criminal Justice and Behavior* 28: 655-694.

Pino, N. W., and Meier, R. F. 1999. "Gender Differences in Rape Reporting." *Sex Roles* 40: 979-990.

Ruback, R. B., Menard, K. S., Outlaw, M. C., et al. 1999. "Normative Advice to Campus Crime Victims: Effects of Gender, Age, and Alcohol." *Violence and victims* 14: 381-396.

Sebba, L. 2001. "On the relationship between criminological research and policy: The case of crime victims." *Criminal Justice* 1: 27-58.

Wadham, J., and Arkinstall, J. 2000. "Rights of victims of crime explain how victims' rights will be affected by the Human Rights Act." *The New law journal* 6943: 1023-1024.

Weinrath, M., and Gartrell, J. 1996. "Victimization and Fear of Crime." *Violence and Victims* 11: 187-197.

Weisman, C. S. 1995. "Armed by Fear: Self-Defense Handguns and Women's Health." *Women's Health Issues* 5: 3-7.

Yee, J. L., and Greenberg, M. S. 1998. "Reactions to Crime Victims: Effects of Victims' Emotional State and Type of Relationship." *Journal of Social and Clinical Psychology* 17: 209-226.

Index

R

S

T

V

W